THE SUPERNATURAL IN TUDOR AND STUART ENGLAND

The Supernatural in Tudor and Stuart England reflects upon the boundaries between the natural and the otherworldly in early modern England as they were understood by the people of the time. The book places supernatural beliefs and events in the context of the English Reformation to show how early modern people reacted to the world of unseen spirits and magical influences. It sets out the conceptual foundations of early modern encounters with the supernatural and shows how occult beliefs penetrated almost every aspect of life.

Darren Oldridge considers many of the spiritual forces that pervaded early modern England: an immanent God who sometimes expressed Himself through "signs and wonders", and the various lesser inhabitants of the world of spirits, including ghosts, goblins, demons and angels. He explores human attempts to comprehend, harness or accommodate these powers through magic and witchcraft, and the role of the supernatural in early modern science.

This book presents a concise, accessible and up-to-date synthesis of the scholarship of the supernatural in Tudor and Stuart England. It will be essential reading for students of early modern England, religion, witchcraft and the supernatural.

Darren Oldridge is Senior Lecturer in History at the University of Worcester. His previous publications include *Strange Histories* (2005), *The Devil: A Very Short Introduction* (2012) and (as editor) *The Witchcraft Reader* (second edition 2008).

THE SUPERNATURAL IN TUDOR AND STUART ENGLAND

Darren Oldridge

Routledge
Taylor & Francis Group

LONDON AND NEW YORK

First published 2016
by Routledge
2 Park Square, Milton Park, Abingdon, Oxon OX14 4RN

and by Routledge
711 Third Avenue, New York, NY 10017

Routledge is an imprint of the Taylor & Francis Group, an informa business

British Library Cataloguing-in-Publication Data
A catalogue record for this book is available from the British Library

Library of Congress Cataloging-in-Publication Data
Names: Oldridge, Darren, 1966– author.
Title: The supernatural in Tudor and Stuart England / Darren Oldridge.
Description: London : Routledge, 2016. | Includes bibliographical
    references and index.
Identifiers: LCCN 2015040289| ISBN 9780415747585 (hardback : alkaline
    paper) | ISBN 9780415747592 (paperback : alkaline paper) |
    ISBN 9781315640839 (e-book)
Subjects:LCSH:Supernatural. | England—Religion—16th century. | England—
    Religion—17th century. | England—Social life and customs—
    16th century. | England—Social life and customs—17th century.
Classification: LCC BL100 .O43 2016 | DDC 130.942/09031—dc23
LC record available at http://lccn.loc.gov/2015040289

ISBN: 978-0-415-74758-5 (hbk)
ISBN: 978-0-415-74759-2 (pbk)
ISBN: 978-1-315-64083-9 (ebk)

Typeset in Bembo
by Apex CoVantage, LLC

For Sharron

CONTENTS

PREFACE

Among the papers of Elias Ashmole, the Restoration courtier and fellow of the Royal Society, is a spell to become invisible. The procedure is surprisingly simple: it involves soaking an anthill in water to produce a "stone of diverse colours", which the magician should carry in his right hand.[1] It is not known if Ashmole attempted this operation; but he was sufficiently impressed by its potential to copy out the instructions by hand, alongside notes on the conjuration of spirits, love magic, and charms to protect his property from thieves.

Modern readers might view Ashmole's projects as excessively ambitious. Many of his contemporaries would have regarded his magical experiments with concern, though for rather different reasons. Ashmole's attempts to raise spirits involved occult forces that were widely assumed to be both potent and real: these facts made such activities hazardous to would-be sorcerers, and problematic in the context of Protestant Christianity. Few doubted that the cosmos was penetrated with unseen powers, and the observable world was merely one part of a vast economy of the supernatural. The newly invented microscope, whose power to illuminate invisible wonders was championed by Ashmole's contemporary Robert Hooke, tended to confirm this view.

This book considers the supernatural assumptions that touched almost every aspect of life in sixteenth- and seventeenth-century England. One of its central themes is the attempt by English Protestants to establish a biblical model of the supernatural world, an enterprise that may be described as "the reformation of spirits". This project was protracted and complex and richly unpredictable in its outcomes. Like Ashmole's plan to become invisible, my own attempt to chart this process combines considerable ambition with perhaps limited prospects of success. Nonetheless, it is hoped that readers will find the broad outlines presented here to be useful, and be led to more specialist texts for the detail that I have sometimes elided. Other scholars will fill the omissions that these pages contain. The current lively interest in all aspects of the supernatural in the early modern period makes me confident that this will be the case.

I have acquired innumerable intellectual debts in writing this book and hope that I have acknowledged them fully in what follows. Thanks are due to my friends, colleagues and students at Worcester, and the marvellous editorial team at Routledge. I am also grateful to the Scouloudi Foundation for their support for my archival research. My deepest thanks go to my partner, Sharron, whose magical attentions kept me safe as I wandered in the kingdom of spirits, and whose love fills me with happiness and wonder. This book is dedicated to her.

Note

1   Bodleian Library, Oxford, MS Ashmole 1406, 97r.

1

INTRODUCTION

What is supernatural?

To write a history of the supernatural is, inevitably, to reflect on the boundaries of the natural world and the forces that operate within it. When the alchemist Thomas Vaughan published in 1650 his history of magic, *Magia Adamica, or, The Antiquitie of Magic*, he was careful to distinguish between good and corrupted forms of the art: the former was a gift of God transmitted from the time of Adam, and the latter a perverse tradition encouraged by the Devil. Thirty years earlier, Walter Raleigh had delineated "natural" and "demonic" magic in his *History of the World* (1616).[1] For these and other early modern thinkers, the history of the occult involved a series of important distinctions: between earthly phenomena and those produced by otherworldly powers, and the various forces and spiritual entities that were active in the world.

A modern historian of these things is obliged to address similarly fundamental issues. The definition of the "supernatural" itself is an obvious place to start. The concept of events "above nature" (*supra naturam*) was accepted in the early Christian church, and the word *supernaturalis* was first used commonly in the thirteenth century. This implied a boundary between ordinary phenomena and direct acts of God. The word emerged in the context of new procedures for canonisation within the medieval church: these required the examination of miracles that were attributed to presumptive saints and that turned on the question of whether such events involved the suspension of natural processes.[2] A true miracle, it was believed, contravened the laws of nature and could be accomplished only by the divine hand that had created these laws. Consequently, the investigation of supposed occurrences of this kind required the demarcation of natural and supernatural phenomena.

Throughout the sixteenth and seventeenth centuries, the idea that only miracles were truly "above nature" was dominant among European intellectuals. In the words of the Elizabethan theologian William Perkins, "a true wonder is a rare work done by the power of God simply, either above or against the power of nature, and it is properly called a miracle".[3] This meant that conventional thinking about the supernatural was, in some ways, similar to that accepted by many westerners today. The overwhelming majority of things were believed to have natural causes, and apparent contraventions of nature were unexpected and extremely rare. This superficial similarity, however, conceals a gulf in understanding between early modern people and ourselves. This was because our predecessors believed in a hidden world of spirits and powers that were active on earth. These included good and wicked angels as well as the "occult" or invisible forces associated with magic. Very few educated people questioned the existence of these things, and those who did – such as the English demonologist Reginald Scot and the political philosopher Thomas Hobbes – placed themselves beyond the mainstream of respectable and credible opinion.[4]

The boundaries between natural and supernatural phenomena have never been securely fixed, and have moved since Raleigh and Vaughan wrote their histories of magic in the seventeenth century. To most of their contemporaries, the activities of spirits, as well as the effects produced by human magicians, were contained within the laws established by God for His creation: they were entirely natural. The fact that people did not understand the means by which angels and demons did remarkable things, such as lifting witches into the sky, made these acts not supernatural but "preternatural": that is, they were accomplished within the laws of nature, but their mechanism was outside human knowledge. Here a modern analogy may be helpful. Scientists today accept that many functions of the human brain are unknown, and some may never be fully understood; nonetheless, they do not assume that such phenomena are "above nature". Early modern thinkers applied similar reasoning to events like the flight of witches: the principles of nature governed earthly phenomena, even when these principles were not understood by human observers. True miracles were the only exception to this rule.

This way of thinking can be illustrated in the writings of Simon Forman, a magician who established a considerable reputation as a healer and astrologer in late Elizabethan and Jacobean London.[5] In 1594 Forman survived an outbreak of plague in the city and became convinced that he could both cure the disease and explain its causes. He was careful, however, to distinguish between the "natural" and "supernatural" origins of the affliction. The former involved the alignment of the planets, particularly Saturn and Mars: the transit of these heavenly bodies was already associated with earthly calamities such as warfare and famine, and this could be extended to pestilence as well. It was possible to anticipate and deal with such natural plagues through the methods of astrology. But at other times plague was sent by God as a judgement or warning to humankind. "If they come of a supernatural cause", Forman explained, "then they come by the will and anger of God and by His command and ordinance, which is above and beyond the course of nature, for He is the lord of nature".[6] A supernatural plague could not be relieved by any natural art or medicine.

To twenty-first-century readers, of course, both of Forman's explanations for plague appear to be supernatural. This reflects the shifting border between the natural and the supernatural in western thought. For the purposes of this book, it will be necessary to define the supernatural in terms broader than those that were used by men such as Forman in Elizabethan England. Scholars of the early modern period often describe the deeds attributed to otherworldly beings such as saints and angels, the Devil and demons, as "supernatural" when they were understood by contemporaries as remarkable but natural events. In effect, this practice extends the category of the supernatural to the preternatural as well. I shall follow this convention. To do otherwise would confine this book to the study of miracles, and exclude many important and fascinating phenomena that today are routinely described as supernatural.

The supernatural in history

English historians writing in the sixteenth century were comfortable with marvels. Both John Bale and John Foxe recorded supernatural events to underline the divine favour enjoyed by Protestant martyrs. In a world ruled by divine providence, men and women could endure appalling executions without pain; and tumults in the sky could mark the significance of their deaths. At the burning of Ann Askew, the heavens "suddenly altered colour, and the clouds from above gave a thunder-clap" to display "the high displeasure of God for so tyrannous a murder".[7] In Foxe's life of William Tyndale, the martyr annulled the power of a magician at a banquet in Antwerp.[8] While the *Book of Martyrs* remains a standard source for writers on the early English Reformation, few if any modern historians take such accounts at face value. This is because the scientific naturalism that dominates western societies – at least at the level of public culture – appears to preclude otherworldly interventions from historical discussion. In the 1960s, E. H. Carr argued that supernatural powers should not be granted a role in shaping historical events; nor should the meaning of the past depend on some higher purpose akin to providence. This was because such beliefs lifted certain events beyond the normal rules of cause and effect on which historians based their interpretations, and undermined the autonomy of their discipline. Religion in history was like a joker in a pack of cards, and for Carr "history is a game played . . . without a joker in the pack".[9]

The Reformation historian Brad Gregory has challenged this approach. Gregory sees a danger in assuming that the supernatural experiences described by women and men in deeply religious past cultures cannot have been real. This assumption, he suggests, resembles the writing of "confessional history" that once dominated accounts of early modern religion, in which scholars produced partisan narratives to support the religious traditions to which they belonged. This practice has been largely abandoned, but historians today often impose secular interpretations on their material and consequently create versions of the past that their human sources would not have recognised. This has a built-in tendency to distort the events that they are trying to understand. Gregory admits that this problem cannot be completely overcome. It can be alleviated considerably, however, by beginning historical enquiries with the question "What did it mean to them?" This obliges historians to suspend their own preconceptions and resist the desire to impose a reductionist theory of "what really happened". It also encourages understanding of the motives of people in the past, which played a fundamental role in shaping historical events.[10]

The approach of this book is broadly consistent with Gregory's views. As far as possible, the question of whether people can truly interact with angels and demons, or whether a martyr's death can produce a God-sent thunderclap, will be set aside. It should be acknowledged, however, that this approach is not without its problems: indeed, it is really a holding position. E. H. Carr's assertion that historians should not, in the pursuit of their discipline, accept the existence of supernatural forces that contravene the ordinary processes of causation remains telling; there should be no joker in the pack. To be a historian is to accept precisely the secular assumptions that Gregory finds problematic – at least when one is doing history. The philosopher Tor Egil Førland has made this point in response to Gregory's argument. He has also observed that the historian's goal is ultimately to explain the past: the question "What did it mean to them?" may be a useful step in this process, but the question "What happened?" cannot be deferred indefinitely. Ultimately, Førland suggests that it is impossible for modern historians to produce interpretations of supernatural events that would be recognised as accurate by those who experienced them: this is a problem, he admits, but it is one that we must live with.[11]

The issue, ultimately, may be one of priorities. To understand completely an incident in the past that was perceived as supernatural, it is not enough to grasp what it meant to those who experienced it: it is also necessary to explain the incident itself.[12] Did God mark the death of Ann Askew with a miraculous storm? Carr and Førland would say that historians should discount this possibility in order to do their job properly; and they are probably correct. Nonetheless, it is usually more helpful to ask Brad Gregory's question: what did the storm mean to those who witnessed it, and to the many more who knew the story through ballads and books? This is because the attempt to describe religious phenomena in naturalistic terms adds little to the kind of explanations that historians normally want: that is, explanations that take seriously the ideas of men and women in the past and acknowledge the role of these ideas in shaping events. Those who wish to explain the religious wars of the sixteenth century, for example, would gain little by concentrating on the psychological and sociological origins of religion. These things may be part of the total picture; but they are hardly a priority. Similarly, the best questions to ask about the supernatural in early modern England are questions about meaning. The supernatural beliefs of Tudor and Stuart people are best understood from within their own frame of reference, and this involves the deferral, as far as possible, of less immediate questions about whether these beliefs were true.

The marvels described by Bale and Foxe, and similar wonders that prolifer-ated in Elizabethan and Stuart England, belonged to a world of meaning that is worth understanding in its own right. This world of meaning also framed other events, such as the reform of popular culture, the rise and decline of witch trials, and the religious conflicts that culminated in the English civil wars. By approaching the supernatural beliefs of the period on their own terms, it becomes easier to explain the actions of the men and women who participated in these events.

Thinking with spirits

How did the world of unseen spirits and magical influences affect Tudor and Stuart thought? Here it is necessary to lay aside modern assumptions about the supposed irrationality and "superstition" of the past. English magicians like John Dee and Simon Forman, experts on angels such as John Salkeld and Henry Lawrence, and demonologists like Richard Bernard and John Gaule lived in a world largely untouched by what would later be called "scientific rationalism"; but this did not make their ideas and arguments irrational.[13] As the historian Stuart Clark has shown, it was possible to adopt carefully logical positions on a subject such as witchcraft within the parameters of early modern assumptions.[14] Nor did belief in spirits preclude sceptical enquiry. Indeed, English writers on *maleficium* − the harmful magic attributed to witches − were normally cautious in their evaluation of the available evidence, while they accepted in principle that occult forces could inflict suffering on individuals and that demons were active in the world.

Generally speaking, the belief that the cosmos was populated by invisible powers expanded the possibilities of early modern thought, while retaining the same kind of naturalistic explanations that are available today. The work of the Stuart psy-chologist Robert Burton exemplifies this point. In his *Anatomy of Melancholy* (1621), Burton proposed a model of mental illness that was based robustly on the known facts of human physiology. Following the medical conventions of his time, he attributed unhealthy states of mind to a surfeit, or imbalance, of the humour known as black bile. It was the action of black bile that produced the groundless fear and sadness that characterised "melancholy". Moreover, this medical explanation extended into experiences that might, if misunderstood, be taken as supernatural. For instance, the melancholy brain could produce distressing hallucinations that suggested the presence of demons; worse still, it might succumb to the kind of despair associated with abandonment by God and damnation. Burton sought to relieve those who suffered from such symptoms by pointing to their probable origin: "to show them the causes whence they proceed, not from devils as they suppose, or that they are bewitched or forsaken of God . . . but from natural and inward causes".[15] He consistently emphasised these "inward causes" of melancholy in order to ease the distress of its sufferers.[16] In his analysis of these things, Burton echoed the views of other Protestant writers: both Reginald Scot and Samuel Harsnett, the future Archbishop of York, observed that melancholy could induce baseless fears and visions of demons.[17]

But Burton's commitment to this-worldly explanations for mental illness was leavened with other possibilities. Like his contemporaries, he was aware that unseen powers could operate through natural processes: indeed, it was axiomatic that God pursued His purposes through the ordinary flow of nature.[18] With divine permission, lesser spirits could also direct natural forces to their own ends. In the case of melancholy, Burton acknowledged that Satan used black bile as an indirect means to trouble the human mind. This humour was "his ordinary engine" for inducing despair, and consequently named "the Devil's bath".[19] Thus the causes of mental illness could be both physical and demonic.[20] Moreover, Burton also accepted that Satan could sometimes intervene directly in human minds. He did so by introducing his own thoughts into a person's imagination. Such thoughts were terrible and shocking, and designed by their originator to produce desperation and fear:

> The Devil is still ready to corrupt, trouble and divert our souls, to suggest . . . ungodly, profane, monstrous and wicked conceits. . . . The Devil commonly suggests things opposite to nature, opposite to God and His word, impious, absurd, such as a man would never of himself, or could not conceive, they strike terror and horror into the parties' own hearts.[21]

Thus, Burton's preference for medical explanations for mental illness was tempered by his knowledge of the Devil's ability to disturb human minds, both indirectly through the mechanism of black bile and directly through the planting of "blasphemous thoughts". Although he returned constantly to the physical causes of melancholy, he nonetheless admitted the influence of otherworldly powers.

It is sometimes claimed that people who lived before the emergence of modern science believed in the supernatural because they were unable to explain physical phenomena. The example of Robert Burton suggests that the situation was rather different and considerably more complex. Burton and his contemporaries did not lack explanations for the world they saw around them; but their acceptance of an invisible realm of spirits meant that their explanations did not necessarily end in the physical world. The ordinary and otherworldly causes of things sometimes coalesced, as in Burton's account of black bile as "the Devil's bath". In this sense there was, in the words of Peter Marshall and Alexandra Walsham, a "supernatural hyper-reality threaded through the natural order of creation".[22] Additionally, invisible powers could act directly in the physical world – like the demonic thoughts that blasted human minds. As a consequence, supernatural beliefs both complemented and extended this-worldly knowledge: they increased rather than diminished the fund of available explanations.

The acceptance of the supernatural could also, of course, complicate attempts to understand the world. When a scholar such as Burton sought to explain the medical and psychological causes of melancholy, he could not ignore the possible agency of invisible spirits; and he was consequently obliged to reach beyond the kind of naturalistic explanations that he normally favoured. Only a determined attempt to exclude such factors from natural philosophy – such as that pursued by Thomas Hobbes in the middle years of the seventeenth century – could produce a fully this-worldly account of human experience. The profoundly religious culture of Tudor and Stuart England, in which the Bible furnished ample evidence of the existence and activity of spirits, ensured that such thoroughgoing naturalism was rare.

The complexity engendered by speculations about the supernatural increased when an extraordinary event could be interpreted in multiple ways. In a plague sermon in Westmorland in 1599, Richard Leake described no fewer than four different explanations that had been advanced for the pestilence, including both medical and magical theories; he then informed his audience that it was a punishment from God.[23] Similarly, a convulsive sickness could be understood as a natural malady or a divine judgement, or both at once; it could also be evidence of bewitchment or demonic possession. The appearance of an angel might be a delusion induced by melancholy or be a messenger from God. Thus it was possible, in the caustic words of Thomas Hobbes, "that the same thing may be a miracle to one and not to another".[24]

The designation of a supernatural event depended on the larger context in which it took place. This often involved a narrative structure – or at least a sequence of occurrences from which a narrative could be made. In the case of divine judgements or warnings, such narratives provided the setting in which remarkable events were understood. On 5 May 1601, for example, Lady Margaret Hoby of Hackness in Yorkshire wrote in her diary an extended description of a two-headed calf. This was the kind of prodigy that featured often in accounts of "signs and wonders" in late Elizabethan and early Stuart England. Hoby was clearly very interested in the creature and had travelled to visit it;

but she did not read any supernatural meaning into the animal's birth. Later that year, however, on 26 December, Hoby recorded the wounding of a young man in a violent brawl; and on this occasion she was emphatic that the incident was a sign from God. The entry in her diary explains why she came to this view:

> This judgement is worth noting, this young man being extraordinarily profane, as once causing a horse to be brought into the church of God, and there christening him with a name, which horrible blasphemy the Lord did not leave unrevenged, even in this world, for [an] example to others.

While the birth of the monstrous calf was, perhaps, a more obvious "wonder", the young man's fate had supernatural significance because of the larger story of his life. As he was a notorious blasphemer, it was probably not lost on Lady Hoby that his injury was also appropriate to his offence: a pikestaff pierced his brain and left him unable to speak.[25]

The physical location of events could also affect their meaning. A strange light reported in a marsh or wood assumed a different significance to the same phenomenon in a graveyard or a church. The unexpected peal of a bell at night might indicate the presence of a demon or a divine summons to repentance, depending in part on the place from which it issued. When a bell tolled mysteriously in a pre-Reformation priory converted to a family home in Earls Colne in Essex around 1628, its evocation of the Catholic past implied a diabolical origin. Accordingly, the godly minister Thomas Shepherd cast out the evil spirit responsible. In contrast, the spectral ringing of bells from a church tower in Ferrybridge in Yorkshire in 1659 was read as a call to the community to amend its ways.[26] Occasionally, it is possible to chart the responses of people in different regions to the same portentous occurrence. On a European scale, Jennifer Spinks has examined the interpretations of a comet sighted across the borders of French and German territories in 1556. She notes that the starry messenger was connected to the fates of particular places from which it was viewed, though the desire to obtain "clear meanings for wondrous signs" was shared across the communities to which it appeared.[27]

While the narrative context and location of an unusual event could shape its interpretation, the prior assumptions of those that encountered it were also important. Here it should be noted that various different, and competing, structures of belief were available in early modern England. The most important formal distinction was between Roman Catholicism and Protestantism; and within both confessions a spectrum of positions was available. Francis Young has argued that "English Catholics were not significantly different from their non-Catholic neighbours in their attitudes to the weird, the invisible and the uncanny".[28] There were, however, nuances in the treatment of supernatural phenomena across the religious divide. Both Protestant and Catholic writers emphasised the role of the Devil as a spirit of temptation, for example, but Catholics tended to give him greater freedom of action.[29] In one area at least, Protestant piety departed dramatically from Catholic teachings on the realm of spirits: the established church denounced as unbiblical the intercessory powers attributed to saints, and therefore it dismissed appearances of "the holy dead" as delusions, counterfeits or demonic masquerades. On the Catholic side, the visions and miracles associated with saints remained a lively and central part of religious life.[30]

Another axis of division was between the beliefs of educated people and those of ordinary men and women. There is some danger in distinguishing too sharply between "elite" and "popular culture" in this period: indeed, several scholars have noted the interpenetration of the two.[31] In some areas of supernatural belief it seems that learned opinion derived from common custom. The practice of divination from the galls of wasps – or "oak apples" – was described in 1579 as "the countryman's astrology, which they have long observed for truth".[32] But the same method was commended by the Elizabethan magus Simon Forman.[33] Similarly, the physician Richard Napier collected cures for bewitchment that circulated in his community, and he may have used them in his practice.[34] It appears, nonetheless, that the supernatural beliefs of ordinary people sometimes diverged from those of their more learned contemporaries. While English theologians emphasised the intangible nature of both good and wicked spirits, these creatures were robustly physical when they appeared in cheap print. The belief in fairies, hobgoblins and imps, and other terrestrial spirits such as "Robin Goodfellow", was increasingly dismissed by educated men in the 1600s. At least one contemporary observer, the historian John Aubrey, associated such beliefs with the illiterate culture of English villagers, and their demise to the advance of education. Aubrey claimed that printed books "have put all the old fables out of doors: and the divine art of printing . . . [has] frightened away Robin Goodfellow and the fairies".[35] The association between fairies and oral culture, and the exclusion of the latter from more-educated circles, was conveyed in references to "old wives' tales" in seventeenth-century books.

It is tempting for modern readers to assume that the distancing of educated opinion from the beliefs of ordinary people marked the advent of scientific rationalism in Tudor and Stuart England. This temptation should be fought. It is more accurate to say that different strands of belief, including the oral traditions that still flourished in much of the country, produced diverse interpretations of supernatural phenomena; the shared acceptance of a world of spirits was largely undisturbed, though different communities populated this world in various ways. The fate of English fairies illustrates this well. While some writers rejected all reports of fairies as delusions or idle tales, others retained the possibility that they were sometimes real but deceiving spirits. Thus, the future James I wrote in 1597 that demons could disguise themselves as fairies to conceal their true nature.[36] In the same vein, John Aubrey referred in 1696 to "those demons that we call fairies".[37] Around 1712 this view was echoed by the owner of an annotated copy of Martin Luther's *Table Talk*, now held in Worcester Cathedral Library: besides Luther's account of a demonic *succubus*, the author noted that fairies were "a sort of devil somewhat partaking of human nature".[38] It is clear that such men did not regard fairies as impossible figments: rather, their assumptions about the cosmos led them to identify them as wicked spirits.

While there was no retreat from supernaturalism in sixteenth- and seventeenth-century England, perceptions of the "invisible world" did change in important ways during the period. Broadly speaking, the official understanding of the unseen kingdom of spirits was simplified, removing all entities that were not found in the Bible. At the same time, a providential model of natural and human affairs became increasingly dominant, emphasising the complete (and often inscrutable) sovereignty of God. Perhaps paradoxically, this was accompanied by an intensification of anxiety about Satan and by the emergence of the prince of darkness as a pervasive spirit of temptation. These developments made an uneven impact on English society as a whole, with many older traditions surviving, and even flourishing, in the religious practices of ordinary people. The changes outlined here flowed from the protracted and complex process by which the Protestant faith was established in England.

The supernatural in the English Reformation

The movement for church reform in the sixteenth century, which during the 1530s acquired the name "Protestant", had at its core two ideas that unsettled traditional ideas about the supernatural: the sufficiency of scripture, and the absolute sovereignty of God. Following the German reformers of the 1520s, the earliest English Protestants insisted on the primacy of the Bible in determining religious truths. In the words of John Frith in 1531, the scriptures were the "perfect touchstone that judgeth and examineth all things".[39] For Frith and the first generation of reformers, the "sure method" of testing the precepts of medieval Christianity against the contents of the Bible produced dramatic effects. The doctrine of purgatory – the place of temporary suffering set aside for souls after death – was mentioned nowhere in the Bible; nor was the power of saints to protect and heal those who offered them earthly devotion. Such teachings were unwarranted additions to Christianity, whose true spirit was preserved in the New Testament; and only the scouring of these accretions could restore the church to its original purity.

As a model for religious reform, the principle of *sola scriptura* – or "by scripture alone" – required a drastic winnowing of the world of spirits. One major casualty was the returning dead. During the late Middle Ages, the church had nurtured the cult of saints, whereby the spirits of the holy dead offered guidance, protection and intercession on behalf of their living devotees, often in return for pious acts such as the completion of a pilgrimage; this cult was associated with the physical relics of the saints, to which were ascribed supernatural power. In the acidic phrase of another first-generation English Protestant, John Bale, the people were thereby "nursed up from their youth in calling upon dead men and images".[40] In parallel with these beliefs, the concept of purgatory meant that the spirits of ordinary women and men also received the attention of the living, who sought remission from suffering on their behalf through the benedictions of the church. The abolition of purgatory as unscriptural erased, at a stroke, all communication between mortals and the dead. This meant not only that the purgatorial anguish of departed souls was no longer acknowledged but also that the appearance of ghosts – which were traditionally believed to be spirits released briefly from purgatory – was dismissed as impossible.

As well as saints and ghosts, a colourful assembly of terrestrial spirits was expelled from the Protestant cosmos. As the church had expanded in the Middle Ages, it had absorbed and accommodated an array of non-Christian entities within a broadly religious view of the world. These beings coexisted with the overtly Christian powers in the realm of spirits, sustained by folk traditions and generally tolerated, or even acknowledged, by members of the medieval clergy. Fairies and hobgoblins inhabited woodlands and remote hills, but could also venture into human dwellings to interact with mortals. Village magic sometimes involved the summoning of fairies, such as those employed by the Dorset "cunning man" John Walsh in the 1560s to find evidence of bewitchment.[41] In a famous passage in *The Discoverie of Witchcraft* (1584), the Kentish demonologist Reginald Scot named over thirty spirits which, he claimed, stocked the stories told by maidservants to children and lingered in the imaginations of credulous adults.[42] For Scot and his Protestant contemporaries, such "bugs" were remnants of an ignorant past. They had infested the long "night of superstition" encouraged by the unreformed church, and they persisted in the imagination of ordinary people. When Samuel Harsnett repeated Scot's list of spirits in 1603, he placed them in the "popish mist" that "had befogged the eyes of our poor people".[43]

The expulsion of fairies, ghosts and saints did not decimate the unseen world, however. This was because the doctrine of *sola scriptura* vouchsafed the existence of some spirits while it abolished others. The activity of good and wicked angels was emphatically endorsed by scripture. In both the Old and the New Testaments, angels appeared frequently to offer assistance, guidance and comfort to mortals. In the Acts of the Apostles, for example, an angel freed Christ's followers from prison (Acts 5:19), and St Paul was informed by an angel that he and his brethren enjoyed divine protection (Acts 27:22–4). Such credentials ensured that angels kept their place in the supernatural universe of reformed Christianity. One recent study of the subject has concluded that "a persistent belief in angels as protectors and ministers was widespread in early modern England"; indeed, they were a "ubiquitous feature" of religious life.[44] Similarly, the Devil and demons were entrenched in the biblical faith of English Protestants. The figure of Satan appeared very seldom in the Hebrew scriptures but assumed a major role in the New Testament; and the expulsion of evil spirits was the most common of the miracles attributed to Jesus. Thus both the Devil and his minions retained their position in the cosmos of the Reformation.

To what extent did angels take the place of medieval saints and did the Devil and demons usurp the role of fairies and "bugs"? The answers to this question are complex and shall occupy several pages of this book. It is clear that Protestants used the activity of good and evil angels to explain many supernatural occurrences that were previously attributed to other powers: the persistent appearance of ghosts, for instance, was often described as demonic trickery. But it is equally true that the reform of the world of spirits made only a partial impact on English culture, and many older beliefs and expectations survived long into the eighteenth century. The sustained campaign to eliminate the cult of saints was not combined with a similar effort to suppress the other spirits of the popular cosmos: rather, ghosts and fairies and their fellows were challenged on an *ad hoc* basis, when reformed doctrines came into conflict with traditional beliefs. Even the suppression of saints did not lead to angels simply assuming their roles. While angels possessed some of the protective and advisory qualities of the holy dead, they lacked the humanity that made the latter such attractive and credible mediators between heaven and earth; nor could they be supplicated as the saints had been, as reformed teaching viewed this practice as idolatrous. The "purification" of the invisible world was, inevitably, difficult and muddled and incomplete.

The complexities of Protestant engagement with the supernatural were illustrated painfully in a text written by the Yorkshire gentleman Edward Fairfax in 1621, following the apparent bewitchment of his eldest daughter, Helen. Fairfax prefaced his account with reflections on the "superstitious ignorance" that dominated the common people: "so many are the strange follies, rooted in the opinion of the vulgar, concerning the walking of souls in this or that house, the dancing of fairies on this rock or that mountain, the changing of infants in their cradles, and the like". Fairfax himself accepted the simplified biblical model of an active God and subordinate angels, both good and bad. So when his daughter succumbed to a trance-like illness in which she experienced visions of otherworldly figures, he was able to accept that her condition was "more than [a] natural disease". The source of her affliction was uncertain, however, as the spirits that haunted her bedside were diverse: they included the spectres of local women believed to be witches, ugly demons, and a "man of beauty incomparable" ringed with light, who claimed to offer spiritual comfort. Fairfax sought advice from the local clergy and spent nights discussing the apparitions with his daughter, before determining that she was the victim of witchcraft through the agency of evil spirits.[45]

The question of how to respond to such assaults related to the second major theme in reformed theology that challenged traditional ideas about the supernatural: the absolute sovereignty of God. In the words of the Oxford professor of divinity Edward Cradock, in 1582, "God only is the protector of the world, no one thing in heaven, or in all the earth, being exempted or privileged from the authority of His jurisdiction".[46] Alongside *sola scriptura*, the acceptance of God's unfettered command of the created universe underpinned Protestant attacks on medieval Christianity: it stripped away the intermediary role of the Catholic clergy and reduced the Mass to a kind of vainglorious magic – or "jiggery popery" – by which priests sought to compel an omnipotent God. As the abolition of intercessory saints underlined, this position also stripped supernatural beings of the power to stay or sway the divine hand. In the Protestant cosmos, all creatures, both spiritual and mortal, were subject to the Lord's will and could do nothing without His permission.

Much flowed from this perspective. The belief in God's complete sovereignty dominated learned attitudes towards witchcraft, for example. From the first English treatise on the subject, Reginald Scot's *Discoverie of Witchcraft* in 1584, all the country's major demonologists agreed that the Devil's involvement in the crime required divine consent. Thus the harm attributed to witches – or, more properly, demons acting with permission from God – always served the Lord's purpose. The appropriate response to this harm was prayerful self-reflection. Richard Bernard set out this conventional view in his advice to jurors in witchcraft cases in 1627: "Seeing God's hand upon us (who does not willingly grieve us, if we provoke him not) this must draw us to a searching of our ways [and] to the acknowledgement of our sins."[47] This approach did not rule out witch trials entirely: after all, deliberate association with wicked spirits was a crime condemned in scripture.[48] But as Bernard and others pointed out, those that God chose to trouble in this way should not make allegations of witchcraft to relieve their suffering. Nor should people look to *maleficia* as a cause of affliction when their own sins were probably responsible: Richard Leake made this point in his plague sermon in 1599, which dismissed those who blamed the epidemic on "the devilish practices of witches".[49] Since witchcraft allegations were based mainly on the harm supposedly caused by suspects, such messages probably contributed to the generally low level of persecutions in England.

On a larger scale, the insistence of reformers on the absolute sovereignty of God produced one of the most characteristic and pervasive ideas of the English Reformation: the doctrine of providence. This held that the divine hand not only guided all earthly and supernatural events but also did so for the benefit of the Lord's servants. Viewed in this light, the universe was a system of benevolence – at least for those whom God chose to favour.[50] In a catechism printed in 1583, the Essex minister George Gifford affirmed the boundlessness of this loving dispensation, which left "no place unto fortune or chance, no not in the smallest things".[51] Arthur Dent comforted ordinary Christians with the same message in *The Plaine Mans Path-way to Heaven* in 1601: "Our Heavenly Father has as great care for the preservation of His creatures as once He had for their creation."[52] In its original formulation, the concept of providence was intended to give comfort to believers in the most general terms: the ways of God were intricate and frequently puzzling, and it was neither possible nor desirable for mortals to seek God's purpose in the details of everyday life.[53] Unsurprisingly, however, this application of the doctrine was eroded as individuals looked for indications of divine favour – or disapprobation – in particular events, especially when these events were remarkable or painful. The idea of "special providences" gave play to this desire: unlike the larger pattern of divine benevolence, a special providence was a particular event that offered guidance to the Christian community or passed judgement on the sins or virtues of individuals.

Providential thinking offered a framework for understanding supernatural events. Reports of occurrences beyond "the ordinary course of nature" were easily assimilated within the system of divine judgements, forewarnings and approbations. In 1642, for example, the schoolmaster John Vicars assembled a collection of "prodigies" recorded in the previous twenty-five years. These culminated in a spectral battle fought in the sky above the town of Aldeburgh in Suffolk:

> There was heard in the air, and evidently seen, a mighty sound of drums beating very loud, after which was also heard at the same time a long and fierce peal of small shot, as of muskets and such like, and then as it were a discharging of great ordnance. . . . But after all this, there was for certain suddenly heard a most joyful noise of sweet music, and of sundry rare musical instruments sounding in a most melodious manner, for a good space together, and at last it all concluded with a most harmonious noise, as it were of delicate ringing of well-tuned bells.

To Vicars the providential meaning of this event was clear. The sounds of battle echoed the nation's collapse into civil war in the summer of 1642, a calamity itself sent by God to punish the moral laxity and irreligion of the preceding decades. The sweet music that followed betokened better times ahead. The war would be brief and yield "a glorious peace and perfect reformation". Thus Vicars ended his account on a note of pious hope and resignation: Christians should "wait on the Lord" for the harmonious outcome He had promised with the music in the sky, which would come "in His due time, and by that way which is best pleasing to His most wise providence".[54]

As well as providing a model for understanding supernatural events, providence could also invest less dramatic occurrences with supernatural meaning. At a general level, the doctrine conferred religious significance on everything that happened on earth. The whole process of history became, in this sense, the unfolding of a spiritual plan. More narrowly, sufficiently dramatic natural incidents could be interpreted as special providences. Thus Margaret Hoby discerned the hand of God in a violent brawl in 1601. In a similar vein, John Vicars found supernatural purpose in ostensibly this-worldly events. Indeed, one of the most striking things about his catalogue of "prodigies and apparitions" was how few truly otherworldly events it contained. Apart from the spectral combat above Aldeburgh, all of Vicars' prodigies were explicable in naturalistic terms, both in his own day and in ours. They included a comet, two dramatic thunderstorms and the birth of conjoined twins. In these and many other accounts of "wonders", the supernatural element depended on the assumptions of the beholders and the framing of a convincing narrative. Thus the doctrine of providence could move in two directions: it could validate reports of events "beyond nature", such as armies clashing in the sky, and also interpret a "fearful storm of wind, lightning and thunder" as a divine judgement.[55]

The tendency to read earthly events as providential was complemented by Protestant biblicism, and especially speculations about the momentous occurrences predicted in the Book of Revelation. When John Bale published the first reformed commentary on this text in English in the 1540s, he presented a theory of history as a struggle between the false church of Antichrist, who had acquired the papacy in the seventh century, and a remnant of true Christians that maintained the uncorrupted gospel. The latest phase of this conflict – equated to the opening of the sixth seal in Revelation – was the ongoing movement to reform the Catholic church, which would culminate in the opening of the seventh seal and the return of Christ.[56] Later English reformers developed similar models of apocalyptic history, and this framework underpinned John Foxe's classic account of the Protestant past in *Actes and Monuments of These Latter and Perillous Days* (1563), better known as the *Book of Martyrs*. Such texts extended the providential understanding of human affairs into the past, and fed expectations of supernatural wonders to come. The astronomical marvels of the age of the sixth seal, when the moon would become "as blood" and stars fall to the earth (Rev. 6:12–3), invited comparison with anomalous events in the skies above Tudor and Stuart England.

The providential understanding of the recent past, and the apocalyptic future, contributed to another feature of the supernatural cosmos of the Reformation: the emergence of new attitudes towards the Devil. Broadly speaking, Satan became both more powerful and less tangible in this period and identified increasingly as a spirit of temptation in this period, and was identified increasingly as a spirit of temptation. This was partly because of the dichotomous framework through which the reformers perceived the world, in which the various forces of Antichrist surrounded the remnant of true believers. As the Lord's enemies multiplied in numbers and might, the influence of their unseen leader also increased. In a sermon in 1655, Francis Raworth likened the Devil to a lion chained to God's hand; but to many English Protestants this chain seemed very long.[57] The waxing of Satan's power also corresponded to a new emphasis on his role as "the father of lies".[58] This accompanied the emphasis on "false belief" that characterised confessional conflict. On both sides of the divide, the seductive power of demonic ideas, usually masquerading as truth, offered the best explanation for the persistence of false religion. It was Satan's policy, observed the preacher Henry Symons in 1657, to rub "our temples with his opium of poisonous suggestions".[59] The Devil and his spiritual train also benefited from the purging of the non-biblical inhabitants of the supernatural world. As specialists in deceit, demons offered a plausible explanation for continuing reports of apparitions that could not be regarded as angelic. Thus, they were sometimes presented as the spirits lurking behind reports of saints, ghosts and fairies, and the innumerable "bugbears" of popular belief.

In their efforts to purge the church of non-biblical accretions, English reformers constructed a simplified model of the unseen world and its role in earthly affairs: God governed a realm of good and wicked angels and exercised unfettered power throughout the universe. This model explained events "beyond nature" and extended spiritual meaning into human history. The intricacies of this vision, and its relationship to the beliefs of the wider population, will occupy the rest of this book.

Notes

1 For histories of magic published in the seventeenth century, see Lauren Kassell, "'All was this Land Fill'd of Faerie', or Magic and the Past in Early Modern England", *Journal of the History of Ideas*, Vol. 67, No. 1 (January 2006), 107–22; for Raleigh and Vaughan, 111–2, 114–7.

2 Robert Bartlett, *The Natural and the Supernatural in the Middle Ages* (Cambridge University Press: 2008), 9–16.

3 William Perkins, *A Discourse of the Damned Art of Witchcraft* (1608), 14.

4 Scot's influence has recently been reappraised by S. F. Davies, who rightly notes that he shared the providential assumptions of most other English demonologists. Nonetheless, Scot's scepticism about magic and denial of incorporeal spirits placed him outside the mainstream of European thought on these matters. S. F. Davies, "The Reception of Reginald Scot's *Discovery of Witchcraft: Witchcraft, Magic, and Radical Religion*", *Journal of the History of Ideas*, Vol. 74, No. 3 (July 2013), 381–401. For the reception of Hobbes, see S. I. Mintz, *The Hunting of Leviathan: Seventeenth-Century Reactions to the Materialism and Moral Philosophy of Thomas Hobbes* (Cambridge University Press: 1962).

5 For an insightful excavation of Forman's career, see Lauren Kassell, *Medicine and Magic in Elizabethan London* (Oxford University Press: 2005).

6 Bodleian Library, Oxford, Ashmole MS 1436, 6*v*.

7 For these and other wonders in Tudor martyrology, see Susannah Brietz Monta, *Martyrdom and Literature in Early Modern England* (Cambridge University Press: 2009), chapter 3, quotation, 62.

8 John Foxe, *Actes and Monuments of These Latter and Perillous Days* (1583 ed.), book 8.

9 E. H. Carr, *What Is History?* (Macmillan: 1961), 74–5.

10 Brad S. Gregory, "The Other Confessional History: On Secular Bias in the Study of Religion", *History and Theory*, Vol. 45, No. 4 (December 2006), 132–49.

11 Tor Egil Førland, "God, Science, and Historical Explanation", *History and Theory*, Vol. 47, No. 4 (December 2008), 483–94.

12 Gregory makes a distinction between explaining things and understanding them, and favours the latter. This is an attractive position, but it is hard to see how the two concepts can remain entirely separate. Understanding the meanings that people attached to events is, presumably, part of the larger project of historical explanation. On this see Gregory, "Other Confessional History", 134, and Førland, "God", 490.

13 Here it is useful to distinguish between rationality and truth. On this I follow Robert Bartlett's suggestion that "rational belief does not mean true belief. It means belief that is in harmony with the evidence and in harmony with other major beliefs". Robert Bartlett, *Trial by Fire and Water: The Medieval Judicial Ordeal* (Oxford University Press: 1986), 161–2.

14 See, for example, Stuart Clark, "The Rational Witchfinder: Conscience, Demonological Naturalism and Popular Superstitions", in Stephen Pumfrey, Paolo Rossi and Maurice Slawinski, eds., *Science, Culture and Popular Belief in Renaissance Europe* (Manchester University Press: 1991).

15 Robert Burton, *The Anatomy of Melancholy* (1621), part 1, section 3, member 3, subsection 1.

16 For Burton's emphasis on the internal causes of mental distress, see Angus Gowland, *The Worlds of Renaissance Melancholy: Robert Burton in Context* (Cambridge University Press: 2006), especially chapter 1, section 9.

17 Reginald Scot, *The Discoverie of Witchcraft* (1584), book 3, chapter 11; Samuel Harsnett, *A Declaration of Egregious Popish Impostures* (1603), 133.

18 This idea flowed from the doctrine of providence, which is discussed in the following section and examined in detail in chapter 2.

19 Burton, *Anatomy*, part 3, section 4, member 2, subsection 3.

20 A tract published in 1653 made a similar point. The author explained that "the presence of the Devil may consist with the presence of a disease, and evil humor. . . . So that learned physicians think that the Devil is frequently mixed with such distempers." *The Black and Terrible Warning Piece* (1653), 4–5.

21 Burton, *Anatomy*, part 3, section 4, member 2, subsection 6.

22 Peter Marshall and Alexandra Walsham, eds., *Angels in the Early Modern World* (Cambridge University Press: 2006), 11–12.

23 Leake is quoted in Mary Abbott, *Life Cycles in England* (Routledge: 1996), 28.

24 Thomas Hobbes, *Leviathan* (1651), part 3, chapter 37.

25 Joanna Moody, ed., *The Private Life of an Elizabethan Lady: The Diary of Lady Margaret Hoby, 1599–1605* (Sutton: 1998), 146, 173–4.

26 For these incidents, see Dolly MacKinnon, "Ringing of the Bells by Four White Spirits: Two Seventeenth-Century English Earwitness Accounts of the Supernatural in Print Culture", in Jennifer Spinks and Dagmar Eichberger, eds., *Religion, the Supernatural and Visual Culture in Early Modern Europe* (Brill: 2015).

27 Jennifer Spinks, "Signs that Speak: Reporting the 1556 Comet Across French and German Borders", in Spinks and Eichberger, *Religion*, 235.

28 Francis Young, *English Catholics and the Supernatural, 1553–1829* (Ashgate: 2013), 2.

29 See chapter 4 for Protestant and Catholic attitudes towards Satan. On the reluctance of the latter to treat the Devil merely as God's executioner of the sinful, see Young, *English Catholics*, 43.

30 For the survival and polemical exploitation of saintly miracles and relics, see Alexandra Walsham, "Miracles and the Counter Reformation Mission to England", *Historical Journal*, Vol. 46, No. 4 (December 2003), 779–815.

31 Alexandra Walsham, for instance, has argued that providential thinking sometimes bridged the gap between reformed theology and English popular culture. For example, shows of collective penitence after natural disasters produced "temporary alliances" between the godly and the larger community. Alexandra Walsham, *Providence in Early Modern England* (Oxford University Press: 1999), 166.

32 Thomas Lupton, *A Thousand Notable Things of Sundry Sortes* (1579), 52.

33 Forman observed that oak apples replete with flies foreshadowed a pestilence. Bodleian Library, Oxford, MS Ashmole 1436, 41*v*.

34 Napier copied a version of the traditional charm against witchcraft "Three biters hast thy bitten", which is examined in chapter 7. Bodleian Library, Oxford, Ashmole MS 1432, VII, 16.

35 John Aubrey, quoted in Richard M. Dorson, *The British Folklorists: A History* (University of Chicago Press: 1968), 6.

36 James VI, *Daemonologie* (1597), book 3, chapter 5.

37 Minor White Latham, *The Elizabethan Fairies: The Fairies of Folklore and the Fairies of Shakespeare* (Columbia University Press: 1930), 141.

38 The author of the annotations was probably John Humphries, who purchased the book in 1708. The passage concerned was "How the Devil Can Deceive People and Beget Children", in Martin Luther, *Colloquia Mensalia* (1652), 386.

39 John Frith, *A Disputacion of Purgatorye* (1531), preface.

40 John Bale, *The Vocacyon of Johan Bale*, ed. Peter Happé and John King (Renaissance English Text Society: 1990), 48.

41 *The Examination of John Walsh* (1566), in Marion Gibson, ed., *Early Modern Witches: Witchcraft Cases in Contemporary Writing* (Routledge: 2000), 28.

42 Reginald Scot, *The Discoverie of Witchcraft* (1584), book 7, chapter 15. Diane Purkiss offers a critical reading of Scot's list of bugs in *Fairies and Fairy Stories: A History* (Allen Lane: 2000), 172–6. The fate of Scot's creatures during the Reformation is examined in chapter 6 of this book.

43 Harsnett, *Declaration*, 135–6.

44 Laura Sangha, *Angels and Belief in England, 1480–1700* (Pickering & Chatto: 2012), 2, 106.

45 Fairfax's narrative, "A Discourse of Witchcraft", was published in the *Miscellanies* of the Philobiblon Society, 1858–9, Vol. 5; quotations, 16, 17, 103.

46 Edward Cradock, *The Shippe of Assured Safetie* (1572), 67.

47 Richard Bernard, *A Guide to Grand-Jury Men* (1627), 10.

48 See, for instance, Lev. 19:31, 20:6; Deut. 18:11; 2 Kings 21:6, 23:24.

49 Abbot, *Life Cycles*, 28.

50 For the prevalence of providential thinking in early modern England, see Blair Worden, "Providence and Politics in Cromwellian England", *Past & Present*, No. 109 (November 1985), and Alexandra Walsham, *Providence*.

51 George Gifford, *A Cathechisme Conteining the Summe of Christian Religion* (1583), f A5r-A5v.

52 Arthur Dent, *The Plaine Mans Path-way to Heaven* (1601), 111.

53 John Calvin, accordingly, presented providence as a source of comfort to Christians while reserving its precise operation to the unknowable wisdom of God. Calvin, *Institutes of the Christian Religion*, book 1, chapter 17, section 9.

54 John Vicars, *Prodigies & Apparitions, or Englands Warning Piece* (1642), 51–3, 56–7.

55 Vicars, *Prodigies*, 31.

56 Bale's commentary was published as *The Image of Both Churches* between 1545 and 1548, during a period of exile in the Netherlands.

57 Francis Raworth, *Jacob's Ladder, or the Protectorship of Sion* (1655), 27.

58 This name was adapted from John 8:44: "He was a murderer from the beginning, and abode not in the truth, because there is no truth in him. When he speaketh a lie, he speaketh of his own: for he is a liar, and the father of it."

59 Symons is quoted in Nathan Johnstone, *The Devil and Demonism in Early Modern England* (Cambridge University Press: 2006), 81.

2

THE FOUNDATIONS OF SUPERNATURAL BELIEF

The world of *Doctor Faustus*

In the shuddering opening scene of the earliest English version of the story of Dr Faustus, the magician stands alone at a crossroads in a dense wood. He marks out a protective circle around him and summons the demon Mephistopheles. There follows a consternation of crashing trees, and the forest fills with a noise like the roaring of lions. Then suddenly a wicked spirit appears, racing around the perimeter of the circle "as if a thousand wagons had been running together on paved stones".[1] In the play that Christopher Marlowe based on the same text, and probably composed around 1589, Faustus conjures Mephistopheles with a florid Latin incantation. The creature comes first as a monster and then, apparently at the sorcerer's behest, in the more palatable guise of a Franciscan friar.[2]

Faustus' liaison in the forest illustrates the elements that underpinned super-natural belief in early modern England and will be considered in this chapter. Both Marlowe's play and the text that inspired it, which survives in a 1592 edition entitled *The Historie of the Damnable Life and Deserved Death of Doctor John Faustus*, were based on allegedly real events.[3] The original Faustus was a student of theology turned fortune teller at Wittenberg in Saxony; his name was linked to the Devil in the 1540s, and the story of his satanic pact, which emerged around 1580, became the centrepiece of the first book based on his life in 1587. The tale was emphatically Protestant: indeed, the Lutheran reformer Philip Melanchthon claimed to have met the magician, and produced one of the earliest accounts of his sinful career.[4] As importantly, the various ingredients of the mature version of the story conformed to the expectations of early modern people: Faustus' encounter with Satan took place in an intellectual, social and physical environment that most Elizabethans would have found realistic.

For modern readers, the most striking supposition in the story is the existence of spirits. This was not only accepted by the original audience for Marlowe's play but also the cause of some anxiety. One performance in Tudor Exeter was abandoned after the conjuration scene, when it was feared that a demon had actually appeared on stage. The godly polemicist William Prynne later reported a similar episode in his tract against the immorality of the theatre in 1632: members of the audience, he claimed, had described to him the manifestation of an evil spirit during the play, "to the great amazement of both the actors and spectators".[5] While the summoning of demons was the most sensational (and risky) feature of Marlowe's work, it contained other conventional assumptions about the supernatural. The most subtle of these was the operation of providence. At his first appearance, Mephistopheles tells an unbelieving Faustus that he has, in fact, no power to conjure him at all: he came because he heard the magician blaspheming God and saw the chance to crush his soul. The demon, in turn, cannot harm anyone unless the Lord permits him to do so: this is made explicit later in the play, when a pious old man proves to be impervious to his assaults.[6] The fate of Faustus and every character in the drama – both human and supernatural – is scripted by the divine hand.

Faustus' encounter with Satan touched on other themes in sixteenth-century religious culture. The scene in the wood in the *Damnable Life* is drenched in the imagery of the apocalypse – the events of the Last Judgement prefigured in the Book of Revelation. Mephistopheles appears first as "a mighty dragon" in the air, echoing the monster in Revelation 12. This is followed by "a monstrous cry in the wood, as if Hell had been opened, and all the tormented souls crying to God for mercy". Few readers would have missed the allusion to the final punishment of the damned.[7] This cosmic symbolism was combined with more mundane but equally familiar details about the location of the action. Faustus summons the demon at a crossroads in a forest, both places that were strongly associated with the supernatural.[8] In Marlowe's play the invocation takes place in "a solitary grove". In both texts the conjuration is performed at night, a time when occult influences were believed to be particularly strong. Marlowe was expressing a common sentiment with uncommon elegance when he called Satan the "regent of perpetual night".[9]

The assumptions that gave life to the story of Faust, making it a believable drama rather than a fantastical piece of entertainment, are also the subject of this chapter. The pages that follow address the intellectual context of supernatural beliefs, as well as the social and physical environment in which these beliefs were experienced and enacted. The first section examines the doctrine of providence, and the second the idea of apocalypse: both provided a religious framework in which otherworldly events made sense, and both conferred a higher meaning to the experiences of individuals and the community at large. The third section considers the operation of spirits and other unseen powers: these penetrated the imaginations, and sometimes the bodies, of men and women who accepted the occult as part of lived reality. The social world in which invisible forces could harm and heal existed beside a natural world that was charged with supernatural power. This is the subject of the last section. Together, these elements made the supernatural an integral part of early modern existence – as real as the sorcerers who occasionally ventured into woods to conjure spirits at night.

"The secret working hand": divine providence

The bargain that Faustus made with Mephistopheles did not quench his desire for salvation. Indeed, the prospect of redemption flickers throughout the magician's story and adds drama – and agony – to his unfolding fate. A good angel attends Faustus in Marlowe's play and promises that true repentance could still rescue his soul; and on several occasions the sorcerer himself appears to acknowledge this truth. But a darker reality is also revealed. In a moment of spiritual rallying, Faustus exclaims, "God will pity me if I repent". At once an evil angel replies: "Ay, but Faustus never shall repent". This response is accurate and icily precise. God could have spared Faustus if he had chosen to repent; but this outcome was not, it seems, part of the divine plan.[10]

Here Marlowe touched on a central theme in English religious culture: the irresistible purposes of God. The doctrine of providence held that the Lord determined all events in the cosmos and did so for the ultimate good of His servants. This process was conventionally understood in two ways. First, the doctrine of "general providence" described the unfolding of divine benevolence in the whole of creation. John Calvin commended this view of the doctrine as a source of comfort for Christians in a perilous and uncertain world. The leading European reformers were considerably more cautious, however, about the second application of the idea: the concept of so-called "special providences". These were specific events that revealed the divine will. Both Martin Luther and Calvin insisted that the details of God's intentions were unknowable – though in practice both they and their followers occasionally discerned divine meaning in earthly occurrences.[11] In England both versions of the doctrine were widely accepted, but they followed distinct patterns of historical development. The concept of general providence was acknowledged throughout the early modern period and remained a cornerstone of religion and science in the eighteenth and nineteenth centuries. The idea of special providences, however, achieved widespread acceptance in the reign of Elizabeth and came to dominate thinking about the supernatural in the middle decades of the seventeenth century; but it entered a long and fitful decline before the advance of scientific naturalism in the late 1600s.

In both manifestations, providential thinking was a complex business. The doctrine could create both reassurance and anxiety. The damnation of Faustus provides an elegant illustration. The magician's downfall clearly served a beneficent purpose: it punished a wicked man and warned others to avoid his sins. This message was pressed home in the final lines of Marlowe's play, which exhorted the wise not to "practice more than heavenly power permits".[12] But the story also implied that Faust, ultimately, had no control over his own life. Those moments in which his redemption seemed possible were, in truth, painful illusions. Still worse, God's orchestration of the whole process appeared to make him the author of suffering: Mephistopheles was merely God's tool. The theologians of Protestant England did not flinch from conclusions of this kind. Nonetheless, the issues raised by such arguments help to explain Calvin's warning against precise speculations in this area. It is easy to sympathise with the preacher Francis Raworth, who observed in 1655 that "a man may easily break his brains in studying the providences of God".[13]

Despite these difficulties, the doctrine of providence touched every aspect of English thought. Indeed, it offered the most comprehensive account of the universe that could be imagined. The divine plan extended both above and below the human world: into the kingdom of spirits and the smallest departments of animal life. As John Wilkins observed in 1649, providence directed "the multitude of affairs among men and angels".[14] It was one consequence of this belief that spirits of all kinds became agents of God, even those – such as Mephistopheles – that fiercely opposed this role. At the other end of the scale, even invertebrates served the divine plan. Preaching in 1615, Bezaleel Carter observed that the Lord commanded "the least worm and creeping thing", such as the parasites that killed King Herod (Acts 12:23).[15] In a treatise on apiary in 1657, Samuel Purchas found divine purpose in the details of insect behaviour. To Purchas, "God's power was no less in creating a little bee than a great lion", and His benevolence was visible "in the smallest and most ordinary matters" of nature.[16]

The doctrine also appealed at all levels of society. For the proselytisers of the English church, the idea of general providence provided a simple and comforting expression of the main theme of the Reformation: the supreme power of God. The concept of special providences was also attractive, not least because it preserved many aspects of traditional religion. As Alexandra Walsham has observed, the habit of seeking signs of divine warning, approval or condemnation had "a deep taproot in the medieval past" and retained a hold on much of the population.[17] Few doubted the assertion of a pamphlet published in 1577 that the Lord could reward the good in this life and scourge the wicked, "so that the residue might better be warned".[18] Moreover, the godly practice of offering public days of repentance after natural calamities recalled the penitential system of the Middle Ages, though such events were stripped of the allegedly magical elements of Catholicism.

The providential understanding of the world permitted accounts of wonderful events and extraordinary judgements, which probably held the imagination of ordinary Christians more than abstract works of religious instruction. A text printed in 1599, for example, described the apparently miraculous speech of a week-old baby before its death: the child repeatedly uttered the words "Oh my Lord".[19] As well as showing the Creator's boundless power, the story dramatised theological ideas: it emphasised the need for constant thankfulness to God and condemned the doctrine of some Anabaptists that infants were untouched by the Holy Ghost. The educational merit of such wonders were not lost on the author: readers would benefit, he noted, from "the astonishment which His divine majesty hath pleased to send us". Judgement tales were equally instructive. Like Protestant sermons, they reminded individuals of their sinfulness and called them to self-examination and repentance. A mysterious pestilence in the vicinity of Worcester in 1598 was presented in this way: according to one account, the disease was "sent us by God to call us to amendment of life". The writer called on individuals to examine their consciences in the light of the calamity, "and then no doubts God will send remorse . . . to draw us to a newness of life".[20]

As these examples suggest, providence also offered a way to deal with misfortune. Faith in God's unfailing and universal benevolence was, undoubtedly, a comfort to men and women faced with affliction: whatever bad things happened, the doctrine promised, all was ultimately for the best. The consoling nature of this idea helps to explain its appeal in the fragile environment of Tudor and Stuart England. It also provides one explanation for the widespread belief in special providences in the mid-1600s, during a period of intense military conflict: the civil wars created extraordinary suffering, with a *per capita* mortality rate that considerably exceeded the world wars of the twentieth century.[21] It was unsurprising in such circumstances for people to seek supernatural explanations for the disasters that befell them, and also to seek the consolation that their suffering would eventually result in good. In a metaphor used often in the period, the divine hand brought "light out of darkness".

At a more basic level, the idea of providence was a response to what theologians call the "problem of evil". This is the problem of explaining why innocents suffer in a world made by a loving and all-powerful God.[22] This not only was a question of abstract theology but was (and remains) a matter of concern to ordinary believers. The Protestant solution was bold. By affirming the absolute sovereignty of God, the reformers insisted that even the most painful and destructive events contained some divine purpose. The implications of this idea were often riddling. As Arthur Dent explained in 1601, God frequently showed love to the faithful by causing them pain: "He woundeth them, that He may heal them. He presseth them, that He may ease them. He maketh them cry, that afterwards they may laugh".[23] Conversely, the Lord sometimes allowed the wicked to prosper on earth in order to test the virtuous, or to punish other wrongdoers; but this temporary indulgence was followed by eternal pain in hell. The paths of divine justice could be snaky, as the preacher George Phillips reminded his audience in 1597.[24] The acceptance of the confounding nature of providence was, perhaps, the only way to square the doctrine with the unpleasant realities of life.

Sudden misfortunes illustrated the unpredictable movements of God's hand. In some cases, it seemed that notorious sinners were aptly visited by calamity: swearers were struck dumb, and drunkards drowned in vats of ale. Thomas Beard filled a volume with such vivid episodes in 1597. Indeed, his material was so plentiful that *The Theatre of Gods Judgements* was divided into sections describing the sudden and atrocious deaths of various kinds of offender, including Sabbath-breakers, blasphemers, magicians and "epicures and atheists". Nonetheless, Beard had to concede that dreadful things also happened to good Christians. Accordingly, he concluded with a chapter on "How the afflictions of the godly and punishments of the wicked differ".[25] In practice, it was exceedingly hard to tell. When a bolt of lightning blasted a God-fearing man in his bed in the Hampshire village of Holdenhurst in June 1613, the printed account of the tragedy sought to discern the Lord's purpose in it. Somewhat ingeniously, the author suggested that the man's death was a warning to sinners. "If this happened unto a man of so upright a conversation", he wrote, "what may befall you that sit day and night at the tavern?"[26]

The inscrutable God that shaped the fate of individuals also supervised whole communities. This was evident in collective blessings and chastisements, such as bounteous harvests or outbreaks of contagious disease. The Hebrew scriptures provided models for the providential government of large groups of people, such as the children of Israel. Like their biblical predecessors, English Protestants were both tested by hardship and succoured by the promise of divine favour – though in many cases the rewards for perseverance came only in the afterlife. John Foxe's monumental account of the church as a fellowship of believers encamped in a hostile world proved enduring. In his *Sermon on Gods Providence* (1609), Arthur Dent affirmed that the Lord's people could expect adversity: "it is agreeable to the justice of God", he observed, "that we be chastened . . . with a fatherly rod, which may keep us in obedience".[27] The image of a flaming bush, miraculously unconsumed by affliction, was a familiar motif for godly communities – both within and beyond the established church – throughout the seventeenth century.

The idea of God's people under providential rule was related to another narrative of divine favour, summarised in the title of an anonymous pamphlet printed in 1591: *The Blessed State of England*. Extending the model of supernatural oversight of the true church, this celebrated "the manifold blessings which it hath pleased almighty God to bestow upon this realm of England".[28] Later writers catalogued the supposed acts of divine mercy that indicated the Lord's special concern for the nation. In 1624, George Carleton, the Bishop of Chichester, framed his history of the reign of Elizabeth as a series of deliverances from internal rebellions and international foes. Here the fate of the queen and the Protestant religion, and the divine protection of both, elided into the story of the whole kingdom. Could anything, the bishop asked, "but the power and protection of God preserve a land from so many, so deadly dangers?"[29] This providential view of the nation was not confined to books. As David Cressy has shown, the story of England's deliverances from peril was celebrated with feasts and bonfires, and the ringing of church bells, on the anniversaries of Elizabeth's accession and the gunpowder plot of 1605.[30]

This providential understanding of the nation had many consequences. At a basic level, it conferred a supernatural meaning on the perceived course of English history. The great events of the calendar – and especially the defeat of the Armada and the gunpowder plot – were presented not merely as moments of national deliverance but as divine interventions. This perception was, of course, robustly Protestant: it excluded those Catholics that resisted the Elizabethan settlement, and it positioned them as both opponents of the kingdom and enemies of God's will. Such a view was by no means straightforward, however. It depended on an alignment between the interests of the English people and their rulers and the wishes of God; and the last of these was a matter dangerously open to debate. Moreover, the Lord's concern for the kingdom meant that it could expect special punishments as well as blessings if it lapsed into disobedience. The belief that the nation had fallen short of divine expectations was widespread in the middle decades of the seventeenth century and provided the most common explanation for the civil wars. In *Gods Call to England* (1680), the Presbyterian Thomas Gouge set out the double-edged logic of national providence: he observed that "the great design of God in bestowing merciful deliverances on a people is to reclaim them from sin", but His retribution for their subsequent transgressions "will be the most dreadful destruction".[31]

Living at the end

Divine providence was linked closely to another staple of supernatural belief: the impending return of Christ to judge the world. It is hard to overstate the importance of this expectation to early modern people. Unlike contemporary westerners, they assumed that human affairs were moving inexorably towards a conclusion; the present state of the world was temporary, and the decisive and permanent condition of humankind would be determined in the future. The climactic event was described by Christ in St Matthew's Gospel:

> When the Son of man shall come in His glory, and all the holy angels with Him, then shall He sit upon the throne of His glory. And before

Him shall be gathered all nations: and He shall separate them one from another, as a shepherd divideth his sheep from the goats. And He shall set the sheep on His right hand, but the goats on the left. Then shall the King say unto them on His right hand, "Come, ye blessed of my Father, inherit the kingdom prepared for you from the foundation of the world". . . . Then shall He say also unto them on the left hand, "Depart from me, ye cursed, into everlasting fire, prepared for the Devil and his angels". . . . And these shall go away into everlasting punishment: but the righteous into life eternal.

(Matthew 25:31–4, 41, 46)

Before the Reformation, this image of the Final Judgement, or "Day of Doom", was painted prominently in almost every English parish church: the blessed passed serenely into the heavenly kingdom as the damned tumbled into an eternity of pain. Nearly all of these images were destroyed in the reign of Edward VI or succumbed to the second wave of iconoclasm that accompanied the civil wars.[32] The idea of the Last Judgement was indelible, however. Indeed, the anticipation of Christ's return was heightened by the religious conflicts of the period: for Protestants and Catholics alike, the division of the church was itself a sign that the end was drawing near.

The sense of impending apocalypse irradiated the controversies of the early English Reformation. Preaching at St Paul's in 1526, the Bishop of Rochester and future Catholic martyr John Fisher described the spread of Lutheran ideas as a sign of the approaching doom: he observed St Paul's warning that "such heresies should rise . . . especially towards the end of the world".[33] Protestant polemicists such as John Frith and John Bale accepted that the last day was nearing but viewed the reform movement as a positive step towards the completion of God's plan. In 1529 Frith anticipated "the great coming of Christ" that would vindicate finally the true followers of the Lord.[34] After the violent reversals in religious policy under Henry, Edward and Mary, an official eschatology emerged, eventually, during the long and relatively settled reign of Elizabeth: this was imprinted firmly in the martyrology of John Foxe, which offered an emphatically Protestant vision of "these last and perilous days".[35]

The framework of apocalyptic expectation was remarkably flexible. The prophetic books of the Bible, and especially the Revelation of St John, were capaciously oblique.[36] They allowed multiple interpretations of the earthly events that would herald the Last Judgement, and infinite recalculations of the time of Christ's return. Consequently, the end was indefinitely suspended in the near future. The imminent winnowing of the saved and the damned could also be understood in personal or collective terms, or both. In the poetry of John Donne in the early 1600s, Doomsday was often addressed as a moment of dreadful reckoning for the author's soul. "What if this present were the world's last night?" he asked, before surrendering in hope to the quiet compassion of Christ.[37] The apocalypse could also be viewed as a moment of national judgement, and thereby allied to calls for religious, political or moral reform. Writing on the eve of the first civil war, John Milton remarked that Christ, "the eternal and shortly-expected king, shalt open the clouds to judge the several kingdoms of the world". He would distribute "national honours and rewards to religious and just commonwealths" – a glory that awaited the people of England only if their religious freedoms and purity were maintained.[38]

For most early modern Christians, the coming doom was a lively and central theme of religious life, perhaps as important as the "immediate judgement" that followed death. Many people shared John Donne's speculation that the end would come in their own lifetime, and as a consequence they would not die at all.[39] The wide availability of scripture, and sermons and printed material that touched on the subject, meant that the imagery of the last day permeated all levels of English society. The deposition in 1562 of Ellis Hawle, the semi-literate son of a carpenter in Lancashire, provides an exceptionally vivid glimpse into the apocalyptic imagination of a plebeian man. Hawle described how he was lifted out of his bed, "as it were in a tuft of feathers with a whirlwind up into Heaven", where he beheld a vision of the Lord:

> I saw our saviour Christ sitting in his royal seat, compassed about with angels, amongst whom me thought I saw one having a book in his hand and looking on it. One asked him whether the time were come. He answered no. From thence I was carried into Hell, where I saw all the torments thereof, and also a place prepared for me if I would not amend my corrupt life, and also a place prepared for me in Heaven if I would follow God's holy will and commandments.

This vision inspired Hawle to distribute his goods among his family and the poor, and to broadcast his prophetic insights. His career as a holy man was cut short when he was sentenced to the pillory "for seducing the people by publishing false revelations".[40]

Hawle's testimony indicates that his foretaste of the coming judgement was intensely personal. He was preoccupied with his own fate at Doomsday and determined to make amends for his previous moral failings.[41] This sense of individual responsibility was evident in other depictions of the apocalypse in popular culture but was sometimes combined with calls for collective reformation. A striking example is the ballad *Englands New Bellman*, which circulated between the mid-seventeenth and eighteenth centuries. The bellman of the title referred to the "passing bell" that was rung in the streets when a person lay on his or her deathbed, but here the image was attached to the whole nation. The opening verse conveyed the urgent, communal warning that characterised the song:

> Awake! Awake! O England,
> Sweet England now awake,
> And to thy prayers speedily,
> Do thou thyself betake:
> The Lord thy God is coming,
> Within the sky so clear,
> Repent therefore, O England,
> The day it draweth near.

The following verses moved between calls for personal repentance and descriptions of the reckoning that awaited the entire land. Individuals were warned to reflect on their earthly "thoughts and deeds", which would pursue them on "that most dreadful day". Then sinners would face the accusations of Satan and fall trembling on the mercy of God. Each verse ended with the call for England itself to repent, as the last day shuddered into view.[42]

What were the effects of these beliefs? The apocalypse provided a cosmic narrative for the struggle of English Protestants against Rome. The language of the last days contained a familiar set of images by which Catholicism, and especially the pope, could be recognised and fought.[43] These included the Antichrist described by St Paul in his first letter to John (2:18) and the many-headed beast of the Book of Revelation (13); these figures were traditionally conflated, and their appearance and overthrow were widely believed to presage the Final Judgement.[44] To take one example, Nathaniel Woodes' play *The Conflict of Conscience* (1581) portrayed the Bishop of Rome as the "Antichrist / figured of John by the seven-headed beast". In a parody of the Holy Trinity, Woodes had Satan introduce the pontiff as "my darling dear, / my eldest boy, in whom I do delight".[45] This message was repeated in countless sermons, pamphlets and ballads.[46] By the 1640s the godly minister Samuel Clarke could note casually that almost every child in the land knew that the pope was Antichrist.[47] This gave anti-popery an eschatological edge: the see of Rome was not merely a hostile power but also a cosmic foe whose downfall would usher the return of Christ.

Apocalyptic speculations also encouraged belief in "signs and wonders". This was because such events were expected in the period preceding the Day of Doom. The visionary texts in the Bible predicted astounding sights as the end approached, such as the "great wonders" and heavenly fire described in Revelation 13:13. Reports of "marvels" acknowledged this context: as a pamphlet observed in 1599, "signs and tokens in the sun, the moon and the stars, monstrous births, and strange marvellous things" signalled the earth's final days.[48]

A report of a beached whale in 1617 began with a description of the supernatural signs that accompanied "this old and declining age of the world".[49] In this way, the literature of wonders both reflected eschatological expectations and seemed to confirm them. The activity of Satan was also amplified as Doomsday loomed, following the traditional belief that he would rage most wildly before his earthly kingdom fell. On a cosmic level, this was expressed in the aggression of the Roman Antichrist. But the Devil also encouraged a multitude of small evils, whose very prevalence appeared to presage his downfall. As the author of a particularly gruesome murder pamphlet explained in 1614, awful crimes were inevitable in "this old impotent bear-pit age wherein we live, [with] the doting world limping on her last legs".[50]

The anticipation of the Last Judgement was a pulse in the background of early modern English culture. This pulse periodically quickened, especially at moments of conflict or political upheaval. This was the case during the Spanish war in the 1580s and the long conflict in Germany after 1618.[51] Eschatological excitement probably peaked during the civil wars in the middle decades of the seventeenth century. It was no coincidence that this period also witnessed a surge in reports of supernatural marvels, as well as intense fears of Catholic insurrections: both fitted the narrative of the last days in those "tottering and staggering times".[52] The belief that Christ would soon return also united the various radical groups that emerged from the wars, despite their disparate political and religious goals. In more settled circumstances, the knowledge that history was drawing to a close enlarged and completed the doctrine of providence: the end of the story was in sight and would embrace not only individuals but the whole cosmos. Christ's return would bring perfect justice to the world and bless the faithful with lives that were "spiritual, immortal, glorious, and free from all infirmity".[53]

The economy of the invisible world

For the experts on spirits in Tudor and Stuart England, the world of human sensory perception was so limited that it missed a large part of God's creation. In 1651, Joseph Hall, the former Bishop of Norwich, observed that the kingdom of angels was so vast that it dizzied the mind. Their number was "next to infinite, and all this numberless number, so perfectly united in one celestial polity . . . makes them a complete world of spirits, invisibly living and moving both within and above this visible globe".[54] Sadly, the company of wicked spirits was equally huge. The contrast between the world revealed to mortal eyes and the supernatural reality was a familiar trope. In 1533 the English translation of Erasmus of Rotterdam's *Enchiridion* distinguished between the perceptible and the "invisible world".[55] The Elizabethan martyrologist John Foxe used the same phrase in the 1570s, and it also provided the title for Hall's book.[56] At the end of the seventeenth century, the antiquarian John Aubrey lamented that much of God's creation was "beyond human reach", and observed that mortals were "miserably in the dark as to the economy of the invisible world".[57]

The reason for this ignorance was, of course, the immaterial nature of spiritual beings. Angels and demons might move constantly among us, but they possessed no physical form. Indeed, they could not even be pictured: strictly speaking, visual representations of spirits were approximations of things that could not be seen in this life. In general terms, educated English Protestants tended to think of the residents of the invisible world as intangible: they felt their presence most often in dreams, or stirrings of the imagination or conscience. Nonetheless, images of spirits were by no means uncommon in cheap print. It was also widely accepted that with God's permission immaterial creatures could make themselves accessible to human perception, at least at one remove. This was achieved through sensory manipulations that produced visions or by the assembly of fake bodies from substances such as air. In the 1590s Edmund Spenser described the latter method in *The Faerie Queene*, in which spirits appear to mortals in forms "framed of liquid air".[58]

Spirits were not the only invisible powers at work in the early modern cosmos. It was believed that a network of unseen forces bound together and regulated the natural world. The most obvious of these was the pull of the moon on the tides. Other parts of the created order exerted a similar influence on one another at a distance. To take a humble example, the flower of the daisy opened and closed in obedience to the rising and setting of the sun: it was this behaviour that conferred its name, as it acted as the "day's eye". A vast and intricate web of similar correspondences affected all parts of God's creation, including the lives of men and women. The position of planets and stars could influence the physical and mental disposition of individuals – a fact that underpinned much of early modern medicine as well as the practice of astrology. Again, to offer a small and simple illustration, it was widely accepted that certain days in the year were propitious or unlucky for particular enterprises. In the second half of the seventeenth century, the polymathic scholar and magician Elias Ashmole noted three days on which a person should not take medicine, as "he shall be in great danger of death". Somewhat more precisely, he marked another ten days when "whosoever eateth any goose . . . shall fall sick in peril of death".[59]

The acceptance of spirits and occult forces had many implications. Perhaps the most profound of these was that people were exposed to invisible powers beyond their own minds. In terms of physical health, something similar is true for westerners today: scientific medicine assumes that unseen entities such as viruses and bacteria can enter human bodies with physical effects. Today it is also acknowledged that external influences, including social and environmental circumstances, can affect states of mind. For early modern people, however, the range and power of the invisible forces in the world was considerably greater. It was possible, for example, for spirits to communicate with individuals, either in dreams or by means of suggestions in the mind. Marlowe dramatised this idea in *Doctor Faustus*: a good angel commends the magician to "think on heaven and heavenly things", while its evil counterpart feeds his desire for honour and wealth.[60] The belief that good and wicked spirits sought to sway human minds was accepted in English angelology and described at first hand in countless spiritual autobiographies.[61]

As well as angels and demons, it was widely believed that other people could affect the mental and physical health of individuals at a distance. Sometimes this was achieved deliberately, as in cases of love magic and witchcraft. But occult effects were also produced by interpersonal conflicts of various kinds, particularly when intensely negative feelings were expressed. A study by Edward Bever has shown that ill feeling between individuals in early modern Europe often created acute and very real distress.[62] The capacity of invisible forces to alter the minds, as well as the bodies, of men and women has led the philosopher Charles Taylor to postulate that individuals in this period had an "unbuffered" sense of self.[63] Unlike contemporary westerners, they believed that they were exposed to external powers that could invisibly instigate thoughts, create emotions or manipulate dreams. Demonic possession and divine inspiration were the most extreme manifestations of this idea, but its effects were felt in everyday life throughout Tudor and Stuart culture.

The ingress of spirits into human minds was extensively documented. In chapbooks and ballads, the crimes of murder and suicide were frequently attributed to demonic temptation. More positively, both Protestant and Catholic devotional writers in the seventeenth century observed that "angel keepers" accompanied Christians throughout their lives. John Bunyan's *Grace Abounding* is perhaps the most affecting account of the sway of invisible powers on an unbuffered self. Bunyan's mind was occasionally illuminated with heavenly insights but more frequently perturbed with the thoughts of demons – and it was sometimes with difficulty that he separated his own cognitions from those introduced from outside.[64] Beyond the interior experience of pious individuals, the idea that spirits vied for the souls of men and women was sometimes expressed in public contexts. One of these was the deathbed. The medieval tradition that angels and demons gathered around the dying endured in the Reformation and occasionally produced reports of spectacular visions – though Protestants denied that such interventions could decide the fate of souls.[65]

Another indication of the prevalence of spirits and occult influence was the various efforts made to repel them. One technique, preserved among the copious magical papers of Elias Ashmole, was based on the apocryphal Book of Tobit. In the biblical story, the angel Azarias instructs Tobit (or Tobias) to catch a fish and remove its heart and liver. The smoke from these parts, the angel explains, can drive away demons, while the gall bladder is a cure for blindness (Tobit 6:2–8). Ashmole's manuscript puts this information to use:

> Though Tobias names not the fish whose heart and liver drove away devils with their smoke, yet the philosophers have found an experiment of the gall [bladder] of any fish, especially if it be had in a box of juniper. If any be hurt by enchantment or vexed with devils or be bewitched, when they go to bed, let it be laid upon coals and the house filled with the smoke thereof, and all mischief shall be expelled.[66]

For those disinclined to fumigate their dwellings, the burial of "witch bottles" offered a popular alternative. These vessels were typically filled with urine and pins and concealed in houses near places of entry for undesirable spirits: doors, windows and hearths.[67] Charms and amulets provided more mobile forms of protection: these could take the form of inscriptions on pieces of paper, or astrological sigils worn around the neck.

Few accounts of human encounters with the unseen world are as detailed and compelling as those preserved in the medical notebooks of Richard Napier, the astrological physician from Great Linford in Buckinghamshire, and his nephew (also named Richard) in the late sixteenth and early seventeenth centuries. The elder Napier was ordained in the established church, but his fear of the pulpit caused him to work as a doctor instead; his practice passed to his nephew at his death in 1634.[68] Both men were social and religious conservatives, but they nonetheless combined an expertise in medical astrology with a lively interest in all aspects of the occult. This helps to explain, perhaps, the careful attention they gave to the supernatural elements that often featured in their client's maladies. This was combined with a holistic approach that led them to record the personal circumstances in which these afflictions occurred.

The consultations recorded by the younger Richard Napier in the period after his uncle's death illustrate, in miniature, the operation of invisible forces in the early modern world.[69] The most basic of these were the astral influences believed to affect physical health and states of mind. All Napier's clients were subject to these powers: disease itself implied an imbalance within the body of humours that were subject to the movement of the stars, and treatments often required the preparation and taking of medicines on astrologically propitious dates. Occasionally, Napier's patients themselves reported the effects of celestial bodies on their wellbeing. In September 1637, for instance, a young man from Leicestershire was "troubled sometimes by fits, with a mopishness and a weakness in his joints which takes him every moon and holds him two or three days".[70]

Other unseen powers were more personal. Several of Napier's patients reported that they were vexed by evil spirits. These sometimes expressed themselves directly in their victims' minds. In April 1634, Ellen Green from Cambridgeshire was "troubled in mind, [and] haunted by an ill spirit whom she sayeth speaketh to her". Later in the same month, another client, Robert Lucas of Charleton, was "troubled in his mind [and] despairing" and wondered "whether he be not possessed with an evil spirit". In these consultations Napier did not record the content of his patients' disturbed thoughts. When he met Jane Towerton of Dorchester, however, he noted her belief that a demon was trying to subvert her religious observances. This creature urged her not "to serve God and say her prayers or go to church". She also claimed that the spirit took visible form, though her description of it as "a black jock" is rather obscure.[71] Towerton's experience echoed the spiritual trials described by Bunyan and other godly Protestants; in more pathological terms, she displayed the symptoms of "religious melancholy" described in the 1620s by Robert Burton.

As this case indicates, the afflictions visited by spirits could extend beyond a distracted mind. The creatures that tormented Napier's clients sometimes chose crudely physical methods. In one unusual case, recorded in June 1634, the family of Joan Hawkins was "much troubled" by a nocturnal phantom:

> Sometimes it [comes] many nights together, yet never did any hurt to them, but makes a noise and throws things about, and plays many unhappy tricks. [It] always comes in the night, and [is] never heard till the candle be out. Upon this they moved their house. It followed them, and . . . haunts them where they are.[72]

Reports of such truculent spirits were relatively uncommon, though a similar creature disturbed the household of John Mompesson in Hampshire in 1662.[73] A number of Napier's patients described a more familiar – and visceral – type of supernatural assault: the intrusion of spirits inside their bodies. On the night of Whitsun Eve in 1634, William Dudley felt something "which came into him . . . as he was in bed". In the following January, Jane Slade from Keysoe in Bedfordshire informed Napier that she felt "something stir in her body with a rising up and down", which she interpreted as a symptom of bewitchment. During his consultation with Ellen Neve in June 1635, the physician noted that she "finds something, as were a live thing, running up and down within her".[74]

As well as the activity of spirits, a number of Napier's patients reported suspicions of witchcraft. These phenomena were sometimes connected, as in the case of Jane Slade, but the involvement of evil spirits was not a prerequisite for allegations of this kind. The common factor in reports of bewitchment was the identification of individuals who, either knowingly or otherwise, were responsible for causing magical harm. The afflictions described were diverse. During a series of consultations in the summer of 1634, Eleanor Aylett alleged that a "company of witches" had caused her to suffer hot and cold fevers and sleeplessness, and sent a spirit that "comes like a fly, roaring and buzzing about her". They had also made her cows give poor milk and stumble about the field. In the same period, Dorothy Green voiced a less dramatic suspicion: she feared that the "ill tongue" of her daughter and another woman had caused her to be "mopish, melancholy and despairing".[75]

In these and other instances of supernatural affliction, interpersonal relationships played a critical role. Indeed, allegations of witchcraft can be viewed as unusually explicit illustrations of a wider rule: that people made one another unwell. In communities that believed implicitly in occult influences, it was accepted that bad feelings could cause disease. It was "an old received opinion", wrote William Perkins in *A Discourse of the Damned Art of Witchcraft* (1608), that an angry gaze could cause physical harm to those on whom it fell.[76] Bitter words could have a similar effect. This belief was captured in the phrase "ill tongue": Napier's patients used these words to describe the effects of cursing, but they also conveyed the sense of verbal conflict between individuals.[77] To be "under an ill favour" was another synonym for bewitchment, with similar connotations. Napier was acutely sensitive to the medical effects of disturbed relationships. He identified these as a source of disease even when witchcraft was not suspected: in August 1637, for example, he observed that the sickness of Mary Drury was "occasioned by grief and discontent from her husband".[78] Unsurprisingly, his interest in the social interactions of his patients was especially marked, and revealing, when their conditions included apparently occult elements.

Sometimes it seems that bad relationships within families led directly to physical and mental sickness. This was presumably the case between Dorothy Green and her daughter. In a more elaborate episode, Joan Fellow of Bletchley was "troubled in mind and light headed" and had not slept for nine nights because she feared that something would come to her bed to kill her. After noting down these symptoms, Napier observed that "her mother-in-law hath used her very unkindly". Supernatural afflictions could also arise from traumatised minds. This probably helps to explain the nocturnal spirit that entered the body of William Dudley: apparently, this creature told him that he was responsible for the death of his wife and would perish himself before his next birthday. Napier recorded that Dudley had been distracted since his bereavement. It is possible that the spirit that moved inside Ellen Neve in 1635 was also connected to her troubled imagination. During their second consultation, the physician observed that she had "grieved very much" since her daughter had been "ravished by a young rogue" at the age of seven.[79]

A misunderstanding is possible here. Napier did not believe that his patients' supernatural afflictions were imaginary or "merely" psychosomatic. He was certainly interested in the social circumstances in which they arose and believed that these circumstances were important; and sometimes he was frankly sceptical of the symptoms that his clients described. When Eleanor Aylett claimed that she was bewitched after bearing her first child, he noted caustically that she "hath had nine children since".[80] But Napier shared many of the occult assumptions of those that he treated. He accepted that bad feelings could cause physical harm and that in some cases this harm was produced through deliberate acts of cursing. As a physician his goal was to restore harmony, both within the body and between individuals and their environments: good social relationships were essential to this, but so also were the disposition of cosmological forces such as spirits and the stars.[81]

Nor were Napier's patients mistaken to believe that unseen powers could affect their health. Historians of witchcraft are sensitive to the role of psychosocial factors in disease: both Robin Briggs and Edward Bever have pointed out that harmful magic really did make people sick, and sometimes even led to death.[82] It is likely that similar mechanisms were at work when people suffered from occult afflictions outside the context of bewitchment. The prevailing belief in a world of supernatural forces was a prerequisite for such effects. The social environment was also important. A weak and unpredictable agricultural economy, combined with high rates of infant mortality and contagious disease, made people sharply aware of the fragility of existence; and life within extended households in small communities heightened the significance of good – and bad – interpersonal relationships. In such conditions it was not surprising that men and women felt exposed to occult forces and often suffered physical and mental distress as a consequence. To revisit the words of John Aubrey in 1696, the economy of invisible powers produced effects that were both visible and real.

The enchanted landscape

While occult forces operated in the social environment, the physical world was also penetrated by otherworldly powers. The landscape of early modern England was alive with spirits. Many believed that wild places – forests, mountains, scrubland and fen – were inhabited by fairies and other "bugs". These could waylay unfortunate travellers or lead them astray with "elf light". Particular landmarks were invested with supernatural influence or viewed as the haunt of spirits of various kinds: these included graveyards, crossroads, ancient trees and natural springs. The legends attached to local features frequently recalled the existence of superhuman beings: rocky crags were deposited by Satan, caves were the abandoned homes of dragons, and standing stones were mortals petrified by God.[83] Plants and trees also possessed occult properties: for those with the right expertise, they could assist in the process of divination, offer magical cures or confer protection against spells and the incursion of harmful spirits.

The supernatural aspects of the English countryside reflected assumptions about the relationship between human settlements and uncultivated land. Cultural historians such as Stephen Wilson and Joep Leerssen have suggested that early modern people perceived the world in terms of civilization and wilderness.[84] According to Wilson, the most important spaces in the pre-industrial environment were the village, cultivated fields and "the wild", the last of which was the residence of unruly and dangerous forces.[85] The otherworldly properties of the landscape also derived from religion. The medieval church had created a network of holy places, often invested with apotropaic powers. Springs and trees associated with the cult of saints frequently acquired their own chapels and attracted pilgrims seeking divine approbation, absolution from sins, or the cure of diseases. Wayside crosses marked the borders of communities and also served as sites for the blessing of crops and the expulsion of evil spirits from the land during annual processions, or "perambulations", led by parish ministers.[86] Beyond these human boundaries, remote chapels staked a Christian presence in the wild: the archangel St Michael was a favoured dedicatee of such outposts, which included a chapel on a high crag on Bodmin Moor and a rocky island at Marazion on the Cornish coast.

The Protestant reformers of the sixteenth century viewed this sanctified landscape with distrust, and were determined to pluck out some of its central features. Underpinning this attitude was the belief that divine power was never attached to particular places: the God of the Reformation was universal. True Christians, wrote the Oxfordshire rector John Prime in 1582, did not need to travel "from shrine to shrine, neither to Rome nor to Jerusalem, nor to any singular place under heaven . . . as if God were more tied to this region than to that".[87] This objection was combined with a hatred of idolatry. The holy places that marked the English landscape were not only the destinations of pious travellers but also objects of supplication; and as a consequence the entire practice of pilgrimage was contaminated with false religion. Wayside crosses were also tainted, as the ritual blessing and purification of fields seemed to be little more than priestly magic. The eradication of such practices required a purging of the countryside.

The assault on the sacred landscape began early in the Reformation and was one of its most enduring accomplishments. Initially, attacks on holy sites were led by individuals: in 1531, for instance, Thomas Patmore, the minister of Much Hadham in Hertfordshire, was accused of removing wax offerings that parishioners had fixed to a tree.[88] By the end of the decade, the king's support for ecclesiastical reform legitimised such actions and lent them the support of law. The injunctions of 1538 impelled clergy to condemn from the pulpit the unscriptural "fantasies" associated with sacred places: these included "wandering to pilgrimage, [and] offering of money, candles or tapers to images or relics".[89] The suppression of pilgrimage, which was enforced with renewed ferocity during the brief reign of Edward VI, plucked many features from the landscape: in some cases whole communities disappeared, such as the hamlet of Kenelmstowe near Halesowen, which once surrounded the holy well of the local martyr St Kenelm.[90] It is a measure of the impact of these reforms that the word "pilgrimage" had lost much of its geographical meaning by the seventeenth century: what was once a physical journey to particular places became primarily a metaphor for the Christian journey through life, immortalised by John Bunyan in 1678 in *The Pilgrim's Progress*.

The countryside was not disenchanted, however. While the suppression of pilgrimage restricted access to divine power, it was still possible for spirits to appear in wild places. The association between Satan and uninhabited land remained strong, not least because of the biblical story of Christ's temptation in the wilderness (Matt. 4:1–4; Luke 4:1–8). For the people of early modern England, the wilderness normally meant a dense and trackless forest.[91] The danger of such terrain was sometimes expressed in symbolic terms, as when the preacher Thomas Adams warned in 1626 that the spirit of falsehood lurked in "the wild forest of paganism".[92] The evil tempter in the woods took more concrete form in cheap print. A pamphlet in 1661 described how a Staffordshire dissenter went at night to meet his co-religionists in a remote house. He was distracted by a strange voice that invited him to "come away, come away, come away", and then accosted by a stranger near the meeting place. The stranger refused to go inside; instead, he took the man by the hand and led him over "thorny hedges and through the boughs of thick maple trees" into the depths of a forest. Here the man found himself alone with the Devil, whose eyes suddenly "glimmered like two counterfeit moons". A great wind shook the trees, and the creature flew off in a burst of flame. The man scrambled back to his home, with a "pale and dismal" countenance, and remained speechless for three days.[93]

While English demons retained their predilection for wild places, there is some evidence that good spirits also frequented locations traditionally associated with otherworldly benevolence. A pamphlet in 1684 displayed both tendencies: this described how a woman in Kent first met a demon disguised as a gentleman "in a solitary place" and then met an angel beside a well.[94] More ambiguous spirits also maintained their ancient haunts. Fairies and imps resorted to hilltops, forests and uninhibited land. In 1566 a cunning man informed the diocesan court at Exeter that he consulted with fairies "upon hills, where there is great heaps of earth"; and in the seventeenth century the scholarly magician Elias Ashmole also assumed that fairies resided near hills.[95] The anonymous author of a text appended to the 1665 edition of Reginald Scot's *Discoverie of Witchcraft* observed that fairies could be found in mountains and woods and that other spirits inhabited caves, mines and "desolate buildings".[96]

As these examples suggest, many reports of spirits in the wilderness tapped into pre-Reformation beliefs. But they should not be viewed as mere survivals of medieval superstition. Rather, they belonged to a lively and evolving collection of early modern ideas about the otherworldly inhabitants of the countryside. The work of Alexandra Walsham has shown how the Protestant faith absorbed and adapted many traditional ideas and added new layers of interpretation to older motifs. The appearance of the Devil in the Staffordshire wood, for instance, offered a providential caution to religious separatists: it was "a warning-piece to all seditious persons, wherein they might view . . . their ill-shaped opinions, and what judgements and examples have lately been upon them for the same". Within a godly understanding of the judgements and mercies of God, it was appropriate to place Satan in the "brambles and briars" of a deep forest, and an angel beside a well; and the addition of new stories to the stock may well have reinforced the supernatural associations of such places.[97]

A similar process of assimilation can be detected in reports of regional spirits. "Black Shuck", the monstrous dog that haunted remote parts of East Anglia, entered contemporary accounts of a lethal storm in Suffolk in 1577. In August that year, an explosion "of rain violently falling, fearful flashes of lightning, and terrible cracks of thunder" left two men dead in the parish church of Bungay and severely damaged the building. At the height of this tempest, it seems that some people witnessed an apparition. In his pamphlet describing the event, Abraham Fleming reported sightings of a black dog running along the aisle; this creature was so dreadful that "the sight whereof, together with the fearful flashes of fire which then were seen, moved such admiration in the minds of the assembly that they thought dooms day was already come". According to Fleming, the beast killed two men, wounded another and then brought similar terror to the neighbouring church of Blythburgh. He presented these depredations as judgements of God, "that we might fear him for his justice, or . . . love him for his mercy". For the victims of this divine chastisement, it appears that the traditional figure of Black Shuck provided its natural agent. Fleming's pamphlet refreshed and perpetuated the legend and established the demonic dog securely in the local landscape.[98]

As well as acknowledging spirits in the countryside, Protestants accommodated other aspects of the geography of the supernatural. In some cases, the legends attached to features in the landscape supported the priorities of the new church. Some standing stones, like the circle at Stanton Drew in Somerset and the "Nine Ladies" at Okehampton in Devon, served as warnings to sinners: they were reputed to be the petrified bodies of Sabbath breakers.[99] In other instances, the topological conventions of medieval hagiography attached themselves to heroes of the Reformation. According to one tradition, a spring formed on the spot in Lutterworth where the bones of John Wycliffe were burned in 1428. Remarkably, it seems that this belief was fostered by Thomas Patmore, the evangelical minister accused in 1531 of despoiling a holy tree.[100] Later in the century, Protestants were prepared to endorse the power of "healing wells": these were interpreted as gifts of divine providence, stripped of older associations with intermediary spirits. Following the discovery of curative springs in Warwickshire in 1579, Walter Bailey observed that God "miraculously revealed wells and springs of medicinal waters", and he contrasted these to the "puddle pits" of Catholic superstition.[101] William Gamage was more cautious in an epigram addressed to the healing well at Malvern in 1621:

> We often read that miracles have ceased,
> Which otherwise seems by thy golden fame,
> (Blazed far and wide: almost to East and West)
> Which cures all, the ulcerous, blind and lame.
> These miracles, God grant, they be not mould
> In the Pope's forge, as counterfeits of old.[102]

Even when Protestants repudiated the thaumaturgical properties of holy sites, this act could itself create new supernatural meanings. In parts of Northern England, the malevolent spirit known variously as "Jenny Greenteeth" and "Peg o' Nell" probably originated in the demonisation of holy wells and streams during the Reformation. In a demonic inversion of the healing spirits that once presided at such places, these creatures caused young children to drown. In one case, a decapitated statue beside a medieval well in the Ribble Valley became known as an image of Peg o' Nell; it is likely that the figure was originally a saint.[103]

While the Reformation absorbed and accommodated many aspects of the supernatural landscape, others appear to have developed (or survived) independently. The magical properties of oak trees provide a good illustration. It was well known that "oak apples" – galls that house the larvae of several species of wasp – were an aid to divination. In 1579, Thomas Lupton explained how this worked:

> If you take an oak apple from an oak tree, and open the same, you shall find a little worm therein, which if it doth fly away, it signifies wars; if it creep, it betokens scarceness of corn; [and] if it run about, then it foreshows the plague.[104]

Given this discouraging set of options, it was presumably best to find a gall with a docile larva, or perhaps not to pick one at all. The green leaves of oak trees could also heal wounds that had festered to the same colour, in an exemplary but unpleasant example of sympathetic natural magic.[105] The ferns that grew at the base of oaks could purge melancholy humours.[106] In popular tales, the tree conferred more extravagant benefits: it was a common location for hidden treasure, such as the "infinite mass of money" revealed in a dream to a Norfolk peddler.[107] More darkly, Reginald Scot listed "the man in the oak" among the monsters that populated English folklore.[108] These and other occult traditions were preserved and circulated in print; and it is reasonable to assume that this process strengthened the magical associations of English oaks.[109]

As the abode of spirits and a repository of invisible powers – both religious and magical – the natural world intersected with the supernatural one. The boundary between the two was especially brittle at night. It was a commonplace that fairies, ghosts and demons appeared most often after dark, either because they were more active at this time or, as Thomas Nashe suggested in 1594, as a consequence of melancholy and distorted vision.[110] Both Scot and Samuel Harsnett noted that the fear of spirits made people wary of venturing outside in the dark, and the latter referred to apparitions as "walking night ghosts".[111] In an age in which candles and firelight provided the only forms of artificial illumination, the onset of night also marked the inevitable incursion of "the wild" into human space. This brought with it the creatures that normally dwelt in remote places: fairies in particular were believed to enter houses at night, either to bestow small favours on their residents or to pinch them in their beds. It is notable that several of Richard Napier's patients were vexed by spirits at night or felt particularly anxious at this time: in April 1634, for example, Thomas Amston was sleepless for fourteen days and "fearful of everything, especially at night".[112] The menace of nightfall was acknowledged in a collect in the Book of Common Prayer: "Lighten our darkness we beseech Thee, O Lord, and by Thy great mercy defend us from all perils and dangers of the night". This was included in the first edition of 1549 and remains part of the Anglican liturgy.[113] In a rather different context, it was also widely believed that magical operations were more potent after dusk. The author of the grimoire printed incongruously with the third edition of Scot's *Discoverie* advised readers on locations that were particularly conducive to sorcery. These were "doleful, dark and lonely, either in woods or deserts . . . or upon the sea shore when the moon shines clear".[114]

The addition of this magical text to Scot's sceptical treatise is a small reminder of the dominance of supernatural attitudes in early modern England. The intellectual, social and physical environment overwhelmingly encouraged the acceptance of otherworldly powers. It is one measure of this fact that the contemplation of the natural world led routinely to the confirmation of supernatural beliefs, just as today it provides evidence of scientific naturalism.[115] The most pervasive force in the early modern cosmos was, of course, an immanent and ever-watchful God, whose presence was revealed both in the ordinary course of nature and dramatic interventions in the world. The most signal manifestations of this deity are considered in the following chapter.

Notes

1 *The Historie of the Damnable Life and Deserved Death of Doctor John Faustus* (1592), 2–3.
2 Marlowe's play survives in two versions. The "A Text" was published in 1604, and the "B Text" in 1616, the latter apparently incorporating substantial additions to

the original composition. Both versions are reproduced in Christopher Marlowe, *Doctor Faustus and Other Plays*, ed. David Bevington and Eric Rasmussen (Oxford University Press: 1995). The references below are from the A Text. Marlowe, *Faustus*, 1.3, lines 1–35.

3 There was apparently an earlier edition of the *Damnable Life*, but no copies survive. On the relationship between Marlowe's play and other versions of the legend, see David Riggs, *The World of Christopher Marlowe* (Faber & Faber: 2004), 231–5.

4 For the genesis of Faustus' story in Lutheran Germany, see Elizabeth M. Butler, *The Fortunes of Faust* (Cambridge University Press: 1952), chapter 1.

5 These incidents are taken from Genevieve Guenther, *Magical Imaginations: Instrumental Aesthetics in the English Reformation* (University of Toronto Press: 2012), chapter 3.

6 Marlowe, *Faustus*, 1.3, lines 45–9; 5.2, 78–80, 113–8.

7 *Damnable Life*, 3.

8 According to the author of a book of conjurations added to Reginald Scot's *Discoverie of Witchcraft* in 1665, "places where three ways meet" were good sites for ritual magic. As the burial place of suicides, crossroads were also associated with the restless dead. Scot, *Discoverie* (1665 ed.), 215.

9 Marlowe, *Faustus*, 1.1, line 155; 2.1, 56.

10 Marlowe, *Doctor Faustus*, 2.3, lines 16–7.

11 Luther argued that mortals could never understand the purposes of a timeless and all-knowing God. In practice, however, he was prepared to endorse specific expressions of the divine will in prodigies such as deformed animals: the "pope-ass" and "monk-calf" of 1523 were celebrated examples. For Calvin's opinions on the general and specific operation of providence, see John Calvin, *Institutes of the Christian Religion*, trans. Henry Beveridge (Hendrickson: 2007), book 1, chapter 17, sections 9–11.

12 Marlowe, *Doctor Faustus*, epilogue, line 8.

13 Francis Raworth, *Jacobs Ladder, or The Protectorship of Sion* (1655), 68.

14 John Wilkins, *A Discourse Concerning the Beauty of Providence* (1649), 41.

15 Bezaleel Carter, *A Sermon of Gods Omnipotencie and Providence* (1615), 20.

16 Samuel Purchas, *A Theatre of Politicall Flying-Insects* (1657), 376.

17 Walsham, *Providence*, 166.

18 *A Most Strange and Rare Example of the Just Judgement of God* (1577), A3*v*.

19 *A Strange and Miraculous Accident* (1599), preface.

20 *True Newes from Mecare and also out of Worcestershire* (1598), A3*v-r*.

21 Approximately 8.6% of the British population died as a result of warfare between 1638 and 1660. This compares to 2.6% during the First World War, and 0.94% in the Second World War. For the calculation of these figures, and the experience of the civil wars more generally, see Charles Carlton, *This Seat of Mars: War and the British Isles, 1485–1746* (Yale University Press: 2011), chapter 8.

22 Euan Cameron has argued that the problem of evil was at the heart of Protestant attacks on "superstition", since magical beliefs and practices were frequently used to deflect misfortune. See Euan Cameron, *Enchanted Europe* (Oxford University Press: 2010), chapter 14. For the providential response to the problem, see Darren Oldridge, "Light from Darkness: The Problem of Evil in Early Modern England", *The Seventeenth Century*, Vol. 27, No. 4 (December 2012).

23 Arthur Dent, *The Plaine Mans Path-way to Heaven* (1601), 117–8.

24 George Phillips, *The Embassage of Gods Angell* (1597), 19.

25 Beard's collection was based on an earlier French text but enlarged with hundreds of new examples; the second edition of 1631 was further augmented. Thomas Beard, *The Theatre of Gods Judgements* (1597), 470.

26 *Fire from Heaven* (1613), Bv–B2r.

27 Arthur Dent, *A Sermon of Gods Providence* (1609), 41–2.

28 *The Blessed State of England* (1591), A2r.

29 George Carlton, *A Thankfull Remembrance of Gods Mercies* (1624), 33.

30 See David Cressy, *Bonfires and Bells: National Memory and the Protestant Calendar in Elizabethan and Stuart England* (Weidenfeld & Nicolson: 1989).

31 Thomas Gouge, *Gods Call to England for Thankfulness after Gracious Deliverances* (1680), 9–10.

32 A complete doom painting survives in the Holy Trinity Church in Coventry, and a medieval Last Judgement is preserved in the west window of Fairford Church in Gloucestershire. For this theme in English ecclesiastical art, see Roger Rosewell, *Medieval Wall Paintings* (Boydell Press: 2008), 72–81.

33 John Fisher, *A Sermon had at Paulis by the Commandment of the Most Reverent Father in God my Lorde Legate* (1526), Epistle to the Reader.

34 John Frith, *A Pistle to the Christian Reader* (1529), lxxii.

35 In 1571 the government instructed cathedrals to keep a chained copy of the latest edition of Foxe's text, confirming it status as an approved account of the unfolding of the end times. The quotation is from the full title of the book.

36 Kevin Sharpe explores the capacity of the Book of Revelation to accommodate diverse interpretations over time in chapter 4 of *Reading Authority and Representing Rule in Early Modern England* (Bloomsbury: 2013).

37 The quotation is the first line of the thirteenth of Donne's "Holy Sonnets", probably composed around 1609 and first published in 1633. See the seventh sonnet for a cosmic treatment of the same theme.

38 John Milton, *Of Reformation Touching Church-Discipline in England* (1641), 89.

39 For Donne's eschatology, see Graham Parry, *Seventeenth-Century Poetry: The Social Context* (Hutchinson: 1985), 66–70.

40 W. P. M. Kennedy, "A Declaration before the Ecclesiastical Commission, 1562", *English Historical Review*, Vol. 47, No. 146 (1922), 256–7.

41 A sense of guilt pervaded Hawle's account. This concerned the hording of wealth and possibly the defrauding of his neighbours. After his vision he pledged "that if any man could come unto [me] whom I owe anything unto, for every penny I would make double amends". Kennedy, "Declaration", 257.

42 *Englands New Bellman. Ringing into all Peoples Ears Gods Dreadful Judgement Against this Land.* The earliest surviving copy was published between 1663 and 1674; another edition was printed around 1740.

43 Kevin Sharpe has noted the role of the Book of Revelation in anti-popery. By the reign of James II, he suggests, the book "had become a Protestant text in England". Sharpe, *Reading Authority*, 77.

44 For the biblical figure of Antichrist on the eve of the Reformation, see Richard Kenneth Emmerson, *Antichrist in the Middle Ages* (Manchester University Press: 1981).

45 Nathaniel Woodes, *An Excellent New Commedie Intitutled The Conflict of Conscience* (1581), Cr.

46 For the pope as Antichrist in popular literature, see Darren Oldridge, *The Devil in Tudor and Stuart England* (History Press: 2010), 107–9; also Christopher Hill, *Antichrist in Seventeenth-Century England* (Oxford University Press: 1971), chapter 1.

47 Samuel Clarke, *A Mirrour or Looking Glasse, Both for Saints and Sinners* (1646), 65.

48 *A Strange and Miraculous Accident*, preface.

49 *A True Report and Exact Description of a Mighty Sea Monster or Whale* (1617), 1.

50 *A Horrible Creuel and Bloudy Murther* (1614).

51 For apocalyptic sentiments during the war against Spain, see Julian Lock, "How Many Tercios Has the Pope? The Spanish War and the Sublimation of Elizabethan Anti-Popery", *History*, Vol. 81, No. 262 (1996).

52 The flood of printed material that followed the collapse of censorship in 1640 also fuelled apocalyptic expectations, as reports of wonders throughout the kingdom created a sense of cosmic upheaval; this in turn encouraged further accounts of marvels. The quotation is taken from *The Black and Terrible Warning Piece* (1654), 1.

53 The quotation is from William Perkins' popular synthesis of reformed theology, *A Golden Chaine* (1591), chapter 49.

54 Joseph Hall, *The Invisible World Discovered to Spirituall Eyes* (1659), 10.

55 Desiderius Erasmus, *A Booke Called in Latyn Enchiridion* (1533), H2*v*-H3*r*.

56 John Foxe, *Christ Jesus Triumphant* (1579), 8*v*, 10*r*.

57 John Aubrey, *Miscellanies upon the Following Subjects* (1696), dedication.

58 Edmund Spenser, *The Faerie Queene* (1590), book 1, 2, verse 45; 3, verse 3.

59 Bodleian Library, Oxford, MS Ashmole 1406, 97*v*. Readers partial to goose should take care on 1 August and the last week of April.

60 Marlowe, *Faustus*, 2.1, lines 15–21.

61 See chapters 4 and 5 for examples of spiritual temptation to good and evil respectively. On the ministry of good and wicked angels to individuals, see Laura Sangha, *Angels and Belief in Early Modern England* (Pickering & Chatto: 2012), 162–3.

62 Edward Bever, *The Realities of Witchcraft and Popular Magic in Early Modern Europe* (Palgrave Macmillan: 2008), especially 20–37.

63 See Charles Taylor, *A Secular Age* (Harvard University Press: 2007), 33–41.

64 John Bunyan, *Grace Abounding to the Chief of Sinners*, ed. W. R. Owens (Penguin: 1987), 11, 27–30.

65 For spirits at the deathbed, see Peter Marshall, "Angels around the Deathbed: Variations on a Theme in the English Art of Dying", in Peter Marshall and Alexandra Walsham, eds., *Angels in the Early Modern World* (Cambridge University Press: 2006), and Darren Oldridge, *The Devil in Tudor and Stuart England* (History Press: 2010), 72–7.

66 Bodleian Library, Oxford, MS Ashmole 1790, 132*r*.

67 For witch bottles, see Ralph Merrifield, *The Archaeology of Ritual and Magic* (B. T. Batsford: 1987), 163–75; and Verena Theile and Andrew McCarthy, eds., *Staging the Superstitions of Early Modern Europe* (Ashgate: 2013), 1–7. For the persistence of the practice after the seventeenth century, see Brian Hoggard, "The Archaeology of Counter-Witchcraft and Popular Magic", in Owen Davies and Willem de Blécourt, eds., *Beyond the Witch Trials: Witchcraft and Magic in Enlightenment Europe* (Manchester University Press: 2004).

68 For Richard Napier the elder, see Michael MacDonald, *Mystical Bedlam: Madness, Anxiety and Healing in Seventeenth-Century England* (Cambridge University Press: 1981). The records of Napier's early consultations are available at *The Casebooks Project* at www.magicandmedicine.hps.cam.ac.uk.

69 The cases described here are taken from MS Ashmole 412 in the Bodleian Library, Oxford. This includes detailed case notes from April 1634 through to August 1635, together with a smaller set of consultations from the autumn and winter of 1637.

70 MS Ash. 412, 259r.

71 Ibid., 115r, 119r, 121r.

72 Ibid., 135r.

73 See Michael Hunter, "New Light on the 'Drummer of Tedworth': Conflicting Narratives of Witchcraft in Restoration England", *Historical Research*, Vol. 78, No. 201 (2005), 311–53.

74 MS Ash. 412, 152r, 169r, 213v.

75 Ibid., 139v, 141r-v, 145r, 157r.

76 William Perkins, *A Discourse of the Damned Art of Witchcraft* (1608), 141.

77 The phrase "ill tongue" was also included in a popular charm against bewitchment. This is discussed in chapter 7.

78 MS Ash. 412, 201v, 255r.

79 Ibid., 150v, 152r, 225r.

80 Ibid., 145r.

81 MacDonald makes this point in connection to Napier's uncle: see *Mystical Bedlam*, 194–5.

82 Robin Briggs, *Witches and Neighbours* (HarperCollins: 1996), 63–6. On the mechanisms involved, see Edward Bever, "Witchcraft Fears and Psychosocial Factors in Disease", *Journal of Interdisciplinary History*, Vol. 30, No. 4 (2000), 573–90.

83 For examples of these and other aetiological legends, see Jacqueline Simpson, "The Local Legend: A Product of Popular Culture", *Rural History*, Vol. 2, No.1 (1991), 25–35, and Alexandra Walsham, *The Reformation of the Landscape* (Oxford University Press: 2011), 499–506.

84 Stephen Wilson, *The Magical Universe: Everyday Ritual and Magic in Pre-Modern Europe* (Hambledon: London 2000), especially chapter 1; Joep Leerssen, *National Thought in Europe: A Cultural History* (Amsterdam University Press: 2001), 26–8.

85 Wilson, *Magical Universe*, 3–4, 10–11.

86 Eamon Duffy, *The Stripping of the Altars: Traditional Religion in England, 1400–1580* (Yale University Press: 1992), 279–80.

87 John Prime, *A Short Treatise of the Sacraments* (1582), A3v-A4r.

88 Walsham, *Landscape*, 117.

89 *Injunctions for the Clergy* (1538).

90 Richard Rex, *Henry VIII and the English Reformation* (Macmillan: 1993), 82.

91 See Keith Thomas, *Man and the Natural World* (Allen Lane: 1983), 194.

92 Thomas Adams, *Five Sermons Preached upon Sundry Especiall Occasions* (1626), 37.

93 *A Wonder in Staffordshire* (1661).

94 These apparitions are described in chapter 5.

95 Marion Gibson, ed., *Early Modern Witches: Witchcraft Cases in Contemporary Writing* (Routledge: 2000), 29; Diane Purkiss, *Fairies and Fairy Stories* (Allen Lane: 2000), 141.

96 Scot, *Discoverie* (1665 ed.), 216.

97 *Wonder*, 2, 6.

98 Abraham Fleming, *A Straunge and Terrible Wunder Wrought Very Late in the Parish Church of Bongay* (1577). For the local context of this episode, see Alexandra Walsham, *Providence in Early Modern England* (Oxford University Press: 1999), 192–4.

99 Walsham, *Landscape*, 502–3.

100 For a detailed examination of this legend, see Alexandra Walsham, "Wycliff's Well: Lollardy, Landscape and Memory in Post-Reformation England", in Angela McShane

and Garthine Walker, eds., *The Extraordinary and the Everyday in Early Modern England* (Palgrave Macmillan: 2010).

101 Bailey is quoted in Walsham, *Landscape*, 433.

102 William Gamage, *Linsi-Woolsie or Two Centuries of Epigrammes* (1621), F3r.

103 Walsham, *Landscape*, 508–9.

104 Thomas Lupton, *A Thousand Notable Things of Sundry Sortes* (1579), 52.

105 Thomas Newton, *Aprooved Medicines and Cordiall Receiptes* (1580), 54v.

106 Bodleian Library, MS Ashmole 1447, VII, 30.

107 The peddler was instructed in his dream to travel to London, where he would hear news of concealed treasure; there he met a man who directed him back to "a great oak tree" that grew not far from his own house. The tale circulated in various publications in the sixteenth and seventeenth centuries. The version quoted here is from *The New Help to Discourse, or Wit, Mirth, and Jollity* (1680), 59–60.

108 Scot, *Discoverie*, 85.

109 The metaphysical qualities of oak trees were referenced in later seventeenth-century traditions. It was claimed that angels fed the future Charles II when he hid in an oak in Boscobel Forest after the battle of Worcester in 1651; the tree was also associated with demons in ballads such as *The Devils Oak* (c 1683).

110 Thomas Nashe, *The Unfortunate Traveller and Other Works*, ed. J. B. Steane (Penguin: 1972), 217, 239.

111 Scot, *Discoverie*, 85; Samuel Harsnett, *A Declaration of Egregious Popish Impostures* (1603), 133, 135.

112 Bodleian, Ash. 412, 135r, 152r; quotation at 121r.

113 For a detailed consideration of the context of this text, see Darren Oldridge, "Foreword: Something of the Night", in Theile and McCarthy, *Staging the Superstitions*.

114 Scot, *Discoverie*, 215.

115 For religious interpretations of the natural world, see Ken Robinson, "The Book of Nature", in T. G. S. Cain and Ken Robinson, eds., *Into Another Mould: Change and Continuity in English Culture, 1625–1700* (1992); also Walsham, *Landscape*, chapter 5.

3

DIVINE INTERVENTIONS

Acts of God

"We infallibly know", wrote the author of a godly pamphlet in 1617, "that God is infinite in power". But this knowledge was remarkably easy to overlook. Indeed, the "perverseness of miserable mankind's natural inclination" meant that people routinely ignored the fact and lived as if they were beyond the Creator's reach. For this reason, God periodically reminded the world of His presence and might. This was sometimes by great storms, floods or fires, and "sometimes by unavoidable infections and plagues and pestilential fevers". In less destructive moods, God sometimes produced extraordinary sights in the heavens or caused the sea to disgorge its monsters. It was a manifestation of this latter kind – a beached whale on the coast of Essex – that caused the pamphleteer to reflect on these things.[1]

This publication expressed the basic assumption that underpinned reports of divine interventions. They were reminders of God's power. For the most scrupulous English Protestants, such demonstrations revealed only God's immanence and majesty and could not be read as particular expressions of the divine will. Some printed accounts of "wonders" observed this rule. When the strangely preserved body of a man was disinterred from the church of St Mary le Bow in London in 1645, for example, the marvel was presented merely as proof that God could "dispose of and order all that He hath created".[2] More commonly, however, such events were held to display the Lord's approval or disfavour, or intimations of things to come. The author of the pamphlet on the whale in 1617 was probably wrong to assume that people were generally unheedful of God's might. The acts of the Almighty were a matter of recurrent concern in a fragile and uncertain environment, and many were eager to discern the intentions that moved the divine hand.

Belief in celestial interventions crossed confessional boundaries. Indeed, the fact of religious division may well have encouraged reports of God's active involvement in the world, as signs and wonders could be read as tokens of religious legitimacy. In 1606 the Catholic Robert Chambers observed that even the scriptures could be distorted by misunderstanding or selective quotation; but the direct actions of God spoke clearly.[3] It appears that the Jesuit missions to Elizabethan England appealed often to such numinous evidence.[4] While the hierarchy of the Church of England was more cautious about the interpretation of heavenly signs, and keen to expose the allegedly fraudulent "miracles" of Rome, English Protestantism was nonetheless imbued with a deep sense of the immanence of God that proved receptive to divine judgements, warnings and deliverances. Even days of national celebration, such as the anniversaries of the accession of Elizabeth and the Gunpowder Plot, were identified explicitly with acts of God to liberate and protect His people.

The expressions of divine power were diverse. They included marvellous tokens from heaven and, more often, events within the ordinary flow of nature. The distinction between "wonders" and less dramatic works of God was never clear and differed from person to person and time to time. As Jerome Friedman has observed, the political upheavals of the 1640s and 1650s bred an appetite for wonders; and this probably meant that unusual events were more readily viewed as marvels in this period than in others.[5] Modern observers may be tempted to classify wonders as events impossible to nature; but on this test very few of the "signs from heaven" described in the period would qualify. There was, in fact, a continuum of divine manifestations in Tudor and Stuart England, from the appearance of spectral armies to small marks of divine favour in daily life. In this chapter I have followed, as far as possible, contemporary representations of these things. The first section considers events that were reported as "signs and wonders" in print – though this designation was sometimes contested. These were presented as deviations from the usual course of nature, with wide public significance. The second section examines smaller acts of God: less dramatic and less public, these nonetheless indicated the presence and purposes of the Lord.

Signs and wonders

In the weeks before Christmas in 1683, the river Thames in London froze over, and a small carnival encamped on the ice. John Evelyn, the horticulturalist and co-founder of the Royal Society, described the scene in his diary in the following month: "I went across the Thames on the ice, now become so thick as to bear not only streets of booths, in which they roasted meat, and had diverse shops of wares, quite across as in a town, but coaches, carts, and horses passed over".[6] This extraordinary fair continued into the beginning of February 1685 and occasioned a small flurry of printed images, comment and versification. One broadside detailed the entertainments on offer on the frozen river:

> There roasted was a great and well-fed ox,
> And there, with dogs, hunted the cunning fox;
> Dancing on the ropes, and puppet plays likewise,
> The like before never seen beneath the skies.[7]

The last line was, perhaps, an exaggeration: the Thames had frozen on previous occasions in the seventeenth century, and the first impromptu festival on the river had assembled itself in 1608. Nonetheless, the "great frost" of 1684 was a rare and spectacular event that disturbed the ordinary course of nature; indeed, the titles of the various tracts that celebrated the occasion – *Great Britains Wonder*, *The Winters Wonder*, and the like – testified to this fact.[8]

The marvel of the frozen Thames illustrated some themes that were central to the understanding of divine "wonders". For a start, the wonderful status of the event depended on the framework of beliefs and expectations through which it was perceived. This fact is, perhaps, particularly evident to modern-day observers because the episode involved extraordinary weather: after all, dramatically cold winters, floods and droughts continue to raise attention in western societies but are normally viewed in naturalistic rather than supernatural terms. This difference in perception is based on wider cultural assumptions. The willingness of early modern people to interpret an event as a wonder rested, ultimately, on the acceptance of divine interventions *per se*; it also depended on the nature of the occurrence itself and the larger significance that could be attached to it. In the right circumstances, relatively mundane natural phenomena might be elevated to the status of wonders. As the crisis between Charles I and his parliament tipped frighteningly close to civil war in February 1642, an unusual tide on the Thames was presented as one of "God's extraordinary heralds" of catastrophe.[9] More gently, the appearance of a robin on the mausoleum erected for the funeral of Queen Mary in 1695 became the "Westminster wonder", betokening the survival of the English church and God's guidance of the nation.[10]

The "great frost" of 1684 also indicates another feature of wonder narratives. As they relied heavily on the assumptions of their beholders, they could be perceived in various ways. Often only one account of a marvellous occurrence survives, but where several have been preserved they show the considerable range of readings that were available, both supernatural and otherwise. The "winter wonder" in London is a good example. Printed accounts of the extreme weather often presented it as a divine intervention. The author of one pamphlet in 1684 affirmed that such events were "the Lord's doings, and ought to be marvellous in our eyes".[11] But the significance of the marvel was open to interpretation. According to one broadside, some feared that it presaged "an approaching sad mortality" like the great plague of 1666. Whether or not this was the case, the author continued, "sin is the cause of all / the heavy judgements that on us do fall", and prayerful repentance the fitting response.[12] In another version, the frozen river was a test of the people's reaction to God's extraordinary deeds. The author of *Londons Wonder* (1684) feared the worst:

> On this mighty river they there did invent
> All kind of vain pastimes to reap their content;
> They acted all rudeness there with one accord,
> And little regarded the hand of the Lord.

The carnival on the Thames was an impious response to the sign that God had sent, which should rather have inspired humility and charity towards the poor. The stalls and entertainments on the frozen river would anger the Lord and "make our sad judgement fall more severe".[13]

The multiple understandings of the great freeze extended to naturalistic explanations. The author of *A Strange and Wonderfull Relation* (1684) rehearsed both natural and supernatural interpretations of "the present unparalleled frost", before siding decisively with the latter.[14] Others ignored the cause of the extraordinary weather entirely, preferring to concentrate on the "humours, loves, cheats and intrigues" enacted on the frozen Thames.[15] The physician John Peter wrote a treatise on the possible medical effects of the unprecedented cold.[16] Perhaps the most nuanced understanding of the event was presented by the Anabaptist merchant Thomas Tryon. In *Modest Observations on the Present Extraordinary Frost* (1684), Tryon interpreted the extreme winter as part of a natural process by which God tested and judged the people: the extraordinary cold would, he believed, begin a cycle of disturbed weather that would cause great suffering. Using nature as His handmaiden, the Lord would thereby correct the "crying abominations" of the sinful population.[17]

The interpretative process involved in the wonder of the frozen Thames was at work in other early modern accounts of divine intervention. These include perhaps the most dramatic act of God reported in seventeenth-century England: the resurrection of Anne Green in Oxford in 1650. Anne Green was a servant in the household of Sir Thomas Read in the village of Duns Tew near Banbury. She became pregnant after a liaison with Read's grandson Jeffrey and discovered this fact only when she suddenly miscarried their child while at work. Subsequently, she was accused of knowingly giving birth to the infant and killing it, and then attempting to hide its body. She was convicted of murder and sentenced to hang in Oxford. After the executioner dropped her from the scaffold, merciful onlookers pulled on her body to quicken her death; and her chest was struck to ensure that the execution was complete. She was cut down and delivered to a company of physicians for dissection. At this point the anatomists detected stirrings of life. A team of medical experts from the university was quickly convened and did all they could to revive the body. In the course of a month, Green made an astonishing recovery; her conviction was rescinded, and she was returned to her family's care.[18]

The execution and revival of Anne Green, no less than the strange winter of 1683–4, was declared a wonder because of the cultural lens through which it was perceived – or rather the various conceptual frameworks through which people made sense of the event. Like the "great frost", multiple versions of the story have survived, and it is possible to observe the influence of various guiding assumptions in presenting the death and life of its protagonist. The first account appeared in the newsbook *Mercurius Politicus* in December 1650, within a week of the execution, followed by a second report in January 1651. This ended with an assertion of the importance of Anne Green's experience, and the hope that "there will come forth a more full and entire relation of her trial [and] sufferings".[19] This call was met by at least three further publications: *A Wonder of Wonders* and *A Declaration from Oxford*, both probably printed in January 1651, and in March a tract attributed to the Oxford scholar Richard Watkins.

These various accounts agreed that Green's escape from death was an extraordinary act of God, and they framed it within the doctrine of providence. This doctrine provided the religious foundation for the story, even for those who viewed it as a remarkable medical event rather than a physical resurrection. The general acceptance of the doctrine was, of course, a prerequisite for this understanding; but other factors also made the episode unusually suitable for a providential interpretation. Green had protested her innocence from the start of her ordeal and declared it again from the scaffold to the audience at her hanging. These claims were supported by the medical authorities who subsequently took up her case, and noted that the child she had borne was extremely premature and probably incapable of life. All of this allowed her survival to be read as divine vindication of her innocence. Indeed, the Justices of the Peace "apprehended the hand of God in her preservation" and reprieved her from a second execution on this basis.[20] This interpretation gained further support from the fact that Sir Thomas Read, her former master, died soon after her recovery. The divine judgement in her favour was, it seemed, balanced by a sign of disapprobation for the household in which she had been wronged.

Within this framework of providential understanding, different readings of the wonder of Anne Green's deliverance were possible. The pamphlets published in January 1651 emphasised her godly deportment throughout her trial, and her humble submission to God's will despite her innocence of the crime for which she was condemned. In this version, Green was a Christian heroine; her conduct and words served "the glorying of God, and magnifying His great name".[21] These texts also raised the possibility that she had returned from the dead. According to the title page of *A Declaration from Oxford*, her words upon awakening were, "Behold God's providence in raising me from death to life". Both publications described her revival as "a deliverance so remarkable, since the ceasing of miracles, that it cannot be paralleled in all ages".[22] Read as a bodily resurrection, her story qualified as a miracle rather than a preternatural marvel, as only a divine suspension of the laws of nature could restore a corpse fully to its former life.[23] Richard Watkins' later pamphlet presented Green's revival in different terms. For Watkins, this "signal act of God's mercy and providence" was accomplished within the bounds of nature.[24] He was primarily interested in the medical aspects of the case, and consequently placed greater emphasis on the treatment that Green received from the physicians in Oxford than on her own pious behaviour.

The various tellings of Anne Green's story preserved its providential significance and observed the "great hand of God in the business". They also agreed on the core factual details. There were, however, some striking additions in the second of the two pamphlets printed in January 1651. The author of *A Declaration from Oxford* claimed that Green saw a vision of Sir Thomas Read's body as she stood on the scaffold, apparently predicting his subsequent death. The same text claimed that she reported heavenly visions after her recovery: "That being (as it were) in a garden of paradise, there appeared to her four little boys with wings, being four angels".[25] It is possible that these claims – which were absent in the other accounts of Green's deliverance – originated in the early stages of her recovery. The second report in *Mercurius Politicus*, dated 9 January 1651, noted that when she recovered her voice, some women had asked her "to relate of strange visions and apparitions . . . in that time wherein she seemed dead". According to the same report, one of Green's doctors asked the women to leave; and his patient subsequently failed to remember anything that had happened during her execution.[26] Richard Watkins later confirmed that this was the case.[27] Nonetheless, there was evidently an appetite for the kind of supernatural details that appeared in the *Declaration*, and these may have derived from her early utterances.

The execution and revival of Anne Green became a wonder – and perhaps even a miracle – through the providential framing of her story; and this wonder was related in various ways through the selective presentation of the evidence to the public. Like the freezing of the Thames thirty years later, the supernatural meaning of the event derived from its interpreters' assumptions. The same was true of the many other divine interventions reported in early modern England, most of which survive in only one version. In terms of their factual content, very few of these would surprise a modern audience – at least no more than Green's survival of the gallows or the savage winter of 1683. As Joad Raymond has noted in the context of Anne Green, this indicates that early modern wonder stories "cannot be dismissed as evidence of credulity".[28] Rather, they reflected the particular repertoire of interpretations that were available at the time, just as our own assumptions influence our understanding of earthly events.

These observations hold true for the various types of wonder that were reported in the Tudor and Stuart period. Broadly speaking, these can be grouped under four headings: disruptions of the external world like the "great frost" of 1682; the appearance of "monsters"; feats of human endurance such as the survival of Anne Green; and spectral apparitions. The first of these included violent storms that served as divine judgements or warnings. A savage hailstorm in Yorkshire in March 1648 was widely perceived as a sign of some kind, though its meaning was uncertain: "none can assuredly tell what it prognosticates", wrote the author of one pamphlet, "but surely such strange and unusual things are signs of some great alterations".[29] This guarded interpretation was probably prudent in the year of the second civil war. The meaning of dramatic weather was more obvious to spectators when it coincided with specific events, and especially so when it appeared to confirm their expectations or political preferences. In 1643 a parliamentarian account of a battle in Devon observed that a dreadful storm accompanied the rout of the king's forces: "an extraordinary storm of lightning and thunder fell upon them, which lightening singed and burned the hair of their heads, and fired the gunpowder in their musket pans".[30] In the same year, a royalist pamphlet detected God's hand in the clearing of a storm at sea that threatened the queen's passage from the Netherlands to Newcastle. This was a "sign from heaven of blessings to come upon the king and queen".[31]

The contentious nature of such interpretations was illustrated starkly after the death of Oliver Cromwell in 1658. A dramatic storm lashed the south of England as the protector lay dying; and this event was predictably attached to the tributes and condemnations that followed his death. In one early panegyric, the poet Edmund Waller observed that "nature herself took notice of his death", and he read her message as robustly positive:

> We must resign; heaven his great soul does claim
> In storms as loud as his immortal fame;
> His dying groans, his last breath shakes our isle,
> And trees uncut fall for his funeral pile.[32]

This verdict was rapidly challenged. In 1659 Richard Watson accused Waller not only of lauding a tyrant but also of falsely reading divine approval in the storm. Indeed, he had "blasphemed God by drawing his providence into the positive contrivance of the usurper's villainies".[33] The intensely divisive nature of Cromwell's politics laid bare the process of interpreting the tempest that accompanied his last days. In the words of Andrew Marvell, the storm was "the great herald" of the protector's death; but what it proclaimed depended on the political sensibilities of its beholders.[34]

Similar issues of interpretation accompanied astronomical marvels such as solar eclipses and comets. In a text translated into English in 1533, the French astrologer-physician Jean Thibaut noted that "comets and eclipses have not been seen without great significance of things to come".[35] Their exact meaning, however, was frequently unclear. The comet seen over England in November 1577 produced a plethora of readings: the scholar Thomas Twyne observed that "every man fancied the events in his own judgement, either as himself would have it or . . . as he feared, or had heard say, or read [about] what had followed the like in former times". Twyne himself took the politic view that it presaged the long reign of the queen.[36] The appearance of a blazing star often coincided with public events that suggested its meaning, though these could change over time. The mathematician John Bainbridge linked a comet in 1618 with the Synod of Dort and hoped that it presaged its successful outcome.[37] This view was revised in the following year, however, when the celestial sign was connected to the death of Queen Anne. Unsurprisingly, people sought meaning in shooting stars during the tumult of the civil war. The comet of 1618 was interpreted, once again, as the harbinger of this conflict in a pamphlet printed in 1642; and in the same year a comet over Devon was presented as a judgement against the impious behaviour of royalist troops.[38]

Warnings and judgements were declared by another major category of early modern wonders: reports of monsters. These included a small but fascinating group of strange creatures discovered in the wild. The terrible serpent that poisoned people and dogs in a wood in Essex in 1614 was, perhaps, the most dangerous such specimen. Unusually, the pamphlet that described this "noisesome and dreadful" beast noted the physical danger that it posed; but more conventionally, it also presented the creature as a judgement against communal sin. The monster in the wood sprang "from the monsters of our sins"; and such creatures would multiply, the pamphlet implied, until people "destroyed the home-bred serpents" of impiety.[39] Less threatening but equally significant were the sea monsters occasionally washed up on English shores. In 1588, according to one later account, "the sea cast forth a horrid monster of a strange shape and bigness upon the coast of Cornwall" to presage the Spanish armada.[40] A pamphlet in 1617 presented a whale beached at Harwich in similarly ominous terms: the long preface explained the history and meaning of such prodigies and called for national repentance in the face of tokens of divine disfavour. The much briefer account of the whale itself, written by another hand, was confined to its anatomical details.[41] Extraordinary sea creatures featured, unsurprisingly, among the wonders reported during the civil wars. In 1642 a sea monster caught and displayed in London – described by one witness as "the Devil in the shape of a great fish" – was read as a warning of potential calamity and a sign that the king and his parliament should work to resolve their differences in peace.[42]

While such exotic discoveries appeared in some accounts of "monsters", the most common subjects recorded in the genre were deformed or stillborn foetuses. Sometimes these were animals. A broadsheet printed in 1531 presented, without comment, two pictures and a brief description of conjoined piglets born in Germany.[43] Some later accounts of such aberrations were framed in providential terms. In 1645 a malformed kitten – "partly shaped like a human creature, and the other part monster like" – was presented among various tokens of divine impatience with the nation's transgressions. Through such prodigies, the author hoped, God would "in His mercy give us all a sight of our sins, and grant us grace to acknowledge them and amend our lives".[44] Less ambitiously, a deformed piglet was displayed in London as a marvellous curiosity in 1676: visitors were invited to admire the creature as one of "the promiscuous productions of nature".[45]

Malformed human infants were, however, the most common "monsters" described in early modern print. This was probably because they presented more fitting material for the kind of providential interpretations that shaped wonder stories: they could be read as especially shocking judgements against human wrongdoing in general and as punishments for particular sins in individual cases. Accordingly, reports of "monstrous births" were most common in the first half of the seventeenth century, when providential readings of earthly events in general reached their zenith. Broadly speaking, "monsters" born to parents with good reputations were viewed as judgements on the community at large. This was the case in a text published in 1595, which noted the "honest life and conversation" of the unfortunate mother.[46] A similar pamphlet in 1617 offered no comment on the parents' lives and presented their offspring as divine retribution for the diverse sins of the kingdom.[47] When the conduct of the parents was held to be questionable in some way, God's hand was more precise. In *Strange Newes of a Prodigious Monster* (1613), for example, the mother was illegitimate and the father a man "of very lewd carriage". Their conjoined twins were, accordingly, portrayed as a judgement on "the sins of adultery and fornication".[48] Ugly narratives of this kind proliferated during the civil wars. *The Ranters Monster* (1652) can stand as an example of the genre. This described a sectarian woman named Mary Adams who allegedly claimed that she was pregnant by the Holy Ghost. Subsequently, the stillborn child that she delivered was "the ugliest ill-shaped monster that ever eyes beheld".[49]

These tragedies depicted as judgements were mirrored by another class of wonder narratives: reports of extraordinary endurance or survival against the odds. At their simplest, such accounts described extreme life experiences as instances of God's confounding power. A broadsheet in 1635 reported an improbably elderly man (apparently 150 at the time of publication) as "the wonder of the age": such longevity, the author noted, proved that "there is nothing impossible unto God".[50]

In other cases, remarkable escapes from death were portrayed as signs of divine favour, either for the individuals concerned or for the cause they espoused. When the royalist Sir Richard Greenville condemned a group of parliamentarians to hang in Cornwall in 1642, one survived the scaffold when the halter on his neck broke free. According to the godly minister Samuel Clarke, this "miracle of God's mercy did so astonish the adversaries that they let him and all the rest depart in safety".[51] One of the condemned men later told his story to the army chaplain Richard Baxter, who surmised that an "invisible power" was involved.[52] Clarke and Baxter recorded another divine intervention that saved the baby of a couple killed by royalist soldiers in Bolton: a woman found that she could breastfeed the orphaned child, despite having been infertile for many years. This marvel, Clarke noted, was "attested by three godly ministers and diverse others of good credit who were eye witnesses of the same".[53]

Perhaps the best-documented case of apparently supernatural human endurance involved a young woman named Martha Taylor, the daughter of a lead miner in the Derbyshire village of Over Haddon. In 1667 Taylor suffered an illness that left her unable, or unwilling, to take food. It was subsequently claimed that she lived for a year on no more than a few drops of syrup each day. The attention aroused by the story led to a series of published investigations and a steady flow of visitors to the Taylors' home. These included the philosopher Thomas Hobbes, who wrote in October 1668 that the girl was "manifestly sick". Hobbes found no evidence of trickery, however, and carefully deferred the question of supernatural agency.[54] Others were less cautious. The godly pamphleteer Thomas Robins presented Taylor's fast as a providential wonder. To support this claim he appealed to her pious demeanour: he noted her desire "to talk and discourse on the scripture . . . for she is very ripe witted concerning the word of God, and takes much delight therein".[55] This propensity attracted visits from the local clergy, who were apparently impressed by her conduct. An anonymous author echoed this sentiment in a detailed treatise in 1669. This confirmed that Taylor's fast was genuine and observed that the Bible was "the standard and rule of her faith and actions". Her survival itself instanced the extraordinary "care and providence of God".[56] Not everyone agreed, however. The schoolmaster John Reynolds favoured a naturalistic explanation: he took Taylor's remarkable abstinence as proof of the human capacity to survive periods of starvation.[57] More cynically, the physician Nathaniel Johnston suspected that she was secretly taking food.[58] The outcome of Martha Taylor's fast is unknown.

Inevitably, this story invites speculation about the relationship between Taylor's "prodigious abstinence" and modern-day eating disorders such as anorexia nervosa. In his pioneering study of this field, Rudolph Bell suggested that some pious women in Renaissance Italy displayed the symptoms of what he called "holy anorexia", a condition analogous to the self-starvation of young women in contemporary western societies. Bell was sensitive to the dangers of medical reductionism, however, and insisted that particular historical *milieux* shaped the two conditions: they were not, he insisted, the same thing.[59] In the case of Martha Taylor, Walter Vandereycken and Ron van Deth have underlined this point. They note the major differences between her behaviour and those of later "anorexics": her fast was conducted in not only a religious context but also a very public one. Unlike those suffering from eating disorders today, who typically attempt to conceal their abstinence, she was conspicuously determined to present her self-starvation to the world.[60] The wider acceptance of wonder stories probably facilitated this kind of display. It is striking that acts of extreme fasting were increasingly patholo-gized in the later seventeenth and eighteenth centuries, as the appetite for such wonders more generally declined.[61]

The distance between past and present is more obvious with regard to the last major class of wonders: the experience of apparitions and visions. Encounters with spirits of various kinds were, of course, based ultimately on the acceptance of the invisible world. God sometimes permitted inhabitants of the unseen king-dom to appear on earth. The simplest reports of this kind merely described sightings of such things: one such pamphlet in 1647 related the regular, inexplicable appearance in a London yard of "a great tall black man (or rather devil)", with eyes like "pewter dishes flaming like fire".[62] More often, the divine purpose that guided such spectres was emphasised. In 1659 the minister and sexton of Fer-rybridge in Yorkshire were summoned to the church belfry by a mysterious peal of bells; there they encountered "four visible shapes of men" illuminated by candle-light. The spirits announced that they had come to reprove "sin and backsliding", and they warned of famine and plague if repentance did not follow. Then the candle guttered and they vanished.[63] Three years later another Yorkshire minister, James Wise of Greenway, received a more extended and opaque series of visions: these included a spirit holding a cross, a winged angel and clouds that transformed themselves into human figures. These manifestations apparently conveyed a divine rebuke to the "rebellion and confusion" that had upturned the nation in the previous decade.[64]

Among the most widely reported apparitions were spectral armies fighting in the sky. These were linked closely to the civil wars: indeed, they were some-times presented as otherworldly re-enactments of its battles. In one early report of the phenomenon, from the Suffolk town of Aldeburgh in 1642, witnesses heard only the noise of an aerial conflict; and some pamphlets in the late 1650s reported the din of canon, muskets and drums without any visible source.[65] The printed accounts always emphasised the cacophony of battle, and this seems to have been the most common way in which people experienced these events. But the clamour was sometimes accompanied by the sight of "incorporeal soldiers". Two months after the Battle of Edge Hill in October 1642, "visions of horror" were reported near the site, as armies bearing the colours of the king and the parliament joined in spectral combat. News of this wonder led the king to send observers to the scene, where they apparently witnessed the spectacle for themselves. A pamphlet on the apparition in January 1643 spelt out its meaning: the Lord was enraged by the tumult and slaughter of the war "and so had permitted these infernal armies to appear where the corporeal armies had shed so much blood". The unearthly combat was "a sign of His wrath against this land for these civil wars"; and the author evidently hoped that it would hasten their end.[66]

The main interest of these and other reported marvels lies in the social world to which they belonged: the existence of an audience that apparently found them credible, and an intellectual context in which they made sense. Those who recorded wonderful events did not, as a rule, assume that their readers would accept them uncritically: on the contrary, they were careful to buttress their accounts with the names of "men of credit" who had witnessed the things they described. The spectral armies at Edge Hill, for example, were certified by named witnesses including a Justice of the Peace and the minister Samuel Marshall. Testimonials of this kind supported news of prodigious events that were not, within the intellectual framework of most early modern readers, inherently incredible. The large and sustained market for such narratives probably indicates their plausibility, as does the fact that they were frequently reported alongside this-worldly events in the pamphlets and newsbooks of Stuart England. The market for wonders depended on a providential view of the world and the acceptance of an unseen realm of spirits. "Signs and wonders" were the most spectacular products of this way of thinking, but probably not the most important: the invisible hand of God was experienced most often in the ordering of human lives.

Special providences

"Since God rules all things in heaven and earth", declared the Suffolk minister Bezaleel Carter in 1615, "nothing comes to pass without His special notice and providence".[67] Such thoughts were probably not on the mind of John Selling, a servant from Putney, when a few months earlier he drove a pickaxe through his master's skull. But Selling would probably have benefitted from the preacher's observation. According to the printed account of the murder in 1614, his crime was exposed through the oversight and "just judgement of God". Selling and two accomplices killed and robbed their master as he slept beside a fire. They then buried the body in a stable, set the victim's horse free in a nearby wood and spread the rumour that he had left on an errand and been waylaid by thieves. The plot unravelled when one of the accomplices confessed. When the second was questioned he quickly broke down and admitted the crime. The whole enterprise was ramshackle and probably doomed from the beginning; but the author of the pamphlet detected a supernatural hand in the business. Murder was a crime, he asserted, that "God in his justice will never suffer to be hid or escape unpunished".[68]

The appeal of divine justice, combined with the sensational nature of the material, made true crime stories of this kind an excellent showcase for "the revenging eye of God".[69] The popularity of the genre was exemplified by the work of the Exeter writer John Reynolds, whose collection of providential narratives, *The Triumphes of Gods Revenge Agaynst the Cryinge and Execrable Sinne of Willfull and Premeditated Murder* (1621), ran through numerous editions in the seventeenth century. Through thirty-five histories of murder that Reynolds supposedly collected during his travels in Europe, the text displayed "the sacred and secret justice of the Lord" in revealing and punishing the crime. The genre was extended in 1685 by Thomas Wright, who compiled thirty accounts of divine detection of both murder and adultery. Henry Fielding continued the tradition in the eighteenth century, with *Examples of the Interposition of Providence in the Detection and Punishment of Murder* (1752). The aim of these texts, and the many similar tales that appeared in broadsheet ballads, was to instruct as well as entertain: they displayed the operation of heavenly justice and sought to deter potential criminals. Reading tales of murder detected and avenged would, Reynolds hoped, maintain people in "charity towards men and the bonds of filial and religious obedience towards God".[70]

One of the best-known and most enduring tales of this kind concerned the "babes in the wood".[71] The origins of the narrative are uncertain, and may well, as Alexandra Walsham has suggested, predate the English Reformation; but the earliest record of the story was a ballad printed in 1595 that typified the genre of providential murder stories.[72] Two orphaned infants in Norfolk came under the charge of their uncle, who planned to kill them in order to obtain their inheritance. He hired "two ruffians" ostensibly to convey the children to relatives in London, but secretly instructed them to kill them *en route*. The men stopped in a wood to commit the deed, but one of them refused; they fought, and the more merciful villain killed his fellow. Then he led the children to a clearing and promised to return with food. The babes wandered in the wood until they were overcome with hunger and lay down to die in each other's arms. Subsequently, their uncle felt "the heavy wrath of God": his conscience was racked, his fields fell barren and his two sons died at sea. His life ended wretchedly in a debtor's gaol. The surviving would-be cutthroat was caught in a robbery and sentenced to death; he confessed his part in the earlier crime before he hanged. The ballad ended with a warning to others with responsibility to orphaned children: they should treat them kindly or feel the punishing sting of God's hand.[73]

The story of the babes in the wood was coloured with small supernatural details. When the children died, a robin covered their bodies in leaves; and their uncle's house – as well as his conscience – was filled with "fearful fiends". It was in the unfolding of the narrative itself, however, that God's purpose was accomplished. The tale made it clear that "God's blessed will" lay behind the detection and punishment of the crime, but this was achieved through the ordinary course of nature: the apprehension of the ruffian for an outwardly unrelated crime, and the series of dreadful misfortunes that struck the uncle. Earthly events of this kind accounted for the majority of "special providences", both in public culture and in private experience. For the devout, they saturated the world with divine purpose; and for their less godly neighbours, they probably offered a framework for organising the facts of unpredictable and often fragile lives into some kind of coherent meaning.

Two pamphlets published in the 1670s described the small movements of God's hand.[74] The first concerned a farmer in Somerset who sold bundles of wheat to his impoverished neighbours at below their market value in the winter of 1673, after a bad harvest had driven prices beyond their reach. In the following year, his own land was blessed with an exceptionally abundant crop. The pamphlet's author found both a theological and a social message in this bounty: he hoped that it would "awaken all to abandon their cruelty and uncharitableness, and to learn to do good . . . for with such things the most high is well pleased, and will recompense the same".[75] The same kind of supernatural economics underpinned the second text. This described the destruction by fire of a barn in Gloucestershire in 1675. When the owner's wife despaired that their household would be ruined as a consequence, her husband cautioned patience and insisted that God would provide. Subsequently, the wheat they managed to salvage from the blaze produced an unusually high yield. Such stories offered a hopeful counterpoint to the true crime narratives that displayed the Lord's vengeance on sinners. In the words of the second pamphlet, they showed that "He is a rewarder, even in this life, of all those that trust in Him".[76]

While these texts illustrate the public culture of "special providences", autobiographical writings indicate the role of such events in individual lives. By their nature, such works were atypical: most ordinary people lacked the inclination, time and ability to produce them. Nor were autobiographies free from the conventional motifs that framed other kinds of narrative. Nonetheless, they offer the best view available of the penetration of supernatural beliefs into private experiences. The autobiography of the Yorkshire gentlewoman Alice Thornton is particularly rich in this respect. Born in 1626, Thornton belonged to a wealthy and well-connected gentry family that stayed loyal to the king during the civil wars. (This fact, incidentally, is a reminder that providential thinking cut across political affiliations.) In her account of her life, Thornton recorded numerous instances of divine protection and judgement. The earliest of these, which she apparently learned from her mother, occurred when she fell and dashed her head against a hearth as an infant. Through her mother's care and the Lord's oversight, she made a full recovery. But as she noted years later, "a great scar still remains and will never be gone, to put me in fresh mind of my great . . . deliverance of Almighty God". As a young woman in 1645, she experienced another medical deliverance, when her family escaped the plague that decimated the Yorkshire town of Richmond. After her marriage, the Lord extended His protection to her husband William: he was close to death from a palsy in November 1665 but was spared by "the graceful father of mercies" as his wife prayed beside his bed.[77]

Perhaps the most painful and immediate of Thornton's accounts of God's mercies towards her concerned the birth of her fifth child in December 1657. Her labour was prolonged and agonising, and culminated in tragedy. Her own words alone can convey the ordeal:

> I fell into exceeding sharp travail [on Wednesday] in great extremity, so that the midwife did believe I should be delivered soon. But lo! It fell out contrary, for the child stalled in the birth, and came cross with his feet first, and in this condition continued till Thursday morning between two and three o' clock, at which time I was upon the rack in bearing my child, with such exquisite torment, as if each limb were divided from other, for the space of two hours, when at length, being speechless and breathless, I was by the infinite providence of God in great mercy delivered. But I having had such sore travail in danger of my life so long, and the child coming into the world with his feet first, caused the child to be almost strangled in the birth, only living about half an hour. So [he] died before we could get a minister to baptize him.

The birth that killed the child also caused lasting harm to the mother. For five months Thornton suffered from lameness and bleeding, losing up to five ounces of blood each day. Her physician advised that she was "deeply gone in a consumption" that could, if sustained, leave her infertile. On his advice she spent a month at the spa in Scarborough, where the waters appeared to relieve her symptoms. She returned home under her sister's care and eventually made a complete recovery. All these events were, to Thornton, acts of God's inscrutable mercy. When she looked back at them, she rejoiced at "His mighty and stretched-out hand of deliverances".[78]

Alice Thornton's representation of these experiences was, of course, shaped by her particular character and circumstances. Nonetheless, it illustrated some wider themes in the operation of providence. As Sharon Howard has argued, her brutal account of childbirth employed familiar motifs of Christian suffering and deliverance: in the context of Stuart England, these included the torture and vindication of Protestant heroines such as Anne Askew, whose story was valorised in the *Book of Martyrs*.[79] Thornton's reflection on her horrific labour echoed these themes: "Though my body was torn in pieces", she wrote, "my soul was miraculously delivered from death". Thornton's memoir also indicates the this-worldly nature of God's activities. She experienced the Lord's power through natural agents: her doctor, for example, recommended the treatment that restored her health, but in so doing he also served the divine plan. The curative waters themselves assumed a similar role: Thornton wrote of the "great cure which the spa wrought on me, for which I most humbly return my hearty and faithful acknowledgement of His mercy". The cure, it seems, was at once natural and divine. In these instances, and countless others in her autobiography, the process of earthly cause and effect was injected with supernatural purpose.[80]

The outward effects of God's guiding hand were combined, for many, with interior experiences of His influence. These "secret workings" were the most intimate expression of God's engagement in individual lives. By their nature such moments were intensely personal; but they could also play a public role by affirming the power of the Holy Spirit for the benefit of other Christians. Spiritual testimonies of this kind were often formulaic; nonetheless, their very tropes and conventions probably reflected the expectations of devout men and women.[81] Frequently, the Lord offered sudden insights or directions through passages of scripture. In one of the spiritual autobiographies gathered by Vavasor Powell in 1652, for example, a woman described how she decided to attend weekday sermons after God touched her heart with the words of Matthew 18:20: "For where two or three are gathered together in my name, there am I in the midst of them".[82] Sometimes the Lord spoke more directly. In *Grace Abounding* (1666), John Bunyan recalled the divine words that blasted him as he was playing a game with friends: "a voice did suddenly dart from heaven into my soul, which said, 'Wilt thou leave thy sins, and go to heaven? Or have thy sins, and go to hell?' " As Bunyan came to understand, such revelations belonged to the Lord's intricate plan for his salvation: they caused him to "look to God through Christ to help me, and carry me through this world".[83]

God's invisible hand was the most common, and paramount, supernatural force at work in early modern England. It could deliver otherworldly marvels – and the acceptance of this fact allowed people to discern "wonders" in the world. But more often the Lord's will was perceived in outwardly unremarkable events and the hidden dramas of the Christian conscience. Other spirits were also abroad, however; and with divine permission they could unsettle the ordinary course of nature and interact with women and men. The activity of these beings is examined in the chapters that follow.

Notes

1 *A True Report and Exact Description of a Mighty Sea Monster or Whale* (1617), 1–2, 4.
2 *Immortality in Mortality Magnifi'd* (1646), 8.
3 Appropriately, Chambers made this point in the dedicatory preface to his translation of an account of the miracles attributed to St Mary at a shrine in Brabant.

Philippe Numan, *Miracles Lately Wrought by the Intercession of the Glorious Virgin Marie* (1606), A4.
4 See Alexandra Walsham, "Miracles and the Counter-Reformation Mission to England", *Historical Journal*, Vol. 46, No. 4 (2003), 779–815.
5 Jerome Friedman, *Miracles and the Pulp Press in the English Revolution* (UCL Press: 1993), especially chapter 2.
6 John Evelyn, *Diary*, 9 January 1684.
7 *Great Britains Wonder: or Londons Admiration* (1684).
8 The perception that this winter was extraordinary was correct: the decades after 1680 marked the coldest phase of Europe's "little ice age", and the winter of 1683 was particularly severe. See Brian Fagan, *The Little Ice Age* (2000), chapter 7, especially p. 113.
9 *A Strange Wonder, or The Cities Amazement* (1642), A3.
10 *The Westminster Wonder* (1695).
11 *Wonders on the Deep; or The Most Exact Description of the Frozen River of Thames* (1684).
12 *Great Britains Wonder.*
13 *Londons Wonder* (1684).
14 *A Strange and Wonderfull Relation*, 1.
15 Examples include *News from Frost Fair* (1683) and *Blanket-Fair* (1684); the quotation is from *An Historical Account of the Late Great Frost* (1684), title page.
16 John Peter, *A Philosophical Account of This Hard Frost* (1684).
17 Thomas Tryon, *Modest Observations on the Present Extraordinary Frost* (1684), 4–5.
18 For Anne Green's survival of the gallows, see Joad Raymond, ed., *Making the News: An Anthology of the Newsbooks of Revolutionary England, 1641–1660* (Windrush Press: 1993), 170–73, 182–4; *A Declaration from Oxford* (1651); *A Wonder of Wonders* (1651); Richard Watkins, *Newes from the Dead* (1651).
19 Raymond, *Making the News*, 184.
20 Watkins, *Newes*, 3.
21 *Declaration*, 4.
22 *Declaration*, title page, 4; *Wonder*, 5.
23 The mere reanimation of a cadaver was a marvel but not a miracle. The test of a true resurrection was the restoration of the personality of the deceased. This was illustrated in one of the legends attached to St Paul, in which the magician Simon Magus attempted to revive a corpse but succeeded only in making its head move; St Paul, in contrast, restored the body fully to its former life. See Jacobus de Voragine, *The Golden Legend*, trans. William Granger Ryan, Vol. I (Princeton University Press: 1993), 343–4.
24 Watkins, *Newes*, 1.
25 *Declaration*, 3–4.
26 Raymond, *Making the News*, 183–4.
27 Watkins, *Newes*, 7–8.
28 Raymond, *Making the News*, 172.
29 *Strange and Terrible Newes from the North* (1648), 2.
30 *Joyfull Newes from Plimouth* (1646).
31 *A True Relation of the Queenes Majesties Returne out of Holland* (1643), 11.
32 Edmund Waller, *Upon the Late Storm, and of the Death of His Highness* (1658).
33 Richard Watson, *The Storme Rais'd by Mr Waller* (1659), Av.
34 For the reading of the storm by Marvell and others, see H. F. McMains, *The Death of Oliver Cromwell* (University of Kentucky Press: 2000), 70–1.

35 Jean Thibaut, *Pronostycacyon of Maister John Thybault* (1533).
36 Thomas Twyne, *A View of Certain Wonderful Effects of Late Dayes Come to Pass* (1578), B1r, B3r.
37 John Bainbridge, *An Astronomicall Description of the Late Comet* (1618), 40.
38 *The Mathematicall Divine* (1642), 6–7; *A Blazing Starre Seene in the West* (1642).
39 *True and Wonderfull. A Discourse Relating a Strange and Monstrous Serpent* (1614), C3r.
40 *Strange Newes of a Prodigious Monster* (1613), A3r.
41 *A True Report*, 10–11.
42 *A Relation of a Terrible Monster Taken by a Fisherman Neere Wollage* (1642), 2, 4.
43 *This Horyble Monster Is Cast of a Sowe* (1531).
44 *Signes and Wonders from Heaven* (1645), 5.
45 *News from St John Street* (1676), 6.
46 *Most Certaine Report of a Monster Borne at Oteringham in Holdernesse* (1595), 2.
47 *A Wonder Worth the Reading* (1617), 7–10.
48 *Strange Newes*, Br.
49 *The Ranters Monster* (1652), 4.
50 *The Wonder of the Age* (1635). This text has been attributed to Thomas Heywood.
51 Samuel Clarke, *A Mirrour or Looking-Glasse Both for Saints and Sinners* (2nd ed. 1654), 16.
52 Richard Baxter, *The Certainty of the Worlds of Spirits* (1691), 163.
53 Clarke, *Mirrour*, 16; Baxter, *Certainty*, 160.
54 For Hobbes' involvement in the case, see Walter Vandereycken and Ron Van Deth, "Miraculous Maids? Self-Starvation and Fasting Girls", *History Today*, Vol. 43, No. 8 (August 1993).
55 Thomas Robins, *Newes from Darby-shire: or the Wonder of all Wonders* (1668), 4. Robins published a second pamphlet on Taylor's fast in the following year, entitled *The Wonder of the World*.
56 H. A., *Mirabile Pecci: or The Non-Such Wonder of the Peak in Darby-shire* (1669), 63, 77.
57 John Reynolds, *A Discourse upon Prodigious Abstinence* (1669).
58 For Johnston's scepticism, see Vandereycken and Van Deth, "Maids", 38–9.
59 Rudolph M. Bell, *Holy Anorexia* (University of Chicago Press: 1985), 86.
60 Vandereycken and van Deth place Taylor among other self-staving young women who presented miraculous fasts as spectacles in sixteenth- and seventeenth-century Europe. These were transitional figures between the religious and public model of extreme abstinence and the clinical model of "eating disorders". Walter Vandereycken and Ron van Deth, *From Fasting Saints to Anorexic Girls: The History of Self-Starvation* (Athlone Press: 1994), chapter 4.
61 See, for example, Richard Morton's designation of self-starvation as a medical condition in 1686: Bell, *Holy Anorexia*, 3–4.
62 *Fearefull Apparitions or The Strangest Visions That Ever Have Been Heard Of* (1647), 2.
63 *The Worlds Wonder* (1659), 8. Dolly MacKinnon considers this incident in the larger context of spectral bell ringing in Protestant England in "Ringing of the Bells by Four White Spirits: Two Seventeenth-Century English Earwitness Accounts of the Supernatural in Print Culture", in Jennifer Spinks and Dagmar Eichberger, eds., *Religion, the Supernatural and Visual Culture in Early Modern Europe* (Brill: 2015).
64 *Two Most Strange Wonders* (1662), 3–11.
65 John Vicars, *Prodigies & Apparitions, or Englands Warning Piece* (1642), 53–8; *A True Relation of a Very Strange and Wonderful Thing That was Heard in the Air* (1658).

66 *The New Yeares Wonder* (1642); *A Great Wonder in Heaven* (1643), 4–5, 7.

67 Bezaleel Carter, *A Sermon of Gods Omnipotencie and Providence* (1615), 12.

68 *A Horrible Creuel and Bloudy Murther* (1614), B2r.

69 *Gods Voice to Christendom* (1693), 12.

70 For Reynolds and the genre of providential murder stories, see Hal Gladfelder, *Criminality and Narrative in Eighteenth-Century England* (Johns Hopkins University Press: 2001), chapter 2. The quotations are from John Reynolds, *The Triumphes of Gods Revenge* (1635 ed.), preface, 457.

71 The ballad was registered by the stationers' guild in 1595 as *The Norfolke Gentleman His Last Will and Testament* and remained in print throughout the seventeenth century. The earliest surviving copy dates from around 1635. A play by Robert Yarrington, *Two Lamentable Tragedies* (1601), was apparently based on the same source.

72 Alexandra Walsham, "Reformed Folklore? Cautionary Tales and Oral Tradition in Early Modern England", in Adam Fox and Daniel Woolf, eds., *The Spoken Word: Oral Culture in Britain, 1500–1850* (Manchester University Press: 2002), 186.

73 *Norfolk Gentleman.*

74 These were *Gods Great and Wonderful Work in Somerset-shire* (1674) and *The Wonderful Recompence of Faith* (1675). The dating and textual similarities of the two publications suggest that they were written by the same hand.

75 *Gods Great and Wonderful*, 7.

76 *Wonderful Recompence* (1675), 8.

77 *The Autobiography of Mrs Alice Thornton of East Newton*, ed. C. Jackson (Surtees Society: 1875), 4, 50, 149–50.

78 Thornton, *Autobiography*, 95–8; quotations 95, 96.

79 Sharon Howard, "Imagining the Pain and Peril of Seventeenth-Century Childbirth", *Social History of Medicine*, Vol. 16, No. 3 (2003), 376–7.

80 Thornton, *Autobiography*, 95, 97–8.

81 Nathan Johnstone makes this point in the context of spiritual autobiographies describing demonic temptation, but it applies equally to moments of divinely inspired insight. See Johnstone, *The Devil and Demonism in Early Modern England* (Cambridge University Press: 2006), 25–6.

82 Vavasor Powell, *Spirituall Experiences of Sundry Beleevers* (1652), 80–1.

83 John Bunyan, *Grace Abounding to the Chief of Sinners*, ed. W. R. Owens (Penguin: 1987), 11, 84.

4

THE DEVIL AND DEMONS

The adversary

As he was at prayer one day in Bedford, John Bunyan sensed a presence behind him and felt a hand tug at his clothes. He had no doubt that the hand belonged to Satan. The evil spirit had laboured for months to distract him from religious duties, making it hard for him to read the Bible or attend the service of communion; he had even cast blasphemous thoughts into his mind. By the time the hand reached out behind him, Bunyan half expected to see the enemy face-to-face. In the event, he was spared this encounter. After a further period of vexation, he was freed from the attentions of his ghostly tormenter by the grace of God. As he subsequently recalled, "the temptation was removed and I was put into my right mind again".[1]

Bunyan's assault by the Devil was by no means unusual. Indeed, the original readers of his spiritual autobiography, *Grace Abounding to the Chief of Sinners* (1666), would have found in it many themes familiar to the Protestant experience of religious conversion. They would also have recognised his depiction of the invisible foe. In early modern England, the Devil was a spirit of temptation, falsehood and unremitting enmity to the children of God. The various names used to describe him emphasised these qualities: he was the tempter, the liar, the deceiver, the enemy and the adversary. In a phrase adapted from St John's Gospel, Satan was "the father of lies".[2] This role involved not merely a love of deception but also a vicious desire to oppose and overthrow all truth. As a consequence, the Devil was the constant opponent of God's church and its true followers – a kind of cosmic leader of the opposition.

The enemy's reach was potentially vast. He was not merely a single spirit but a host of malevolent entities. As the Essex minister George Gifford noted in the

1580s, there are "great multitudes of infernal spirits, as the holy scriptures do everywhere show, but yet they do so join together in one that they be called the Devil in the singular number".[3] As importantly, the adversary could rely on human instruments to serve his will, either knowingly or as the dupes of his various intrigues. As the spreader of insidious falsehood, he could influence large numbers of people at a distance, as he had corrupted the progeny of Adam and Eve. This task was made easier by the "spiritual blindness" that had afflicted humankind since the Fall. In the words of John Milton in *Paradise Regained* (1671), Satan was "a liar in four hundred mouths".[4]

These qualities largely explain the prevalence and distinctive nature of demonism in Tudor and Stuart England. For Protestants, the father of lies was a powerful presence in a world that seemed awash with spiritual deception. It was the Devil's first stratagem, the Suffolk minister William Gurnall noted in 1655, to allure people with sham religious beliefs: "he hangs out false colours, and comes up to the Christian in the disguise of a friend".[5] As a consequence, Satan's instruments were often sincere but fatally misguided followers of religion. The delusions of the Church of Rome were explained in these terms: Satan presented a poisonous counterfeit of Christianity as the real thing. The success of this method demonstrated both his subtlety and his sway over human affairs. Satan reigned in disguise as an "angel of light" (2 Cor. 11:14) and was constantly seeking new ways to exploit the spiritual weakness that afflicted his subjects.

As a spirit of falsehood, the Devil was also an insidious presence in the lives of devout men and women. The interior spirituality of Protestantism encouraged an intense relationship with the enemy: personal faith brought with it the personal experience of temptation. This was sharpened by the fact that the Church of England stripped away the ritual defences against the adversary that had permeated medieval religion: holy water, the sign of the cross, the ringing of bells to disperse demons, and the exorcism of infants at the font. Henceforward, only God's grace could protect Christians from the enemy's wiles. As the London minister William Gouge remarked in 1619, the assaults of a spiritual foe could be repelled only by spiritual armour.[6] The internalised experience of Satan both extended his power and hid him from view: the Protestant Devil was pervasive but normally invisible, and spread his influence through "poisonous suggestions".[7]

These qualities made Satan a remarkably complex and versatile figure. Sometimes he was associated crudely with religious opponents. It is not hard to find Protestant tracts depicting the Roman clergy as satanic, particularly at times of anti-popish agitation such as 1642 and 1689.[8] Both Catholic and Protestant polemicists found a description of their foes in the Book of Revelation: "Behold, I will make them of the synagogue of Satan" (3:9). Equally, however, the adversary's love of deception meant that he could not be identified solely with the external enemies of true religion: he threatened to corrupt all Christian faith from within. This knowledge led many believers to a painful and continual struggle against the tempter. In 1652 one godly writer recalled how she "lay under very great temptations and was ready to despair, and for several nights could not take any rest in my bed".[9] In more general terms, devotional writers warned that the enemy constantly scrutinised the thoughts and desires of individuals for signs of spiritual weakness. It was within the human heart, Richard Sibbes wrote in 1634, that "Satan builds his nest and forges all his designs".[10]

If the experience of Satan was intensely personal, it also occurred within a social context. At its most simple, awareness of the Devil's power was amplified whenever the enemies of true religion appeared to be ascendant. The author of one early seventeenth-century pamphlet described the calculation with unusual bluntness: "I am verily persuaded that God had never fewer true servants . . . than are in these our days; and surely it is to be feared [that] where God has least, the Devil has most".[11] In the *Book of Martyrs*, John Foxe observed that the true church "would mightily be impugned, not only by the world but by the uttermost strength and powers of all Hell". These included "the rulers of this world, with their subjects publicly and privately".[12] On the Catholic side, the exiled priest Thomas Hide appealed to the persecuted remnant of the old faith to resist the Devil's party. He warned in 1579 that Satan was "always stirring against the united members of Christ".[13] Both Catholic and Protestant churchmen sought to instruct, and fortify, the men and women in their communities against demonic temptation. Nathan Johnstone has argued that within the established church this became the primary focus of English demonism. Stripped of the ritual power to protect their flocks from the Devil, Protestant ministers offered guidance and help in the daily struggle to escape his snares.[14]

The first part of this chapter will focus on the battle against demonic temptation. This produced some of the most remarkable pastoral writing of the sixteenth and seventeenth centuries, as well as affecting personal testimonies from those assailed by the enemy. As Satan often inveigled his "poisonous suggestions" into the minds of individuals, their accounts of temptation also reveal a great deal about the psychology of early modern people. The second part considers the Devil in popular culture. Here his role as a tempter and deceiver was also prominent, though he was also given to physical manifestations. Popular literature also stressed Satan's role as a punisher of wickedness – often in bloody and dramatic ways. Finally, the chapter reviews an uncommonly direct expression of the adversary's activity: the bodily possession of men and women, and his expulsion at the hands of Protestant and Catholic exorcists.

Temptation

In 1643 a young man in London was recovering from a "fearful and dangerous sickness". He was visited during his convalescence by a friend, who read to him some words of scripture and then joined him in singing the thirteenth Psalm. As they reached the beginning of the last verse – "I will give thanks unto the Lord" – the youth suddenly recalled the blasphemous words of Job's wife to her husband when he was afflicted with disease: "Curse God and die!" (Job 2:9). As he later remembered, "Satan stood at my right hand, tempting me to blaspheme the great and fearful name of God . . . and thus he forced so vehemently on my mind that I had no power to resist him". Before he could say the words, it seems that the youth collapsed into a delirium; and for days afterwards he was convinced that he had cursed God and was consequently damned.[15]

This kind of sudden mental incursion was the most dramatic evidence of Satan's power over human minds. It was widely accepted that the Devil could instil his own thoughts into the consciousness of his victims. These infernal cognitions often came without warning and blasted the mind with terrible force. The enemy "can set our hearts afire so suddenly", Thomas Cranmer warned in his catechism of 1548, "that we shall not know from whence such sudden fire and sparks do come".[16] In the reign of Elizabeth, William Perkins observed the same phenomenon. "Among other temptations", he wrote, "the Devil doth mightily assault some men by casting into their minds most fearful motions of blasphemy". These experiences were so shocking that they moved their victims to astonishment and despair.[17] The Oxford minister Thomas Bolton likened the Devil's cognitive strikes to flashes of lightning. He noted in 1634 that these incursions could be distinguished from ordinary thoughts by their sudden and violently sinful nature and the overwhelming force with which they engulfed the mind.[18]

These ideas belonged to an intellectual context that has now disappeared, and one that requires an effort of imagination to reconstruct. Few modern readers will accept that demons can plant their own thoughts in a human consciousness; the modern reader will assume instead that such experiences arose from the psychology of the individuals concerned. As a result, the question of whom or what was responsible for these "fearful motions" has lost its metaphysical dimension. For Tudor and Stuart thinkers, however, the existence of satanic thoughts meant that people were not necessarily accountable for the wicked ideas that entered their minds. William Perkins distinguished between "natural" sinful thoughts, which arose "inwardly from the flesh", and those "conveyed into the mind by the Devil". The latter belonged entirely to the enemy, and would not implicate those that received them unless they engendered "some degree of delight or assent".[19] Robert Bolton made the same distinction, and described the relief that this doctrine brought to men and women who were blasted by Satan's cognitive thunderbolts.[20]

The borderline between natural and demonic thoughts was often murky, however. This was because humankind was so utterly depraved by the Fall that the seeds of demonic temptation normally found fertile soil. It was a theological commonplace that the flesh was weak; and for Protestants and Catholics alike, the prevalence of "false religion" indicated that the intellect was equally prone to corruption. Human bodies and minds were, therefore, exceptionally responsive to the Devil's wiles; indeed, they were his natural allies. In his enormously popular catechism of 1590, Perkins noted that the "natural man" was consumed with the propensity to sin: this condition was like "a leprosy that runneth from the crown of the head to the sole of the foot". In their every inclination, individuals were "moved and stirred to that which is evil".[21] In this sense Satan was "the prince of this world" (John 12:31) and counted everyone among his subjects. Viewed from this perspective, it was only God's grace that was truly foreign to human nature; and without God's intervention, people would always assemble in the enemy's camp.

These ideas permitted a spectrum of responses to demonic temptation. At one end the sufferers could ascribe the wicked thoughts and desires that they experienced entirely to the Devil, and at another they could feel intimately and painfully associated with the tempter's suggestions. Nathan Johnstone has argued that godly English Protestants inclined strongly towards the latter end of this spectrum. Their encounters with the enemy made them confront their own spiritual weaknesses in "a self-conscious and often sustained engagement with the experience of sin, guilt and the demonic".[22] At the same time, however, it should be noted that the independent status of the Devil's voice allowed the expression of ideas that could not be easily articulated in other ways. It is striking that the authors of spiritual autobiographies often credited Satan with radical arguments for unbelief: John Bunyan, for instance, described how the Devil told him that Christians had no more reason to accept the divine origin of their scriptures than Muslims.[23] In such cases it seems that the struggle against the tempter allowed the rehearsal – and defeat – of arguments that pious men and women were reluctant to attribute to their own imaginations. Similarly, the Devil could express desires that seemed violently unnatural to those that experienced them, such as thoughts of infanticide or self-harm.[24]

The engagement of godly Protestants with the spiritual enemy was described in a collection of testimonies published in 1652 as the *Spirituall Experiences of Sundry Beleevers*. These accounts were recommended as "heart knowledge" by Vavasor Powell, the London preacher and future reformer of the church in Wales. The anonymous authors sometimes recalled how the Devil allured them to public sins: one man described his temptation to gambling, then tobacco and then alcohol, before Christ rescued him from the tempter's snares. More often, the testimonies described inner struggles to overcome religious anxieties. One woman was troubled by "doubts and questions" concerning the scriptures and was subsequently assailed by waves of demonic suggestions. These were repelled only briefly by the resurgence of her faith: "as soon as the Lord had enabled me to refuse one temptation, the Devil assaulted me with another, so that I had scarce time to fetch my breath, one temptation following so close upon another". She was finally convinced that she had committed the sin of blasphemy against the Holy Spirit, which is described as unforgivable in St Mark's Gospel.[25]

These accounts indicate a profound sense of personal responsibility for sin. During his lapse into drunkenness, the man gave "the full reins" to his will. The woman was overwhelmed by her own unworthiness before God: indeed, her narrative implies that this awareness precipitated her spiritual crisis. At the same time, the testimonies suggest that knowledge of the external nature of demonic temptation could sometimes bring relief. The woman's fear that she had blasphemed the Holy Ghost was allayed by her awareness of the Devil's interventions in her mind: "I had not sinned willingly", she wrote, "for I found it to be an affliction to me to be tempted with evil thoughts touching the Lord, though I consented not to them". In other testimonies, the writers ascribed particularly dreadful or unnatural desires to the enemy: he suggested suicide to some and enticed one woman to contemplate her husband's murder. In these cases it seems that knowledge of the tempter's activity helped his victims to make sense of unspeakable impulses and to confront and overcome them.[26]

Among the most striking recollections were the dreams that men and women had about the Devil. These were soaked with imagery of Satan from the Bible and popular tradition, and often contained meanings that their recipients held on to later in their lives. As a youth, one man dreamed that he was in a green meadow with "a great red dragon" and a beautiful child. He held the child in his arms as the dragon approached and then fled with it for safety to a nearby hill:

> I feared that the dragon would catch me, but my strength being come to me I got up to the top of the hill, and the dragon made up the hill after me. . . . [At] the top of the hill there appeared a brightness from heaven, which gushed forth like a flash of lightning, and split the dragon in pieces, at which I rejoiced exceedingly.

The child revealed itself to be Christ, who had come to earth "to save that which was lost". As well as the dragon and child in the Book of Revelation (12:1–6), the dream echoed the legends of saints such as Margaret of Antioch, who was devoured by a dragon and burst free in a flash of celestial light. In another testimony, a woman recalled how she was carried in a dream to a place "of fire and shrieking, and a great deep ditch" above a "burning lake". She was guided to safety by the Lord in the form of a child, and awoke to the knowledge that Christ would lead her away from the enemy.[27]

The demonic experiences of devout Protestants emerged, of course, within the conventions and expectations of reformed religion. These experiences were well documented and have attracted scholarly speculations about "the Protestant Devil". English Catholic encounters with Satan await detailed investigation. Some conjectures are possible, however. Francis Young has observed that the kind of introspective piety that encouraged intense experiences of temptation was present in Counter Reformation Catholicism.[28] It is also likely that Catholics experienced a sense of renewed conflict with the enemy during the Reformation, and were as mindful as their confessional opponents of the tempter's earthly power. This is certainly implied in the work of the Elizabethan Jesuit Robert Parsons. In *The First Booke of the Christian Exercise* (1582), Parsons observed that spiritual warfare was integral to Christian life: the devout were called to combat with "the world and the Devil, which do never cease to assault him, now by fair means and now by foul, now by flattery and now by threats, now alluring by pleasure and promotion, now terrifying by affliction and persecution". Satan was content to possess souls "quietly" while they rested in conventional living but was stirred to rage against individuals who made a stand for true faith. In an insight that few godly professors would have challenged, Parsons remarked that God's children could expect the tempter's fiercest attention in return for their heavenly crowns.[29]

Parsons also accepted the adversary's role as the spreader of false religion. In a reversal of Protestant polemics against Rome, he described Satan as "the head lord and master of all heretics".[30] "The Devil's chief chaplains" on earth were the adherents of his counterfeit faith. As the vanguard of satanic deception, the reformed churches had inevitably spawned still further and more dreadful perversions of Christianity: sects that challenged the doctrines of the Trinity and the divinity of Christ.[31] These arguments were framed within the Catholic understanding of the authority and succession of the church of St Peter; they also followed the logic of confessional demonism, which attributed religious errors to the enemy's deceptive wiles. It is likely that Satan's role as the seducer of sincere but misguided believers was a commonplace across confessional frontiers. The Devil's ability to tempt and deceive was also a staple of popular literature, suggesting that this model of demonic activity reached beyond the concerns of a devout minority. At the same time, popular representations of Satan were more diverse than "the ghostly enemy" portrayed in religious polemics and devotional texts.

The Devil in popular culture

In September 1624, William Lilly, the future astrologer, attended the death of his master's wife in London. As he attempted to relieve her sickness, she told him a story about her first husband's encounter with an evil spirit. The man had been travelling in Sussex when he lodged at an inn. It was his misfortune to be given a room where, a few months earlier, another guest had cut his own throat. For many years afterwards, he heard a voice in his mind that directed him to kill himself in the same way. This tempting spirit was so powerful that the man sometimes cried out loud: "I defy thee, I defy thee". One day his wife overheard these words and asked him what they meant. He confided in her, and she decided to seek a remedy from the celebrated magician Simon Forman. Forman crafted a golden sigil for the afflicted man to wear around his neck; he did so for the rest of his life and was never subsequently tormented by the evil voice. Lilly's mistress had inherited the sigil and kept it with her through her last sickness. She bequeathed it, along with the story of its origin, to her servant before she died.[32]

The tale illustrates an understanding of evil spirits that partly complemented and partly undermined the reformed theology of Satan. Like the tempter that assailed the authors of godly autobiographies, the creature was an invisible presence in its victim's mind; its assaults also resembled the "sudden and vehement motions to do evil" described by Thomas Cranmer and later writers.[33] The impulse to suicide, moreover, was a trope in Protestant accounts of demonic temptation.[34] But in other ways the spirit that assailed the first husband of Lilly's mistress was quite unlike the Protestant Devil. It was apparently attached to a particular place, where it entered its victim rather like a supernatural disease. Most reformed theologians dismissed the belief that spirits were confined to physical locations; and the idea that demons lurked in particular spots to ambush unwary visitors ran counter to the whole concept of satanic temptation. The victim's response to his affliction was also profoundly at variance with reformed religion. Instead of relying on divine grace to drive the tempter away, he paid a sorcerer to do the work. Even more contentiously, this operation was a success.

The surviving papers of Simon Forman, the magician who accomplished this task, also suggest similarities with and divergences from the Protestant view of the Devil. Alongside his other activities, Forman composed three treatises on the natural and supernatural causes of plague; and in this context he adopted a carefully biblical approach to Satan's power. He noted that the enemy was sometimes commanded by God to punish the wicked and otherwise acted within limits imposed by divine providence. When the adversary acted on his own presumption, he was motivated by hatred towards the Lord's servants: a good Christian could expect his attention, as "he hath great envy and malice at a man when he seeth that he observes the will of God".[35] At the same time, Forman believed that it was possible to expel evil spirits through magical operations. He copied out spells for this purpose and forged sigils that could drive demonic temptation from a person's mind. In this respect he resembled the healers that William Perkins condemned for using "counterfeit means" to relieve the victims of demons.[36]

As these examples indicate, the Protestant understanding of Satan was only one among a variety of representations that circulated in Tudor and Stuart England. The idea of an invisible tempter was well established; but this was combined with a lively tradition of portraying the enemy in more crudely physical forms. Other tensions arose from the core themes of reformed religion. The orthodox view that all people deserved damnation unless they were delivered by divine grace sat uneasily with common-sense assumptions about the Devil's role: it assumed that everyone was by nature in thrall to the prince of this world, whereas popular belief assigned this status only to obvious sinners. Similarly, the idea that a person could escape the adversary's attentions by "living well" implied a religion based on works rather than faith. The resort to magical remedies for Satan's darts was, of course, equally reprehensible.

The Devil's role as a tempter was a constant theme in cheap print. Like the husband of Lilly's mistress, those prone to suicidal thoughts were presented as his victims. In 1662 the suicide of George Gibbs, a sawyer from Houndsditch, occasioned a godly ballad on "the Devil's cruelty to mankind". This presented Gibbs' death as the culmination of an extended period of demonic temptation and warned others to resist the enemy's traps:

> The Devil, he said, did tempt him long,
> and many times before,
> For all he did resist him strong,
> he never would give him ore,
> Thus have you heard the doleful end,
> of Gibbs, which is too true,
> And take this council from a friend,
> for fear you after rue.

The ballad extended its treatment of the demonic impulse to suicide to other manifestations of Satan's power. Its audience was advised to avoid the broad path that led to Hell and shun the company of swearers and others that served the adversary's will. A woodcut below the title showed two figures kneeling before a dragon beside an upturned cup of wine.[37] In some other accounts of the temptation to suicide, the Devil appeared visibly to his victims. In 1657 a pamphlet described how William Pool, a Quaker apprentice from Worcester, was visited by "the prince of darkness . . . in the shape of some goodly personage". Eventually this figure led Pool to the river where he drowned himself.[38] Here Satan was embodied in his two favoured roles – as a tempter and an angel of light.[39]

While the demonic impulse to suicide was a staple of cheap literature, the tempter played an even bigger part in accounts of murder. Here he featured as the secret instigator of the crime. The woodcuts that accompanied murder pamphlets and ballads often included a demon whispering in the villain's ear. Satanic temptation was a motif in reports of bloody crimes, such as the story of a Sussex miner who slit his wife's throat in 1595.[40] There was a brisk market for similar horrors throughout the seventeenth century. In most cases the Devil played a brief and invisible role; indeed, his presence was sometimes the only religious content in texts written primarily for gruesome entertainment. Occasionally, however, the enemy appeared in person at the heart of the narrative. A chapbook in 1674 recounted the visit of stranger to a woman in Shadwell. The figure appeared inexplicably in her room, holding a purse and a knife. In a voice that was "low but shrill [and] insinuating", he claimed that he had come to relieve her poverty. He remarked that "she had a most insupportable charge of children, and that she should never be happy till she had lessened their number". He gestured towards her youngest child, asleep in its bed, and offered her the knife. The woman fled the house in horror and cried out for help. At this moment two of her neighbours "saw the likeness of a tall man in black habit come down [the] stairs, and so into the street by them, but he did not seem to walk as men do, but rather glide along like a shadow".[41]

As a tempter to suicide or murder, the Devil in these texts played a role consistent with Protestant theology. Indeed, the story from Shadwell resembled the autobiographies of godly Christians who successfully repelled the enemy's entreaties.[42] In other cases the representation of Satan departed more thoroughly from orthodox expectations. The Devil sometimes appeared as a savage black dog. In 1577 such a creature killed two men in the parish church of Bungay in Suffolk.[43] A "fiend of Hell" was reputed to haunt Newgate gaol in the shape of a black dog.[44] A pamphlet in 1641 described how a dog-like monster, "all as black as pitch", attacked a group of Catholics as they recited the rosary in a London alehouse. One of the servants ran outside, "quaking and shivering at what she had seen". Some of those nearby claimed that the creature was only a dog, but the pamphlet's author disavowed this explanation: "without all doubt it was either the Devil or some strange monster that disturbed them, [sent] from the Devil".[45] In these cases it appears that the figure of Satan combined with a trope of traditional culture. Monstrous dogs featured in contemporary legends; and such creatures were also described in early allegations of witchcraft.[46]

These tales of satanic monsters were placed in a Protestant context. The Catholics accidentally summoned the devil-dog through their devotions, exposing the nature of their misbegotten religious practices. Here the Devil acted as kind of supernatural avenger, punishing wrongdoers and the enemies of true religion.[47] This was possible under divine providence, as the Lord could use Satan to succour His children by smiting their foes. It was also consistent with the Devil's traditional role as the scourge of the wicked. In the second edition of *The Theatre of Gods Judgements* (1631), a history of the providential justice meted out to "notorious sinners", the godly author Thomas Beard included a chapter on the punishment of evildoers by demons. For instance, Satan appeared as a gaming companion to a soldier much "given to play, swearing and drinking"; first he won the man's money, and then he "carried him away with him into the air".[48] Such tales provided gaudy warnings against impiety; but their repetition threatened to dilute, or even undermine, the orthodoxy that all people were the Devil's slaves until they were rescued by Christ.

It is striking that in popular literature the Devil appeared most often as the punisher of infamous sinners. In a mid-seventeenth-century ballad he approached a Norfolk farmer who was hording corn at the expense of his neighbours. He offered the man an inflated price for his crop, struck a bargain and agreed to come and collect the corn. When he arrived, he raised a storm that smashed the farmer's barns and scattered his harvest away.[49] A chapbook in 1678 reported a similar act of demonic retribution. In this case a farmer refused to pay a labourer a decent wage for mowing his oats and then rebuked the poor man when he offered in desperation to do the work anyway. Ill advisedly, the farmer exclaimed "that the Devil himself should mow his oats before he should have anything to do with him". That night his field was consumed in flames, and he subsequently found that the oats had been cut in meticulous circles, "as if the Devil had a mind to show his dexterity in the art of husbandry". He was too frightened to gather the crop.[50] A ballad in 1684 described a more direct form of satanic punishment. This recorded how a notorious sinner named "Dirty Doll" was beaten and killed by the Devil in Southwark. In these and many other texts, it was clear that the fiend assailed his victims because of their wicked lives. Indeed, the chorus of *Dirty Dolls Farewel* implied that Satan's attentions could be avoided by dealing fairly with one's neighbours:

> Make conscience in your ways,
> And do to no man wrong,
> For cursed cheats and false deceits
> Do never prosper long.[51]

Occasionally, godly writers sought to correct this impression with more orthodox narratives of the Devil's methods. In his sequel to *The Pilgrim's Progress* (1678), John Bunyan told the fictional story of a wicked man destined for damnation. Bunyan's "Mr Badman" enjoyed earthly prosperity and died comfortably in his bed, only to lift his eyes in the flames of Hell. The message was that Satan normally left the wicked alone, allowing them to live "at peace and quiet with sin".[52] It was not easy to sell this counter-intuitive idea, however, and the Devil continued to plague obvious evildoers in popular literature long into the eighteenth century.[53]

The tension between official and popular ideas about the Devil was particularly clear when the fiend appeared in fictional entertainments. These often presented him in fleshly guise rather than as an invisible tempter. This quality allowed him to suffer numerous humiliations: he was variously beaten, castrated and farted at in ballads that circulated in the seventeenth century.[54] It was also common for wily mortals to outwit him. In one comic tale, a man promised to show the Devil a creature that he could not name in return for seven years' prosperity. Then he dressed his wife in feathers and lime and led her backwards on all fours to the arranged meeting place. The Devil examined the creature and conceded that he could not name it, adding that its face had "monstrous cheeks" and was "wondrous grim".[55] While the fiend in this and similar stories was threatening but incompetent, elsewhere he was almost benign. This was evident in the jocular tales that grew around the figure of Mother Shipton, the legendary Yorkshire prophetess, in the period after the Restoration. Shipton's character was progressively demonized, but she remained essentially good: she called on the Devil to help her deal with unkind neighbours and assist her in "merry pranks".[56]

Even the legend of Dr Faustus, the iconic magician who gave his soul to Satan in return for earthly power, existed in popular variants that compromised its religious message. Cheap print provided several examples of mortals who entered pacts with the enemy to gain prosperity without going to Hell. Like the tale of the man who disguised his wife as a beast, these turned on deceptions that foxed the prince of darkness. The closest parallel to Faustus was Peter Fabell. A scholar "of great learning, including many mysteries", Fabell conjured a demon that served him in return for the promise of his soul. The fiend could claim this prize, he pledged, upon his death and burial within the parish church or anywhere else outside. As a further inducement, Fabell promised to serve Satan's interests on earth, bearing "more souls along with me to Hell than twenty of your cunning devils". He deceived the adversary on both counts. At the end of Fabell's life, the Devil came to chastise him "for neglecting his business". But Fabell's soul was safe, as he had arranged for his body to be interred in one of the church walls.[57]

The circulation of such tales does not, necessarily, indicate the failure of Protestant demonism to penetrate popular culture. Indeed, the story of Peter Fabell coexisted with the more orthodox legend of Dr Faustus in early seventeenth-century cheap print.[58] Nor is it possible to know how readers responded to either text. Nonetheless, the popularity of Fabell and other demon-baiting heroes indicates that godly depictions of satanic temptation were only one among a diversity of representations of the Devil. The fact that darker portrayals of the enemy in popular literature normally showed him as the tormenter of notorious sinners, rather than the insidious "prince of this world", tends to confirm this impression. At the same time, the conventions of reformed religion were often present in popular tales about Satan. Even Peter Fabell turned at last to the redemptive power of Christ: in words that echoed the spiritual autobiographies of the godly, he told the Devil, "He that redeemed my soul hath taken it to keep, thou canst not have it".[59] More crudely, anti-Catholicism was a recurrent theme in popular accounts of the Devil; and the doctrine of providence was pervasive.

The intersection between reformed faith and traditional beliefs about evil spirits was evident in another area of the Devil's activity: his possession of human bodies. This was, perhaps, the most complex of all demonological phenomena, as well as the most wrenchingly unpleasant. The idea that demons sometimes seized physical control of men and women was impeccably biblical: indeed, the gospels attested that exorcism was central to the ministry of Jesus.[60] As a consequence, many Protestant clergy accepted the continuing reality of demon possession; so too did the Jesuit missionaries that proselytized in parts of Elizabethan England. More broadly, the concept was entrenched in popular belief and featured prominently in allegations of witchcraft. As the most public demonstration of Satan's power, it was not surprising that possession provoked intense discussion; the practice of exorcism also generated controversies between Protestants and Catholics and within the established church itself.

Possession and exorcism

The symptoms of demonic possession were well defined, and remarkably con-sistent, throughout the early modern period. The victims – or "demoniacs" – were gripped by contortions and spasms that violently distorted their bodies. These were sometimes accompanied by swellings that seemed to move beneath their skin. The possessed youth William Sommers, for example, experienced in 1597 a "variable swelling or lump" that rippled "up and down between the flesh and skin through all the parts of his body".[61] The voice of the possessed person was either uncommonly guttural or shrill, and it seemed to emanate from the depths of the person's body. The behaviour of sufferers was equally striking. Displays of piety, or holy objects, moved them to violent hostility or pain. They yelled blasphemies and expressed obscene desires, and often they uttered a kind of tormented glossolalia. In the words of the sceptical demonolo-gist and future Archbishop of York Samuel Harsnett, a typical demoniac would "gnash her teeth, startle with her body, hold her arms and hands stiff, make antic faces, gurn, mow, and mop like an ape, tumble like a hedgehog, and mutter . . . words of gibberish".[62]

The possession experience could arise in various contexts, including two that demand particular attention. The first of these was demonic temptation. For devout Christians assailed by "satanic" suggestions, the Devil's activity could produce a kind of temporary possession. When the enemy blasted the mind of John Bunyan with terrible desires to blaspheme, he felt that "surely I am possessed of the Devil".[63] In some cases it appears that Satan's incursions into the minds of pious individuals led to bodily possession. This was probably the case with a devout young woman in London in 1691, who progressed from "strange distractions" to violent cursing in the voice of a "hellish fiend".[64] In these and similar cases, it appears that possession was part of the larger spiritual war that God permitted the enemy to wage against His children: as Nathan Johnstone has suggested, it was "an extreme form" of temptation.[65] In normal conditions the struggle was fought invisibly within the victim's mind; in cases of full possession, the Devil prolonged and extended his interventions to seize greater control, and the sufferer required the assistance of other people to throw him off. This model helps to explain the preponderance of pious men and women among demoniacs. By framing possession in the larger context of Christian combat with Satan, it also encouraged some Protestant clergy to act as exorcists.

The second context in which bodily possession occurred was ostensibly very different. It was widely believed that witches could cast evil spirits into the bodies of their victims. This concept was prominent in the case of Alice Samuel of Warboys in Huntingtonshire, who was hanged for witchcraft in 1593.[66] It also underpinned the allegations of *maleficium* against an elderly woman in Norfolk in 1600. In this case, the suspect died shortly after her accuser, a possessed young woman, scratched her on the face in an attempt to lift the bewitchment.[67] In these and other episodes, it seems that the invading spirits were identified closely with the "imps" that featured often in English witchcraft accusations. Unlike the psychological intrusions that characterised temptation, these creatures were introduced bodily into their hosts. They could be ingested with food proffered by the witch, or breathed into their victims through sinister kisses.[68] The moving lumps observed on the bodies of the possessed were, it seems, sometimes identified with these supernatural parasites. In 1645 the East Anglian witch trials encouraged by Matthew Hopkins and John Stearne exposed popular fears of this form of sorcery. According to her accusers, Joyce Boanes of St Osyth in Essex used imps to control the bodies of her victims. Another alleged witch warned John Stearne that one of her imps would get "into his throat" and fill his stomach with toads.[69]

Perhaps surprisingly, these different concepts of possession were sometimes combined. This was certainly evident in the cases involving the godly exorcist John Darrell during the 1580s and 1590s. In 1596 a pious adolescent named Thomas Darling claimed that he had been cursed by an old woman he met in a wood near his uncle's house in Staffordshire. Subsequently, Darling experienced violent fits and visions of a monstrous green cat. As his condition worsened, he engaged in a series of verbal confrontations with the spirit that possessed him, which he clearly regarded as the Devil. These combined the tropes of the Protestant struggle against temptation with the belief that he was bewitched. On one occasion he demanded that the enemy reveal the name of the witch that had sent him into his body. When Satan refused and threatened to make him suffer instead, Darling rebuked him with a pious flourish:

> "Do thy worst. My hope is in the living God, and He will deliver me out of thy hands." Having spoken these words he was cast into two several fits; which being ended, he desired the standers-by to join with him in humble and hearty prayer, and so fell upon his knees, praising God, for that he had somewhat revealed his enemy Satan unto him.

When the spirit was finally expelled, it departed in a form that resembled a witch's imp. Darling declared that a mouse had bolted from his mouth and scurried into "the farthest part of the parlour".[70] This blending of Protestant zeal with traditional witch beliefs was repeated in the possession of William Sommers in 1597. In both cases, John Darrell, the minister who dispossessed the afflicted youths, viewed their deliverance as "the rare and great work of God" to glorify His church.[71]

Religious zeal and the fear of bewitchment provided contexts in which possession experiences made sense. At a deeper level, however, the medical and psychological causes of the condition remain obscure. As most readers would probably reject the existence of malevolent spirits that can occupy human bodies, it seems necessary to consider naturalistic explanations for the phenomenon. Two such explanations circulated widely in early modern England. Particular instances of possession were sometimes attributed to physical or mental disorders. Indeed, medical explanations were normally offered in the early stages of the condition: the diagnosis of "falling sickness" – now recognised as a form of epilepsy – was often made, and some victims were initially treated for melancholy. The other common explanation was fraud. Like other forms of bewitchment, it was possible to feign some of the symptoms of possession; and fraudulent cases of possession were occasionally exposed. In 1603 Samuel Harsnett combined both explanations: he claimed that the condition could be faked with "a little help of . . . epilepsy or cramp".[72] The preponderance of children and adolescents among the possessed lends some credibility to the idea that the condition was often a counterfeit: young people could gain attention and a kind of authority in the adult world by assuming the role of demoniacs.[73]

Illness and fraud can explain some of the manifestations of demon possession. But they are inadequate, on their own, to account fully for the phenomenon. While it is plausible to claim that some possessions were fabricated, this cannot explain many others in which the onset and symptoms of the condition appear to have been involuntary; equally, medical theories of the affliction cannot do justice to the elaborate and culturally specific words and deeds of the possessed. The concept of "cultural performance" offers a more complete explanation. In this model, both the demoniac and those that participated in their diagnosis and cure were actors in a social drama. They assumed roles that were implicitly sanctioned within their communities, and mutually reinforcing. "Whether unconsciously or not", Brian Levack has argued, the possessed and their deliverers were "following scripts that were encoded in their respective religious cultures".[74] This interpretation acknowledges the importance of the family of the afflicted person as well as the exorcist and the sometimes-large crowds that witnessed dispossessions. It also helps to explain why exorcism often produced "cures" – as the social script ensured the recovery of the possessed and their reintegration into normal life.[75] Finally, the idea of cultural performance explains the lived experience of possession and exorcism without explaining it away.

The social drama of possession was staged in a larger religious and political context. The ability to expel demons was contested, at various times, between Protestants and Catholics and between Protestant factions within and beyond the Church of England. This was because the act of exorcism not only relieved the suffering of the possessed but also conferred legitimacy on those that performed it. In the gospels Jesus gave "authority over unclean spirits" to his disciples (Matt. 10:1).[76] For many, this dispensation implied that exorcism was one of the signs of the true church. In 1590 the Jesuit Robert Parsons interpreted Christ's words in this way; and the Catholic mission to England in the last quarter of the sixteenth century used the power of exorcism to demonstrate the authenticity of the Roman priesthood.[77] Some members of the Church of England made the same claim. These included the martyrologist John Foxe and a number of clergy on the more zealously evangelical wing of the church.[78] "If the Church of England have this power to cast out devils", wrote George More in 1600, "then the church of Rome is a false church, for there can be but one true church, the principal mark whereof (as they say) is to . . . cast out devils".[79] For all sides, exorcism was a mark of ministerial authority; it was also a means of securing conversions and an exceptionally dramatic way to confront and overcome the prince of this world.

The most dramatic Catholic exorcisms were undertaken, in secret, during the Jesuit mission to England in the 1580s. These involved the household of Sir George Peckham of Denham in Buckinghamshire. In a letter to Robert Parsons in 1586, the lead exorcist, William Weston, described the remarkable success of this aspect of his ministry, both in relieving those afflicted with unclean spirits and in advancing the cause of his faith. He noted that news "of these events is spreading throughout the land", and some supporters were even calling for exorcisms to be performed in public. In a remarkable vignette from his memoirs, Weston recalled that on one occasion searchers visited a house while a possessed girl was in the entrance hall. "As soon as she saw them", he wrote, "she glared and ground her teeth, and said that one of the searchers had a thousand devils hanging from the buttons of his coat". This so unnerved the visitors that they made only a perfunctory search of the property, allowing the escape of several priests. This odd moment of demonic providence only stayed the discovery of Weston's activities: he was arrested in August 1586 and imprisoned until his exile in 1603.[80]

The apparent success of Catholic exorcisms raised questions for their confessional opponents. Clearly, the ability of priests to cast out demons could not be interpreted as a sign of the authenticity of their calling; and therefore alternative explanations were required. One possibility was satanic deceit. In this version the possessions were genuine but involved a double bluff: the demoniacs were temporarily relieved of their suffering at the hands of the priests, but this was merely a ruse on the Devil's part to encourage more people to join the Church of Rome. The future James I proposed this explanation in 1597.[81] A less baroque theory was that the whole phenomenon was faked. In the early 1600s Samuel Harsnett investigated the exorcisms led by William Weston some fifteen years earlier. The result was a mockingly partisan treatise on "popish impostures" that included statements obtained from some of the supposed demoniacs at Denham. One of them, a servant in the Peckham household named Sarah Williams, described how she was instructed by the Jesuits on the behaviour expected of a person taken by demons. She later tried to resist the harsh treatment she received at the hands of her supposed deliverers, but they presented this as a sign of her possession:

> She attempts to take to her heels, and run away from them, [but] the common voice was, "It was not Sarah, but the Devil." . . . She smiles, and it must not be she that smiles, but the Devil. She weeps, and she was [told] that it was not herself that wept, but the Devil. So as she said, she was at her wits end, fearing (as it seems) so much as to mutter, hum, or spit, for fear the priests should make it not her own spitting, but the Devil's.

In Harsnett's interpretation, the whole affair was a cruel deceit by Weston and his confederates. The Devil never came to Denham. The priests directed and cajoled their victims "like puppets in a pageant", and exploited the credulity of their audience to win false credit for the relics and formulae they used to rout a pretended foe.[82]

By the time that Harsnett exposed the allegedly fraudulent Jesuit exorcists, the practice of casting out demons was also contentious within the established church. Some ministers believed that demoniacs could be delivered by steadfast prayers to God, without the rites and sacred objects associated with traditional exorcism. In 1563 the "famous and godly preacher of the gospel", John Lane, cured a possessed young woman from Chester in this way.[83] Some twenty years later, John Darrell attempted to cast a small company of demons from the body of Katherine Wright in Mansfield. He brought her only temporary relief, however, as the unclean spirits returned.[84] In 1596 Darrell dispossessed the devout adolescent, Thomas Darling of Burton; and a year later he helped to cure the bedevilled children of the Starchy family in Cleworth in Lancashire. In these episodes, he believed, the Lord confounded the claims of both papists and sceptics by using godly preachers as His instruments.[85] Darrell's career ended with the spectacular dispossession of William Sommers of Nottingham in 1597. This led to an investigation of the witches allegedly responsible for Sommers' affliction; and the collapse of these proceedings eventually brought Sommers himself, and his godly deliverer, under suspicion of fraud. In 1598 Darrell was examined by an ecclesiastical commission in Lambeth. Katherine Wright and William Sommers were summoned as witnesses and testified that their possessions were faked. Darrell was convicted, somewhat improbably, of conniving in their impostures and was ejected from the ministry.[86]

As Marcus Harmes has recently argued, Darrell's downfall was part of a larger battle for legitimacy within the English church. Both Samuel Harsnett and his patron, the future Archbishop of Canterbury Richard Bancroft, viewed dispossession as "an affront to episcopal authority" and used its suppression to further their oversight of the clergy.[87] The fallout from the Darrell affair was acrimonious and long. In 1599 Harsnett published a violently hostile account of the "exorcising imposters", including the confessions of Sommers and Wright.[88] Darrell and George More, his associate in the dispossession of the Starchy children, produced defences of their activities in the following year. The ministers and their supporters maintained that the physical contortions of the possessed were impossible to feign and that Sommers' testimony had been coerced.[89] As the print war raged, the practice of godly dispossession went on: in 1603 the minister Thomas Pierson witnessed the cure of a possessed youth in Northwich in Cheshire, an event that lasted several days and occasioned sermons and fasts.[90] In an attempt to contain such activities, the ecclesiastical canons of 1605 required clergy to obtain a licence from their bishop before attempting a dispossession. This probably restrained the practice but also reinforced its association with the "hotter sort" of English Protestants. The supporters of dispossession in the 1620s and 1630s belonged mainly to this wing of the church; and it was no accident that John Darrell's account of the cure of William Sommers was reprinted during the clamour for godly reformation in 1641.[91]

The idea of possession featured on another front of religious conflict in the wake of the civil wars. The emergence of separatist congregations claiming direct inspiration from the Holy Spirit, and especially the Quaker movement of the 1650s, stirred debate about the nature of ecstatic experiences. Predictably, some enemies of the Quakers discerned in their spiritual transports a particularly devious variant of demon possession: this combined the physical symptoms of the condition with fake revelations. The victims of this experience were shaken by dark spirits but believed they were filled with God's light. In 1655, Edmund Skipp, the vicar of Bodenham in Herefordshire, suggested that the spiritual raptures described by some Quakers were satanic deceits.[92] In the same year, John Gilpin, a former Quaker from Kendal, gave an account of his own bodily transports in these terms. After attending a series of meetings describing the inner light of the spirit, Gilpin suddenly received this light in a physical blast: "I began to tremble and quake so extremely that I could not stand upon my feet, but was constrained to fall down upon my bed, where I howled and cried . . . in a terrible and hideous manner".[93] For a time Gilpin believed that he was touched by the Holy Ghost, but he came to see that he was actually gripped by demons. These spirits returned periodically in the guise of angels of light, until he was finally freed by returning to conventional forms of Protestant devotion.

The dissemination of such accounts was, of course, part of the larger struggle for religious authority after the civil wars. For most participants in this struggle, Satan was the unseen mastermind of heresy, building his kingdom through the propagation of false but enticing beliefs; the charismatic experiences of some separatists were, to their enemies, merely grotesque embellishments of this larger strategy. In his role as the adversary, the Devil was an exceptionally versatile figure, as central to the thinking of Protestant dissenters and Catholics as to orthodox divines; his devotion to lies also made him a beguiling and insidious foe. Christians did not face him alone, however. They were supported in the visible world by the ministers and leaders of their respective religious traditions, sustained by the providence of God; and in the unseen world they were surrounded by a vast company of good angels that sought to protect and deliver them from the enemy's snares.

Notes

1 John Bunyan, *Grace Abounding to the Chief of Sinners*, ed. W. R. Owens (Penguin: 1987), 29, 31.
2 John 8:44: "He was a murderer from the beginning, and abode not in the truth, because there is no truth in him. When he speaketh a lie, he speaketh of his own: for he is a liar, and the father of it".
3 George Gifford, *A Discourse of the Subtill Practises of Deuilles by Witches and Sorcerers* (1587), Dr.
4 John Milton, *Paradise Regained* (1671), book 1, line 428.
5 William Gurnall, *The Christian in Compleat Armour* (1655), 98.
6 William Gouge, *The Whole-Armor of God* (1619), 20–1.
7 The phrase is taken from the Kentish minister Henry Symons in 1657, quoted in Nathan Johnstone, *The Devil and Demonism in Early Modern England* (Cambridge University Press: 2006), 81.
8 The ballad *A New Song of Father Petre and the Devil* (1689), for example, has the pope and two monks entreating Satan with the words "Save us, good father".
9 Vavasour Powell, *Spirituall Experiences of Sundry Beleevers* (1652), 135.
10 Richard Sibbes, *The Saints Safetie in Evil Times* (1634), 6.
11 *A True Report and Exact Description of a Mighty Sea-Monster* (1617), 2.
12 John Foxe, *Actes and Monuments* (1583 edition), book 1, 24.
13 Thomas Hide, *A Consolatorie Epistle to the Afflicted Catholikes* (1579), E2*v*.
14 Johnstone, *The Devil*, 61–2.
15 A. W., *The Young-Mans Second Warning-Peece* (1643), 4. In a previous reference to this episode, I mistakenly relocated it to a church. I would like to attribute this error to satanic intervention, but sadly I cannot.
16 Cranmer is quoted in Johnstone, *The Devil*, 72.
17 William Perkins, *The Combat Betweene Christ and the Divell Displayed* (1606), 8.

18 For Bolton's account of satanic thoughts, see Darren Oldridge, *The Devil in Tudor and Stuart England* (History Press: 2010), 64–6.

19 Perkins, *Combat*, 8.

20 Oldridge, *The Devil*, 65.

21 William Perkins, *The Foundation of Christian Religion, Gathered into Six Principles* (1590), section II.

22 Johnstone, *The Devil*, 129.

23 Bunyan, *Grace Abounding*, 27; for other examples see Oldridge, *The Devil*, 66–7.

24 Louise Jackson has detected this role for demonic temptation in some confessions to witchcraft in Suffolk in 1645. See Louise Jackson, "Witches, Wives and Mothers", in Darren Oldridge, ed., *The Witchcraft Reader* (Routledge: 2nd ed. 2008). For another interpretation of the Devil's voice, see Jacqueline Pearson, "Then she asked it, what were its sister's names?": Reading Between the lines in Seventeenth-Century Pamphlets of the Supernatural", *The Seventeenth Century*, Vol. 28, No. 1 (2013), 67–9.

25 Powell, *Spirituall Experiences*, Epistle, 143–5, 309–11. The unpardonable sin is described in Mark 3:29.

26 Powell, *Spirituall Experiences*, 142–3, 146–7, 168–9, 273, 279, 311, 354, 357–8.

27 Powell, *Spirituall Experiences*, 364–6, 370–2.

28 Francis Young, *English Catholics and the Supernatural, 1553–1829* (Ashgate: 2013), 40.

29 Robert Parsons, *The First Booke of the Christian Exercise* (1582), 227, 242–3, 279.

30 Robert Parsons, *The Seconde Parte of the Booke of Christian Exercise* (1590), 353.

31 Robert Parsons, *A Treatise Tending to Mitigation Towardes Catholike-Subiectes in England* (1607), 140, 267.

32 Lilly recorded the story in his autobiography, which was eventually published as *Mr William Lilly's History of His Life and Times* (1715), 11–2. Unsentimentally, he sold the sigil for 32 shillings.

33 Johnstone, *The Devil*, 72.

34 In a literary exploration of the theme, Edmund Spenser described a tempter that led its victims to suicide in *The Faerie Queene*; see book 1, canto 9.

35 Bodleian Library, Oxford, MS Ashmole 1436, 11r.

36 William Perkins, *A Discourse of the Damned Art of Witchcraft* (1608), 175.

37 This image may refer to the worship of the world and its sensual pleasures, or possibly the Catholic Mass. *The Divils Cruelty to Mankind* (1662).

38 *A Sad Caveat for All Quakers* (1657), 8–9.

39 The text also portrayed Satan as the nurturer of sectarian heresy. It was his policy, the author warned, "to overthrow the gospel by the gospel" through the encouragement of Quakerism.

40 For this and similar murders see Oldridge, *The Devil*, 99–102.

41 *A Strange and Wonderful Relation from Shadwel, or the Devil Visible* (1674), 5–6.

42 Some of the authors in Vavasour Powell's *Spiritual Experiences* were tempted to suicide by visions of the Devil. The woman in Shadwell sought help through the prayers of her neighbours, and her story was attested by members of the local clergy. Powell, *Spiritual Experiences*, 273, 354; *Strange and Wonderful Relation*, 6.

43 See chapter 2 for the larger context of this event. The printed account described the creature as "a black dog, or the Devil in such a likeness". Abraham Fleming, *A Straunge and Terrible Wunder* (1577).

44 *The Blacke Dogge of Newgate* (1596), Cr.

45 *A Relation of a Strange Apparition* (1641), 1–3.
46 The first English witchcraft pamphlet, *The Examination and Confession of Certaine Wytches* (1566), described a spirit "in the likeness of an evil favoured dog", and "a thing like a black dog with the face of an ape". This creature was also conflated with Satan. Marion Gibson, ed., *Early Modern Witches: Witchcraft Cases in Contemporary Writing* (Routledge: 2000), 20, 22.
47 This message was pointed in the year of the pamphlet's publication, when a Catholic rebellion in Ireland inspired reports of the massacre of English settlers. Some of those attacked by the monster were identified as Irish.
48 Thomas Beard, *The Theatre of Gods Judgements* (2nd ed. 1631), 577.
49 *A Warning Piece for Ingroosers of Corne* (c. 1647–65).
50 *The Mowing Devil: or Strange News out of Hartford-shire* (1678), 3, 4–5.
51 *Dirty Dolls Farewel* (1684).
52 John Bunyan, *The Life and Death of Mr Badman* (Hesperus Press: 2007), 173, 174.
53 The difficult message of *Mr Badman* may help to explain why Bunyan produced a more conventional sequel to *The Pilgrim's Progress* in 1682.
54 See Oldridge, *The Devil*, 27, 87–9, 123–4.
55 This story existed in at least two versions. It was included in the collection of ballads *Merry Drollery Complete* (1670) and also circulated as a broadsheet entitled *The Politick Wife, or The Devil Outwitted by a Woman*. The quotation is from the latter.
56 See Darren Oldridge, "Mother Shipton and the Devil", in Angela McShane and Garthine Walker, eds., *The Extraordinary and the Everyday in Early Modern England* (Palgrave Macmillan: 2010).
57 *The Life and Death of the Merry Devil of Edmonton* (1631), Bv.
58 Around 1640 a broadside ballad based on the Faustus legend was published as *The Just Judgment of God Shew'd on Doctor John Faustus*.
59 *The Life and Death*, Bv.
60 Exorcism was the most common miracle attributed to Christ. The gospels record the following instances: Mark 1:32–4/Luke 4:33–7; Mark 5:1–20; Mark 9:14–29; Matt. 12:22–3/Luke 11:4; Matt. 9:32–3; Luke 8:2; and Mark 7:24–30.
61 John Darrell, *A True Narration of the Strange and Grevous Vexation by the Devil of 7 Persons in Lancashire* (1600), 15–6.
62 Samuel Harsnett, *A Declaration of Egregious Popish Impostures* (1603), 136.
63 Bunyan, *Grace Abounding*, 28.
64 *The Distressed Gentlewoman; or Satan's Implacable Malice* (1691).
65 Johnstone, *The Devil*, 102.
66 In this case, the afflicting spirits entered the witch's body after they fled her victims. *The Most Strange and Admirable Discoverie of the Three Witches of Warboys* (1593), Ir.
67 The sources for this episode are reproduced in C. L'Estrange Ewen, ed., *Witchcraft and Demonianism* (Heath Cranton: 1933), 190–3.
68 This was the method by which Edmund Hartley was accused of infecting the members of the Starchy family in Lancashire. For an account of this episode see Kathleen R. Sands, *Demon Possession in Elizabethan England* (Praeger: 2004), especially 154.
69 *A True and Exact Relation of the Severall Informations, Examinations, and Confessions of the Late Witches* (1645), 4, 29–31.
70 *The Most Wonderfull and True Storie of a Certaine Witch Named Alse Gooderige of Stapen Hill* (1597), 11, 37.

71 For Darrell's contentious career, see Marion Gibson, *Possession, Puritanism and Print: Darrell, Harsnett, Shakespeare and the Elizabethan Exorcism Controversy* (Pickering & Chatto: 2006). The quotation is from *The Doctrin of the Possession and Dispossession of Demoniakes*, attached to Darrell's *True Narration*, 1.

72 Harsnett, *Declaration*, 136.

73 For the role of children in cases of possession, see J. A. Sharpe, "Disruption in the Well-Ordered Household: Age, Authority and Possessed Young People", in Paul Griffiths, Adam Fox and Steve Hindle, eds., *The Experience of Authority in Early Modern England* (Macmillan: 1996).

74 Brian P. Levack, *The Devil Within: Possession and Exorcism in the Christian West* (Yale University Press: 2013), 29.

75 On the medical efficacy of dispossession, see Sands, *Demon Possession*, 10–12.

76 There is a parallel passage in Mark 3:15.

77 Parsons, *The Seconde Parte*, 310.

78 For Foxe's role in the exorcism of Robert Brigges in 1574, see Sands, *Demon Possession*, 65–71.

79 George More, *A True Discourse Concerning the Certaine Possession and Dispossession of 7 Persons in One Familie in Lancashire* (1600), 5.

80 William Weston, *The Autobiography of an Elizabethan*, trans. Philip Caraman (Longmans, Green and Co: 1955), 26, 30.

81 James VI, *Daemonologie* (1597), 71–2.

82 Harsnett, *Declaration*, 53, 148.

83 Sands, *Demon Possession*, 21–8; quotation, 22.

84 The main source for this episode is the hostile account compiled by Samuel Harsnett. For Wright's recovery and subsequent re-possession, see Harsnett, *A Discovery of the Fraudulent Practises of John Darrell* (1599), 304–5.

85 Darrell, *Doctrin of the Possession and Dispossession*, 69–70.

86 Marion Gibson argues persuasively that Darrell's prosecution was unfair, though it was conducted within the conventions of ecclesiastical law: see *Possession, Puritanism and Print*, especially chapter 5.

87 Marcus Harmes, "The Devil and Bishops in Post-Reformation England", in Marcus Harmes and Victoria Bladen, eds., *Supernatural and Secular Power in Early Modern England* (Ashgate: 2015); quotation, 189.

88 Harsnett, *Discovery*, 51.

89 *A Detection of That Sinnful, Shamful, Lying and Ridiculous Discours of Samuel Harshnet* (1600), 122–3, 141–2.

90 Jacqueline Eales, "Thomas Pierson and the Transmission of the Moderate Puritan Tradition", *Midland History*, 20 (1995), 81–2.

91 For the involvement of puritan-minded clergy in dispossessions in the period before the civil war, see Oldridge, *The Devil*, 159–61; for godly critiques of episcopal interventions in this area, see Harmes, "Bishops", 191–3.

92 Edmund Skipp, *The Worlds Wonder, or The Quakers Blazing Starr* (1655), 24, 42–4.

93 *The Quakers Shaken, or A Warning Against Quaking* (1655), 3.

5

ANGELS

The guard of God's children

Towards the end of his life in 1691, the minister Richard Baxter attended an unusual meeting with a small group of his London flock. The subject of the gathering was "a gentleman of considerable rank" – Baxter concealed his identity in the written account – who in recent months had succumbed often, and with some enthusiasm, to the sin of drunkenness. The man's younger brother was a member of Baxter's congregation, and he and his wife had raised their concerns with the venerable pastor. Their testimony touched on more than intemperance, however. On every night that the gentleman returned to his chamber to sleep off his excesses, he was awakened by a rapping noise on his bedstead. When he stayed at his brother's house, the sound was heard by other members of the family, who began to watch over him as he slept in an attempt, unsuccessfully, to detect its source. The invisible knockings became so common and disturbing that the man and his family met with Baxter, who determined that a spirit of some kind was warning him to change his ways. In his subsequent reflections on the affair, the minister wondered "what kind of spirit this is that hath such a care of this man's soul. . . . Do good spirits dwell so near us? Or are they sent on such messages? Or is it his guardian angel?" He reserved the matter to the hidden wisdom of God, "who keepeth such things from us, in the dark".[1]

Baxter's uncertainty was understandable. It was rare for angels to manifest themselves so directly – though reports of angelic visitations appeared in cheap print during the seventeenth century. English Protestants were generally wary of visions of angels, which were associated with popery and the subterfuges of the Devil. On the whole, angels were not expected to reveal themselves to the physical senses at all: in the delicate phrase of Joseph Hall, the Caroline Bishop of Norwich, they embraced humankind with "unfelt hands".[2] Nonetheless, it is striking that Baxter did not question the good intentions of the spirit that tapped at the drunkard's bed, and on this basis surmised that it was an angel. In warning an errant Christian of the dangers of sin, it certainly behaved like a member of the heavenly host. It was the duty of angels to protect and nurture human souls and to guide them away from sin. As William Perkins had written in the reign of Elizabeth, they were "the guard of God's children".[3]

If Baxter was right, the spirit in his parishioners' bedroom was a rare outward manifestation of an unseen kingdom of angels. Few doubted that the cosmos was populated by an immense company of good spirits. This belief was underpinned by biblical authority: as Perkins reminded the readers of *A Golden Chaine* (1591), ten thousand times ten thousand angels stood before God in the vision of Daniel (Dan. 7:10), and the members of this host served as "ministering spirits" to all faithful Christians.[4] But despite their ubiquity, angels were an ambivalent presence in the English church. At a basic level, it was unclear whether they could even be portrayed in images. While the reformers condemned depictions of God as invitations to idolatry, many representations of the heavenly host were allowed to remain in parish churches.[5] The veneration of angels was denounced, alongside appeals to ministering spirits to intercede with God. But the festival of St Michael, or Michaelmas, was preserved in the calendar. There was similar uncertainty about the concept of "guardian angels", members of the heavenly guard assigned for the care of particular individuals. For much of the sixteenth century the idea was tainted with Catholic associations, but some English thinkers later incorporated "angel keepers" within a reformed scheme of heavenly oversight.[6] Accordingly, Baxter could imagine the spirit tapping at the bed frame to be a guardian angel.[7]

There was also, inevitably, some tension between the scholarly conception of angels and their portrayal in wider culture. The first part of this chapter considers the ministry of God's heavenly guard in Protestant angelology, as well as the expectations of ordinary people. It argues that a reformed understanding of angels was established in English culture at large, though theologians were less inclined to describe angelic encounters in material terms than the authors of popular texts. The second section examines the participation of angels in the religious conflicts of the period. Here they assumed a more belligerent role, as spiritual allies in the battles of the Reformation.

The ministry of angels

Like the intercession of saints and the interventions of magicians, the benevolent acts of angels afforded protection in a world that could seem desperately insecure. Early modern writers often noted the need for such protection. In his bestselling guide to godly living, *The Plaine Mans Path-way to Heaven* (1601), Arthur Dent described how Christians were shielded from the dangers of daily life by an invisible company of angels.[8] More specifically, Joseph Hall observed the "many perils" that threatened the lives of young infants, and he attributed their survival to the care of the heavenly guard. How is it, he asked, "that little children are conserved . . . but by the agency of angels?" Adult life could be fragile too. In a resonant metaphor, Hall likened human experience to a journey through a wilderness concealing cutthroats and thieves: for those who feared God, the passage was safe because they were "invincibly guarded" by angels.[9] For generations of English preachers and devotional writers, the thirty-fourth Psalm provided the standard text on this comforting doctrine: "This poor man cried, and the Lord heard him, and saved him out of all his troubles. The angel of the Lord encampeth round about them that fear him, and delivereth them".[10]

The desire for such spiritual defence was probably sharpened by the theological innovations of the Reformation. The abolition of the cult of saints and the apotropaic power of the sacraments had removed traditional sources of supernatural protection. In their absence, the ministry of angels meant that Christians were not alone in a hostile world. The Church of England did not permit direct appeals for angelic assistance, but it was acceptable to ask God for protection through the agency of His celestial guard: indeed, a prayer "For the help of God's holy angels" was included in the church primer of 1553.[11] In the mid-seventeenth century the godly minister John Gumbleden provided an exemplary formulation in a printed prayer: "O most merciful saviour, my petition is that thine holy angels may be commanded to guard me, to protect me, to minister unto me while I live, and while I am within the danger of Satan".[12] It is impossible to know if such carefully phrased entreaties were widely used. That people appealed directly for angelic support is suggested by the most famous cry of this kind in Renaissance literature. At the first appearance of his father's ghost on the battlements at Elsinore, Hamlet exclaims: "Angels and ministers of grace defend us!" The prince calls again for angelic protection when the apparition returns, this time in more crafted but also more personal terms: "Save me, and hover o'er me with your wings, / you heavenly guards!"[13]

The angelologists of early modern England provided many more real-life illustrations of the need for celestial protection. Occasionally, these conveyed the urgency of individuals facing moments of sudden distress. Isaac Ambrose recorded a particularly jolting example in his *Ministration of and Communion with Angels* (1661). This concerned a man who stayed at a London inn without knowing that another resident had died of a pestilence only days before, and that a woman succumbed to the same disease on the night he arrived. The next day he discovered his plight:

> He arose in the morning, took some repast, and went about his occasions; but at his return in the afternoon, as he was going into the inn a friend called him back, and told him the truth. In the midst of the discourse, he saw the gates shut before his eyes, and presently was written upon them, *Lord*

have mercy on us. This had minded him of God's providence and promise: *Surely he shall deliver thee from the noisome pestilence, for he shall give his angels charge over thee.*[14]

The fact that Ambrose ends his account with these words, with no indication of the man's fate, only sharpens the urgency of his tale. More often, the literature of angels offered more comfortable reports of deliverance from peril. In 1658 the London minister Thomas White described how one of his friends had almost drowned in a pond as a young girl. She was saved when a man in a nearby house was unaccountably disturbed by a sense of unease, and wandered down to the water and found her.[15] A few years later Ambrose used the story to illustrate the protection extended to children by angels, who presumably caused the man to walk to the pond.[16]

This story typified the subtle nature of angelic operations. For men like Ambrose, God's agents were "secret physicians".[17] Often they acted through small movements of the heart or mind; and the guidance of their "unfelt hands" was in many cases appreciated retrospectively. Writing in the early eighteenth century, George Hammond invited individuals to review the apparently fortuitous moments in their lives and detect therein the "watchful care" of heavenly spirits.[18] More dramatic manifestations were not expected, and apparitions of angels were rare – at least in the scholarly literature on the subject. In the words of Joseph Hall, "the trade that we have with good spirits is not now driven by the eye but is like to themselves, spiritual".[19] Angels conferred strength in moments of distress and perseverance at times of temptation or doubt. When they intervened more directly in human lives, it was usually in the form of dreams or a "small voice" in the mind.

This spiritualised view of angels was, of course, analogous to the internalised understanding of the Devil described in chapter 4. If demons marshalled stirrings of temptation in human minds and flesh, God's ministering spirits encouraged fortitude against them. The Baptist theologian Henry Lawrence developed this view with particular rigour and clarity in 1646, in his aptly entitled treatise *Of Our Communion and Warre with Angels*. In the infancy of the church, Lawrence observed, good angels had appeared frequently to the outward senses to communicate divine revelations. Now, however, they operated "especially, and above all, in relation to our spirits and inward man, tacitly and in a spiritual way . . . suggesting good things, and provoking us to our duties in holiness and obedience". He noted that evil spirits were also determined to work at this level: indeed, their apparitions were now almost as rare as those of the heavenly guard. They set their snares for the spirit instead of the body. Consequently, good angels were deployed to assist men and women in their struggle with demonic temptation. Lawrence was upbeat in his assessment of the spiritual forces involved: the angels were stronger than demons, "and their love higher than the others' malice".[20]

Perhaps the most common accounts of angelic assistance were reported from the deathbed. The belief that celestial figures gathered around the bodies of the dying, and conveyed their souls to heaven, was embedded in medieval Christianity. Indeed, David Keck has suggested that this was the most widespread image of angels in the pre-Reformation church.[21] The idea of angelic assistance in the hours before death survived in Protestant England, though direct appeals to these ministering spirits were discouraged.[22] Rather, the heavenly guard assembled to comfort the departing spirit and to strengthen its resolve against the assaults of Satan. In the last words of a godly minister preserved by Henry Smith in 1591, the man declared, "the Devil doth not amaze me, because the angels pitch about me".[23] The idea that heavenly spirits lifted the souls of the redeemed to the Lord also survived. At the conclusion of John Bunyan's *Pilgrim's Progress* (1678), angels conveyed Christian and Hopeful to the celestial city on the hill.[24] Two years later, Bunyan described the ethereal music that accompanied the death of a pious man. This was, he explained, "the melodious notes of angels who were sent of God to fetch him to heaven".[25]

As Bunyan's text illustrates, some Protestant writers retained the possibility that angels could manifest themselves directly to human senses, albeit in exceptional circumstances. The 1583 edition of Foxe's *Actes and Monuments* included the story of an angelic visitation to the Suffolk martyr Robert Samuel, as he was chained to a post and starved in the days before his execution:

> After he had been famished or pined with hunger two or three days altogether, he fell into a sleep, as it were one half in a slumber, at which time one clad all in white, seemed to stand before him, which ministered comfort unto him by these words: "Samuel, Samuel, be of good cheer, and take a good heart unto thee. For after this day shalt thou never be either hungry or thirsty."

Foxe left open the question of whether the angel appeared in a delirium or revealed itself to Samuel's outward senses, though he and later writers seem to have accepted that the martyr was comforted by a ministering spirit.[26] Other accounts of angelic encounters offered more tangible proofs. According to Thomas White in 1658, a Warwickshire man was converted to the cause of godly religion by a series of visions accompanied by a heavenly voice. At the end of this visitation, "he had a blow given him on his side, as with a dagger, the mark whereof he carried with him to his grave".[27] Isaac Ambrose repeated the story in his treatise on angels. He added another instance of the physical intervention of good spirits that was both topical and politic in the early years of the Restoration: the future Charles II was, he supposed, guarded and fed by angels during his period of hiding after the battle of Worcester in 1651.[28]

Beyond the work of scholarly writers, there is evidence that people accepted the possibility of apparitions of angels. Among the correspondence of the Jacobean minister Daniel Featley is an account of his advice to Sir Thomas Wise, a West Country gentleman who believed that a female spirit had visited him at night. The spectre had unlatched the door to his bedchamber and moved to the foot of his bed. Terrified, Wise had offered a prayer to God and abjured the figure to come no closer; it then stood silently for half an hour before fading away. Wise first consulted an archdeacon, who suggested that his visitor was an angel. Then he turned to Featley for advice, only to be told that it was an evil spirit. Featley based this judgement on the known attributes of angels, which he set out in four points. First, ministering spirits no longer appeared to the outward senses, since the age of "miraculous revelations" had ended. Second, "angels are never sent but with some message, and to accomplish some extraordinary service, whereas this spirit only made a chamber show". He then pointed out that the Holy Ghost had given Wise the strength to pray and instruct the figure to stay away, at which point it had stopped moving. Finally, he claimed that "it is a thing unheard of that an angel should appear in the perfect likeness of a woman". Wise should be grateful to God, he observed, that his demonic visitor had not come in a more terrible shape. He should also examine his conscience for whatever sin had occasioned the apparition, and amend his ways accordingly.[29]

If Featley's advice echoed the conventionally cautious attitude of Protestant theologians towards angelic visions, Sir Thomas Wise and the archdeacon were probably not alone in believing that angels might sometimes appear on earth. Some considerably less respectable testimony supports this view. The conjuration of angels was a feature of ceremonial magic in sixteenth- and seventeenth-century England, and those involved apparently believed that "celestial creatures" could present themselves to the outward senses. The memoirs of the astrologer William Lilly described a magician named Evans who in the 1620s summoned an angel to find the deeds to some property that one of his clients had lost. After observing the appropriate rites, Evans made the angel appear to receive his commands; it quickly returned "with the very deed desired, laid it down gently upon a table where a white cloth was spread, and then being dismissed, vanished". Among several features of this surprising transaction, it is notable that Evans was a minister in a Staffordshire parish at the time – though he was subsequently obliged "to fly for some offences very scandalous".[30]

The disreputable Evans was not the only churchman who sought to summon angels. In the late seventeenth century, the antiquarian John Aubrey claimed that Richard Napier, the physician and minister of Great Linford in Buckinghamshire, conversed with the angel Raphael as part of his medical practice. The angel offered prognoses for Napier's patients and also imparted knowledge of future events. It was by this means, Aubrey claimed, that Napier predicted that John Prideaux would become Bishop of Worcester.[31] More scandalously, the Berkshire minister John Pordage was removed from his benefice in 1654 for allegedly professing heterodox doctrines and conjuring angels.[32] Pordage admitted to encounters with "pure angelical spirits", which appeared to his "inward eye" in luminous forms "full of beauty and majesty, [and] sparkling like diamonds".[33] But he denied that he had summoned these creatures by illicit means. Pordage and his followers embraced a mystical version of Christianity that largely eschewed the practical aspects of angelic conjuration, such as medicine and the recovery of lost goods. It is probable nonetheless, as Joad Raymond has argued, that Pordage used astrological magic to produce some of his visions.[34] This is suggested by his association with Elias Ashmole, the gentleman alchemist and astrologer who presented him to his living in the 1640s.

Owen Davies has noted that angels featured only infrequently in the operations of more humble magicians, or "cunning folk", in the sixteenth and early seventeenth centuries. The publication of English editions of magical treatises in the mid-1600s, however, democratized some branches of scholarly magic; and as a result angelic conjurations entered the "cunning trade".[35] The most common device for summoning angels was a crystal ball, or some other reflective surface, in which the image or message of the spirit could manifest itself. In 1696 John Aubrey described one such vessel that was then in the possession of Sir Edward Harley of Brampton Bryan in Herefordshire. One of its previous owners, a miller from Norfolk, had used it to solicit medical advice from angels: this appeared on its surface either as recipes or images of herbs.[36] In this case it seems that the angels communicated directly to the magician; more often, an intermediary was used to decipher the images that appeared in the stone. This was normally a young boy or girl, as children were believed to possess the purity required to read the celestial dispatches.[37]

The angels in popular literature were more direct in their dealings with humankind. A pamphlet published in 1605 described how a young man from Antwerp was falsely accused of robbery while travelling on his uncle's business in Germany. He was sentenced to hang and left on the gallows for five days. When his uncle discovered what had happened, he went to the scene and found the youth miraculously alive. It had "pleased Almighty God", his nephew explained, "to preserve me by placing a stool under my feet, which to you is not perceived, upon the which I stand, and the angel of the Lord from heaven hath fed me here five days".[38] A more homely tale from 1659 related the good fortune of a Lincolnshire shoemaker who was cured of a consumptive illness by a mysterious stranger. In return for a glass of small beer, his visitor gave him the recipe for a medicine that enabled him to walk unaided for the first time in four years. The pamphlet concluded that the stranger – an old man dressed in purple and white, and mysteriously untouched by the rainstorm in which he arrived – was an angel sent to restore the man's health.[39]

In their robust physicality, stories such as these challenged the assumptions of godly angelologists like Henry Lawrence and George Hammond – though they would not, perhaps, look out of place in the compendium of marvellous interventions assembled by Isaac Ambrose. In other respects, the ministering spirits of cheap print conformed broadly to Protestant expectations. Indeed, the stranger who cured the shoemaker in 1659 met most of Daniel Featley's criteria for an angel. He was a grave and pious man on an extraordinary mission, and he insisted on several occasions that the recipient of his medical advice should serve and fear God above all things. For his part, the shoemaker was presented as a Christian professor: he was reading a godly tract when the stranger tapped at his door, and when he was asked about his illness he declared that he was in "the hands of Almighty God, to dispose of him as He pleased". For these and other "weighty reasons", the pamphlet reported that a meeting of local clergy had determined that the man had truly encountered an angel.[40]

Other godly pamphlets effectively externalised the good and evil spirits described by Henry Lawrence, presenting angels and demons as physical companions to human beings. *The Kentish Miracle* (1684) was a dramatic example of this tendency. The text described a destitute but God-fearing woman named Mary Moor, who was accosted by a finely dressed man who offered to take her and her children into his master's service. It emerged, however, that his terms required her to renounce the Bible and the church and to condemn religion as "the delusions of deceitful clergy". She chose to stay poor rather than accept this bargain. Subsequently, she came to a well and drew some water for her children. Another stranger approached and asked why she was there. She explained her circumstances, and he responded with celestial beneficence:

> The angel (for so he was) replied, "Blessed be thou, servant of the Lord . . . for great is thy faith, and the Lord has heard thy prayers, and will provide for thee, and will relieve all thy wants. Turn thee round and up that stone, and thou shall find something to buy bread for thee and thy babes." Upon which she went and took up the stone, where she found thirty shillings in a paper, and these words written: "Blessed are all those that believe in God, for He will never leave or forsake them."

The angel then told her to stay firm in her faith and called on the people of England to repent their sins as the Day of Judgement neared. To prove his words, he instructed her to bring witnesses to the same place the next day. She brought three ministers, who also saw the angel alongside a retinue of heavenly spirits, and subsequently set their names to her testimony.[41]

The tendency to physicalise spiritual conflicts was also evident in ballads that mentioned angels. In one late illustration, *The Children's Example* (1700), a young girl was first tempted by the Devil in a churchyard and then consoled by an angel. The angel returned when the child fell ill and died, escorting her soul to heaven.[42] A more savage fate awaited the anti-hero of *Strange News from Westmoreland* (1663).

This told the story of a man who killed his wife in a drunken temper, causing his screaming children to draw their neighbours to the scene. The murderer denied his crime. At this point a sweet-complexioned stranger appeared at the door. The visitor denounced the man's various sins and declared judgement against him. He then called on the Devil to execute the sentence: the fiend appeared as a terrible monster, snapped the perpetrator's neck and vanished. The stranger announced that his business was done; but before departing he told the witnesses that "to love each other well . . . is the way to get to heaven". They drew the obvious conclusion that he was an avenging angel sent by God.[43]

The depiction of angels in cheap print permits a tentative evaluation of the ministry of these spirits in popular culture. Clearly, the audience for these texts did not share the suspicion of angelic visions that characterised Protestant theology on the subject. It also appears that traditional motifs permeated the popular literature of the heavenly host. Angels continued to fulfil roles that were established before the Reformation: as healers and advisors, workers of wonders, and avengers of the innocent and comforters to the dying.[44] Even the geography of their manifestations echoed older beliefs. The angel beside the well in 1684 recalled the appearance of good spirits – including saints – beside holy water places in the Middle Ages. (Correspondingly, the intrusion of the Devil in a graveyard in *The Children's Example* reflected traditional expectations of the geography of spirits.) Nonetheless, it would be rash to assume that the angels in small godly books merely preserved ancient beliefs beneath a veneer of reformed religion. It is striking, for instance, that they did not respond to direct prayers from the faithful: rather, they appeared independently as agents of God. When the religious beliefs of their beneficiaries were described, they conformed to approved styles of Protestant piety. Mary Moor, for example, practiced the kind of unadorned and patient devotion that had been recommended by generations of English reformers.[45]

Interestingly, it also seems that pamphlets based on angelic apparitions were comparatively rare. This tends to support the view, advanced persuasively by Laura Sangha, that angels did not merely replicate the roles once performed by saints in English popular culture: they would surely have enjoyed a much higher profile if this had been the case. The abolition of direct appeals for intercession – both to saints and to angels – meant that God's "secret physicians" could not provide the kind of immediate protection that was previously associated with the holy dead; nor could they attract the same level of personal devotion.[46] The angels of popular literature were broadly consistent with reformed theology, despite their stubborn insistence on physical manifestations. The identity of English angels was further sharpened by their involvement in confessional conflict: this placed ministering spirits on both sides of the struggle between Protestants and Catholics that defined early modern religious culture.

Confessional angels

Suspended above the most searingly confrontational image of the English Reformation, the title page of John Foxe's *Actes and Monuments* (1563), is a scene of heavenly concord. Flanking the figure of Christ seated in judgement, two bands of winged trumpeters sound the music of the last days. The angels are the only figures in the pictorial scheme that break its spacial dichotomy between the saved and the damned, which places Protestant worshippers and martyrs on the left and the idolatrous flock of Antichrist on the right. The celestial players are a reminder of the shared heritage of the two sides. But this traditional portrayal of heaven was emphatically not a symbol of potential reconciliation. On the contrary, it underlined the conviction that there was one true and timeless revelation, and the reformed ministry was its custodian. By definition, the rival church of Rome could not share this status: it was at best an earthly folly and at worst a false creed that led to hell. Catholics applied the same confessional logic. Within this way of thinking, the angels that adorned Foxe's book could serve only one side or the other: they were the invisible guard of the one true church.

The affiliation of Foxe's angels was shown in the episode, already described, when a ministering spirit comforted Robert Samuel through the torture that preceded his martyrdom under Mary Tudor. Angels maintained their role as the protectors of God's true children in the Elizabethan and early Stuart church. William Perkins noted their particular affinity with the Protestant clergy, with whom they shared the role of serving and disseminating the word of God. As "ministering spirits sent out for the good of them which shall be saved", he wrote, angels took a special interest in those "which shall both be saved themselves and save others also".[47] Accordingly, they guarded the clergy against their many earthly and spiritual adversaries. They gave them physical strength to pursue their calling, and spiritual fortitude to resist the temptations and false doctrines with which they had to contend. In 1601 Arthur Dent affirmed the kinship between angels and devout members of the English church. True Christians were "angel's fellows, descended of the highest house, of the blood royal of heaven".[48] They could count on their spiritual kin to assist them against their earthly foes.

For Perkins and Dent, these heavenly protectors were not merely partisans in the confessional struggles of their age: they were assigned exclusively to those whom God had chosen to save. The hidden hands of angels preserved only the elect. This doctrine was developed systematically by the Protestant angelologists of the seventeenth century. In 1646 Henry Lawrence cited the words of St Paul to the Hebrews: that "ministering spirits" were sent to the "heirs of salvation" (Heb. 1:14). This privilege, he concluded, was reserved only to them. It was equally clear to Lawrence that the heirs of salvation were redeemed members of the Protestant community.[49] Isaac Ambrose began his own treatise on angels with the same text, and he insisted on the same interpretation. The care of angels, he observed, was a glorious demonstration of God's love for the elect; and their indifference to the reprobate consigned them miserably to the falsehoods and snares of the Devil.[50]

Naturally, however, English Catholics also found defenders in the heavenly guard. In a mirror image of Foxe's account of the death of Robert Samuel, angels were reported at the scene of Catholic executions in the later sixteenth century. According to one sympathetic witness, the Jesuit Edmund Campion declared from the scaffold in 1582 that his death was "a spectacle unto my Lord God [and] a spectacle unto His angels". A verse attached to the account confirmed the presence of celestial witnesses at the gallows: "Men, angels, saints, and all that saw him die / forgot their grief, his joys appeared so nye". A second poem affirmed that the community between Campion and the angels would continue in heaven, where he joined them in everlasting song. The author reversed the apocalyptic imagery of the *Book of Martyrs*, declaring that "an angel's trump" was a fit accompaniment to the priest's death.[51]

Catholics were generally less cautious about angelic visitations than their confessional counterparts. In part, this attitude derived from the tradition of medieval visionary experience; but it also reflected the needs of a community excluded from secular authority, for which supernatural interventions were an important source of validation. In this context, it is notable that angels were mainly associated with religious instruction during the reign of Mary Tudor, when the status of the church was secure.[52] More direct manifestations of angelic favour were a powerful weapon when the old faith came under attack. By the late sixteenth century, when recusant congregations were increasingly persecuted, supernatural revelations were presented as signs of true religion. In the direct language of the exiled priest Richard Bristow in 1574, heavenly visions were a "sure and infallible way . . . to find out who has the truth, we or the Protestants".[53] In 1600 the Catholic missionary Thomas Hill endorsed this view, and used reports of visions to win English converts. "In these days", he wrote, "I know diverse and sundry papists (as you call them) who have seen undoubtedly wonderful visions . . . with sufficient and irrefragable testimony".[54]

Angels featured often in such revelations. In the most celebrated early example, Elizabeth Barton, "the holy maid of Kent", was apparently directed by ministering spirits to warn Henry VIII against seceding from Rome.[55] According to the hostile account of Thomas Cranmer, Barton claimed to have received some of these communications in a letter written in gold, "feigning the same to have been delivered to her by an angel from heaven".[56] She also instructed one of her associates, on the advice of an angel, to destroy an English translation of the New Testament.[57] Perhaps the most incendiary of Barton's visions also involved a member of the heavenly host. In this she witnessed the king attending Mass and preparing to receive the consecrated bread; but an angel took it from the priest's hand and gave it to Barton instead. The result of such otherworldly interventions was predictable. Barton was made to confess to fraud, and every sympathetic account of her visions was destroyed – including at least one book and numerous copies of the angelic letter.[58] She was hanged for treason in 1534.

Another young Catholic woman was involved in a dramatic encounter with angels during the reign of Elizabeth. In 1580 Elizabeth Orton of Flintshire experienced a series of visions, apparently mediated by celestial spirits. In one, an angel appeared as a "goodly fair bird, having the body of a sparrow hawk, the face of a man, the beak of a pigeon, and feathers of diverse colours". This creature spread its wings over her breast and touched its bill to her face, then declared itself to be a messenger from God. Another angelic visitor was more homely:

> Standing by the fire in the old hall . . . amongst the rest of our family, there appeared unto me a goodly old man all in white, who after he had made two or three turnings before my face, returned to the new parlour, from whence he was come as we thought, whither also I followed him to see what he did. But missing him there, I made haste towards the upper chamber, where I hoped to find him. And lo, suddenly no small number of wax candles burned in my sight. . . . The foresaid old man himself again approached near me. I was afraid, but he comforted me, saying, "Be not afraid, for here is none will do thee hurt".

The spirit confirmed that it was sent by God and presented her to an apparition of Christ and the apostles, together with St Anne and the Virgin, whose face was "brighter than any crystal".[59] The emphatically Catholic nature of Orton's revelations – which included a visit to purgatory – ensured a stinging official response. Like Elizabeth Barton before her, she was obliged to renounce her own visions as fraudulent in Chester cathedral.

The authorities were probably right to fear such disruptive angels. The cases of Elizabeth Orton and the maid of Kent displayed the subversive potential of divine messengers. Elizabeth Barton was briefly an important figure: she enjoyed audiences with bishops, and even the king himself, before the increasingly unguarded content of her revelations brought her down. On a smaller stage, it appears that Elizabeth Orton posed a threat to the established church on the Welsh borders: she was not originally from a recusant family, and the audience for her visions included conforming members of the local laity.[60] It also appears that angelic apparitions could help to sustain established Catholic communities. Visions of angels were among the "popish impostures" exposed by Samuel Harsnett in the recusant household at Denham in Buckinghamshire in the late 1500s.[61] In the seventeenth century, English members of religious orders, such as Mary Ward and Catherine Burton, experienced angelic visitations that confirmed their faith.[62]

The role of angels in Catholic piety was usually less dramatic, of course. The publication of English translations of continental texts encouraged devotion to heavenly spirits, and especially guardian angels, for whom Pope Paul V created a feast day in 1608. In Gaspar Loarte's *Exercise of a Christian Life* (1579), readers were encouraged to appeal for angelic assistance as part of a daily round of supplicatory prayers. These appeals were made directly to members of the divine company. A translation of Jeremias Drexel's *The Angel-Guardians Clock* in 1630 provided a book-length treatment of these themes. Drexel's supplicants sought guidance and protection from the "watchful guardians" of their souls, and hoped "to enjoy their everlasting society". The work also asserted a decisively Catholic relationship between humankind and angels. Prayers for intercession were offered by name to the archangels Michael, Gabriel and Raphael, and collectively to the nine orders of the celestial guard. An appeal to St Mary addressed her as the "queen of angels". The prayers themselves sought protection for the leaders of the church and the religious orders – and also, at a more intimate level, against the perils of disease and "sudden and unprovided death".[63]

The participation of angels in the conflict between Protestants and Catholics was replicated in disputes within the established church. Some Protestants objected to the retention of Michaelmas in the religious calendar.[64] On the more ceremonial wing of the church, the invisible presence of angels at the Eucharist was used to justify a decorous style of worship. This tendency reached its zenith in the work of some Laudian divines in the 1630s: Robert Shelford, for instance, impressed the need for parishioners to cover their heads "lest the holy angels in the congregation should be offended at the women's irreverent carriage with bare heads and long hair, and at the men's hats on their heads".[65] Contrasting attitudes towards angels were expressed most dramatically in the fabric of parish churches. During the first waves of official iconoclasm under Henry VIII and Edward VI, many images of angels were defaced or destroyed; but many others survived unmolested. This was partly the result of ambivalence about whether depictions of angels *per se* contravened the Mosaic injunction against "graven images", which enjoyed the status of the second commandment in the English Bible, or whether they should be removed only when they encouraged veneration. No doubt it also reflected the cost, both emotional and financial, of destroying such precious things. These qualms were cast aside by the godly iconoclasts of the civil war. The extraordinary journal of William Dowsing in the winter of 1643–4 records what one historian has called a "war on angels".[66] In a single day in December 1643, Dowsing's men "pulled down two mighty great angels with wings" in the chapel of Peterhouse College in Cambridge, alongside "about a hundred cherubim and angels".[67]

Perhaps surprisingly, the hardening resistance to representations of ministering spirits was accompanied, in some godly circles, by the acceptance of the idea of guardian angels. In 1613 John Salkeld, a former Jesuit seminarian, tacitly affirmed the existence of such beings; and the anti-puritan controversialist Richard Montagu explicitly endorsed them in 1624.[68] On the opposite wing of the Protestant community, the Baptist Henry Lawrence affirmed in 1646 that individuals had "particular angels . . . deputed to them as tutors and keepers".[69] He was followed (and plagiarised) by Robert Dingley, who placed the concept of angel keepers at the heart of his *Deputation of Angels* (1653). Crucially for both men, guardian angels belonged only to members of the elect.[70] As a consequence, their presence became an invisible sign of divine grace, and was integrated into the search for indications of election that characterised the "experimental" Calvinism of the godly in Stuart England.

From the middle decades of the seventeenth century, then, belief in guardian angels united a remarkable diversity of men and women, from the puritan wing of the English church to members of the recusant community. Faith in these protecting spirits also cut across the period's political divisions: the parliamentarian Robert Dingley shared his commitment to guardian angels with firm royalists such as Alice Thornton.[71] This reflected the flexibility of the concept, as well as the openness of the biblical texts on which it was based. In an age of insecurity and conflict, the idea that individuals had supernatural helpers assigned to their care was also, we may assume, deeply comforting. Adapting the words of the ninety-first Psalm, Henry Lawrence conveyed this sense of reassurance in 1646: "They shall always bear us in their arms, that no evil shall befall us".[72]

Notes

1 Richard Baxter, *The Certainty of the Worlds of Spirits* (1691), 61–2.
2 Joseph Hall, *The Invisible World, Discovered to Spirituall Eyes* (1659), 43.
3 William Perkins, *Of the Calling of the Ministerie* (1605), 67.
4 William Perkins, *A Golden Chaine, or The Description of Theologie* (1591), Q3r.
5 Alexandra Walsham examines the ambivalence of English Protestants on this issue in "Angels and Idols in England's Long Reformation", in Peter Marshall and Alexandra Walsham, eds., *Angels in the Early Modern World* (Cambridge University Press: 2006).
6 See Peter Marshall, "The Guardian Angel in Protestant England", in Joad Raymond, ed., *Conversations with Angels: Essays Towards a History of Spiritual Communication, 1100–1700* (Palgrave Macmillan: 2011); Laura Sangha, *Angels and Belief in England, 1480–1700* (Pickering & Chatto: 2012), 108–13.
7 Interestingly, Baxter also entertained the more controversial possibility that the spirit might be "the soul of some good friend" returning to warn the errant gentleman. He did not, however, suggest that it was a demon.
8 Arthur Dent, *The Plaine Mans Path-way to Heaven* (1601), 125–6.
9 Hall, *Invisible World*, 27, 38.
10 Psalm 34:6–7.
11 Sangha, *Angels*, 45–7.
12 John Gumbleden, *Christ Tempted: The Divel Conquered* (1657), 86.
13 *Hamlet*, Act 1, Scene 4, line 39; Act 3, Scene 4, lines 103–4.
14 Isaac Ambrose, *The Compleat Works* (1674), 134. The italics are in the original text.
15 Thomas White, *A Treatise of the Power of Godlinesse* (1658), 415.
16 Ambrose, *Works*, 121.
17 Ambrose, *Works*, 134.
18 Marshall, "Guardian Angel", 310.

19 Hall, *Invisible World*, 63.
20 Henry Lawrence, *Of Our Communion and Warre with Angels* (1646), 42, 45.
21 David Keck, *Angels and Angelology in the Middle Ages* (1998), 203.
22 On the survival and adaptation of this belief, see Peter Marshall, "Angels around the Deathbed: Variations on a Theme in the English Art of Dying", in Peter Marshall and Alexandra Walsham, eds., *Angels in the Early Modern World* (Cambridge University Press: 2006).
23 Henry Smith, *Three Prayers, One for the Morning, Another for the Evening: The Third for a Sick-man* (1591), 22.
24 John Bunyan, *The Pilgrim's Progress*, ed. Roger Pooley (Penguin: 2008), 159.
25 John Bunyan, *The Life and Death of Mr Badman* (Hesperus: 2007), 153.
26 John Foxe, *Actes and Monuments* (1583 ed.), book 11, 1728. Thomas White retold the story in 1658, and it was included among the examples of angelic assistance "to our outward man" in Abrose's *Ministration* (1661). Ambrose, *Works*, 134–5.
27 White, *Treatise*, 411–13.
28 Ambrose, *Works*, 134, 137–8.
29 Bodleian Library, Oxford, MS Rawlinson D 47, 43r-v.
30 Bodleian Library, Oxford, MS Ashmole 421, 189r-v, 232r. See chapter 7 for the conjuration of angels in ritual magic.
31 John Aubrey, *Miscellanies* (1696), 133–4.
32 For Pordage's trial and subsequent career, see Joad Raymond, "Radicalism and Mysticism in the Later Seventeenth Century: John Pordage's Angels", in Raymond, *Conversations*.
33 John Pordage, *Innocencie Appearing through the Dark Mists of Pretended Guilt* (1655), 75.
34 Raymond, "Radicalism", in Raymond, *Conversations*, 319.
35 Owen Davies, "Angels in Elite and Popular Magic, 1650–1790", in Marshall and Walsham, *Angels*, 302–3.
36 Aubrey, *Miscellanies*, 130.
37 Davies, "Angels", in Marshall and Walsham, *Angels*, 305.
38 *A True Relation of Gods Wonderfull Mercies* (1605), 6.
39 *The Good Angel of Stamford* (1659), 5–6.
40 *Good Angel*, 2–3, 6.
41 *The Kentish Miracle: or A Seasonable Warning to All Sinners* (1684), 4, 6.
42 *The Children's Example* (1700).
43 *Strange News from Westmoreland* (1663).
44 On the ministry of angels to the dying, see Peter Marshall, "Angels around the Deathbed: Variations on a Theme in the English Art of Dying", in Marshall and Walsham, *Angels*.
45 Moor's repudiation of the demonic tempter, for example, followed the style of Protestant spiritual autobiographies. *Kentish Miracle*, 5.
46 For a comparison between medieval saints and Protestant angels, see Sangha, *Angels*, chapter 2, especially pp. 42, 45–50.
47 Perkins, *Calling of the Ministerie*, 68.
48 Dent, *Plaine Mans Path-way*, 125.
49 Lawrence, *Communion*, 19.
50 Ambrose, *Works*, 107, 10.
51 Thomas Alfield, *A True Reporte of the Death & Martyrdom of M. Campion* (1582), Cr, E1r, E3v, F1v.

52 For the educational emphasis of Marian angelology, see Sangha, *Angels*, 132–5.

53 Richard Bristow, *A Briefe Treatise of Divers Plaine and Sure Waies to Finde out the Truth* (1574), 32*v*.

54 Thomas Hill, *A Quartron of Reasons of Catholike Religion* (1600), 39.

55 For Barton's career, see Diane Watt, *Secretaries of God: Women Prophets in Late Medieval and Early Modern England* (Cambridge University Press: 1997), chapter 3.

56 Thomas Cranmer, *Miscellaneous Writings and Letters of Thomas Cranmer, Archbishop of Canterbury*, ed. John Edmund Cox (Cambridge: 1846), 65.

57 Alexandra Walsham, "Catholic Reformation and the Cult of Angels", in Joad Raymond, ed., *Conversations with Angels* (Palgrave Macmillan: 2011), 276–7.

58 Watt, *Secretaries*, 57–8, 69.

59 Barnaby Rich, *The True Report of a Late Practise Enterprised by a Papist* (1582), C1*v*, D1*v*-D2*r*.

60 On this point, see Peter Marshall, *Beliefs and the Dead in Reformation England* (Oxford University Press: 2002), 134.

61 Samuel Harsnett, *A Declaration of Egregious Popish Impostures* (1603), 274.

62 Walsham, "Catholic Reformation", 281–2.

63 Jeremias Drexel, *The Angel-Guardians Clock* (1630), 51, 61–2, 65.

64 Sangha, *Angels*, 103.

65 Shelford is quoted in Sangha, *Angels*, 99.

66 Trevor Cooper, "Brass, Glass and Crosses: Identifying Iconoclasm outside the Journal", in William Dowsing, *The Journal of William Dowsing: Iconoclasm in East Anglia*, ed. Trevor Cooper (Boydell Press: 2001), 94.

67 Dowsing, *Journal*, 21 December, 1643.

68 Marshall, "Guardian Angel", 298–300.

69 Lawrence, *Communion*, 20.

70 Sangha, 109–12; Marshall, "Guardian Angel", 302–5.

71 Thornton thanked God for sending "His guardian angel to watch over me and mine for my good preservation ever since I was born". *The Autobiography of Mrs Alice Thornton of East Newton*, ed. C. Jackson (Surtees Society: 1875), 4.

72 Lawrence, *Communion*, 22.

6

GHOSTS AND GOBLINS

"Doubtful spirits"

Among the surviving papers of the astrological physician Richard Napier is a series of notes, written around 1635, which summarise the cases that he dealt with over his long career. The author grouped them by the afflictions of the patients concerned. The first category was for those "haunted by spirits". There were entries for almost every year between 1601 and 1619, and a smattering of cases from the 1620s and early 1630s. Brief notes were appended to some of the dates: on 12 October 1602, "a house haunted at Beckley in Suffolk", and on 17 December 1608, a person "haunted with fairies". Beneath this list was a small group of cases entitled "Apparitions", and a few pages later there was a much larger set headed "Figures of Witchcraft", including a note on one patient "stricken with some ill spirit".[1] The catalogue of afflictions indicates the extent of occult incursions in the lives of men and women in the early decades of the seventeenth century. The spirits that vexed Napier's patients were, it appears, a recurrent and disruptive presence in the early modern period.

For those who took a more theological view of these things, the nature of these creatures was a matter of some interest and concern. The various "bugs" of traditional culture – including the spirits and fairies that troubled Napier's clients – were not easily accommodated within a biblical cosmos: to borrow a phrase from the godly minister Richard Baxter, they were "doubtful spirits".[2] Predictably, Protestant thinkers tended to explain such creatures as part of the larger artifice of the Church of Rome. According to the Elizabethan Bishop of Lincoln, Thomas Cooper, the various agents of Antichrist had "bewitched the world, now these many years, by spirits, ghosts, goblins, and many vain apparitions".[3] An editorial note attached to Edmund Spenser's *Shepheardes Calendar* (1579) reminded readers of the provenance of the fairies and elves that populated some of its pages: they were originally invented by "bald friars and knavish shavelings . . . that sought to [coddle] the common people in ignorance".[4]

This allegation, though common, was no less fanciful than Spenser's poem. Ghosts and goblins were not invented by medieval churchmen; nor did they play a particularly important part in English religion before the Reformation. Rather, they appear to have belonged to an assembly of pagan and semi-Christian spirits that mingled among the saints and angels of the medieval church. In some cases, these were contained quite successfully within the framework of orthodoxy: apparitions of the dead, for example, could be explained as souls freed briefly from purgatory. Fairies, elves and goblins, and the various "startlebugs" of traditional culture were occasionally classified as demons; but more often they seem to have hovered undisturbed at the margins of official religion, just as they lived in the woods, hills and marshes beyond human habitation.[5]

This chapter considers the fate of these beings in the reformation of spirits. The first section is devoted to ghosts, as the returning dead were the subject of particular controversies in Tudor and Stuart England, and retained a lively presence in the period's popular literature. The second section examines the more amorphous collection of spirits that some contemporary writers described as "bugs". These included the overlapping categories of fairies, hobgoblins and imps, alongside more exotic but elusive creatures like "the man in the oak". None of these entities had a secure berth in scripture, and consequently all were effectively abolished by the Protestant authorities. The fact that they fill a whole section of this book testifies to their remarkable and complicated persistence.

Ghosts

Reports of ghosts, wrote Thomas Cranmer in 1547, were fantastical tales conceived to deceive adults and frighten children. They "ought to be taken as old wives' fables [and] the words of liars". The reason was simple and pithily expressed in a marginal note to the archbishop's text: "for souls departed the body cannot walk here on earth". This conclusion arose from the Protestant repudiation of the doctrine of purgatory and from the adoption of a radically simplified model of the afterlife. For medieval churchmen, purgatory provided a temporary residence for human souls pending the last judgement; and in this interim state, the spirits of the dead were occasionally permitted to return to earth. In contrast, the reformers envisioned permanent barriers between the saved and the damned and the living and the dead. Enlarging on a passage from the Wisdom of Solomon, Cranmer asserted that "the souls of the righteous are in the hand of God, and the souls of sinners are straight after their death carried away. . . . The soul therefore, after it be departed from the body, cannot wander here amongst us."[6] This remained the position of the Church of England in the sixteenth and seventeenth centuries.

In the memorable words of Peter Marshall, ghosts became "illegal immigrants across a border that was supposed to remain sealed and impermeable until the end of time".[7]

Unlike the saints, or "holy dead", the ghosts of ordinary people had played a relatively small role in medieval Christianity. Appearances of the humble dead were, nonetheless, acknowledged by the English church before the Reformation and occasionally featured in exemplary tales that affirmed the existence of purgatory and the power of sacraments to relieve the suffering of its inhabitants. In one affecting narrative from the late fourteenth century, the spirit of a woman returned to her lover to request the celebration of masses for her soul. The man cut some hair from her head, which in death had turned from golden to black; and as the masses were performed, he saw that each hair recovered its original hue.[8] Tudor Protestants were keen to mock such tales. Preaching at Hampton Court in 1578, William James denounced a cluster of illusions that had sustained the Roman church: these included "the insufferable pains of purgatory", and myths "of walking spirits [and] of ugly and fearful ghosts".[9] In a similar vein, the Archbishop of York, Edwin Sandys, dismissed in 1585 the Catholic belief that the spirits of the dead could instruct the living. Rather, these "pale and grisly witnesses" were props of the pope's deceitful kingdom.[10] This point was reiterated often in the seventeenth century. The Shropshire minister Robert Horne was expressing a commonplace in 1619 when he remarked that the Roman church was "kept going by necromancies and . . . apparitions of the dead, all damnable and fabulous".[11]

The allegation that the English recusant community actively sustained ghost beliefs was a considerable exaggeration. English Catholic writers were generally circumspect on the subject, not least because they did not wish to lend credence to their enemies' claim that they nurtured superstition. Most of the defences of the concept of purgatory published in the sixteenth and seventeenth centuries did not mention the returning dead at all; nor did Catholic ghost stories place particular emphasis on the doctrine or the practice of prayer for the dead.[12] In 1565 the future cardinal William Allen referred somewhat cautiously to ghosts in his *Defense and Declaration of the Catholike Churches Doctrine Touching Purgatory.* Allen observed that the spirits of the dead could sometimes return to earth, and he cited the example of Moses' appearance at the transfiguration of Christ. While asserting the reality of such manifestations, however, he noted that they were "rare and marvellous works of God" and was keen to distinguish them from the "fantasies" of superstitious men and women.[13]

For Allen's Protestant contemporaries, of course, even these qualifications were unacceptable, as they believed that human souls were consigned irreversibly to another state after death. This doctrine did not, however, rule out all the activities of the "disorderly dead". In theory at least, some Protestants acknowledged that corpses could be possessed by demons. This proposition was less contentious than the claim that spirits could return from purgatory: indeed, it did not touch on the fate of human souls at all. In his treatise on witchcraft in 1597, the future King James made this point explicitly: he noted that demons could occupy cadavers because such unpleasant manipulations did not involve their departed souls. Evil spirits could animate the dead flesh of both the saved and the damned, and use corpses to enter the homes of the living.[14] The Norwich physician Sir Thomas Browne echoed this view in 1645: he rejected the possibility that the souls of the dead could appear on earth, but he accepted that evil spirits could animate corpses in order to copulate with witches.[15]

This caveat did not, in practice, soften the Protestant prohibition on the returning dead. Occasionally, reports of revived cadavers appeared in England. As part of his pastoral advice to a gentleman who had seen a spirit in his bedchamber, the Jacobean minister Daniel Featley described a case from France in which the Devil possessed the corpse of a hanged woman in order to seduce a man at night: the man awoke to find the lifeless body beside him, with the imprint of the noose around its neck.[16] The majority of English churchmen were sceptical that Satan could exercise this power, however. It also appears that the people of Tudor and Stuart England were seldom troubled by roaming corpses, although such creatures had been described in some late medieval chronicles. A pamphlet in 1659 reported that a dead sailor rose from his grave on the shore to demand reburial further inland; but this unruly spirit – or possessed cadaver – was apparently put to rest when its former shipmates acceded to its request.[17]

While such literal appearances of the dead were rare, it appears that reports of ghosts persisted in the early modern period. This fact was acknowledged in the preface to the English translation of the standard Protestant text on the subject, Ludwig Lavater's *Of Ghostes and Spirites Walking by Nyght* (1572): this observed that "there be many, even nowadays, which are haunted and troubled by spirits", and hoped that Lavater's text would offer them comfort and guidance.[18] The persistence of such experiences was recorded in pamphlets throughout the seventeenth century, as well as in a small number of personal testimonies that historians have studied in depth.[19] The spectres in these accounts were apparitions rather than revived bodies, and they frequently retained the character of known individuals; they were also associated closely with people and places they have known in life. According to the Cambridge philosopher Henry More in 1659, reports of such spirits were "numerous and frequent in all men's mouths".[20]

The persistence of spectral apparitions, alongside historical accounts of the phenomenon, obliged English Protestants to provide alternative explanations for sightings of ghosts. Predictably, many medieval reports were attributed to the lies of Rome, occasionally supplemented by priests dressing in sheets to spook their unwary parishioners. Various natural explanations were deployed to explain contemporary encounters with spirits of the dead. Since hauntings were frequently reported at night, the effects of poor and shadowy lighting were often cited; deficient eyesight was another possible cause. These factors were especially potent when combined with a fearful imagination. When "fear and weakness of the sight . . . meet together", Lavater noted, "then men fall into strange and marvellous imaginations, believing things utterly false to be very true".[21] Black humours could also produce hallucinations. In 1621 Robert Burton identified ghosts among the "thousand ugly shapes" that fantasy presented to the melancholic mind.[22]

Such this-worldly explanations did not, of course, exhaust the resources available to Tudor and Stuart thinkers. The existence of angels and demons meant that these spirits could masquerade as ghosts. Lavater left open the possibility that angels sometimes appeared in the guise of the dead; but the deception involved made it more likely that evil spirits were responsible. English writers strongly favoured this interpretation. Cranmer admitted that people sometimes heard the souls of the dead apparently calling out to them; but he warned that "these words proceed out of the fraud and deceit of the Devil".[23] In one of the fullest treatments of the subject in Elizabethan England, the London preacher Henry Smith expanded this argument. Just as Satan appeared as an angel of light, he "can change himself into the likeness of a man much more". He spread fear and falsehood among unwary Christians by assuming the shape of the dead. This was, Smith observed, one of the most perilous counterfeits of the enemy, which he practiced "to draw us from the word of God, to visions and dreams and apparitions, upon which many of the doctrines of the papists are grounded".[24]

These theoretical positions were applied to the ghostly experiences of real men and women. In 1583 Henry Howard, the Earl of Northampton, described the apparent manifestation of a gentleman's ghost to his surviving daughters. He noted, however, that this was a cruel deception by Satan, who "lurking under the names and titles of the dead . . . may set snares for the living".[25] In the early seventeenth century the Cornish gentleman Sir Thomas Wise sought the advice of the minister Daniel Featley on apparitions in his household, including the spectral figure of a woman that appeared at his bedside. Featley determined that the spirit was a demon, and he advised Wise to scrutinise his conscience for any sin that might have caused the Lord to permit the creature to disturb him.[26] Satanic deception remained the orthodox explanation for sightings of the dead throughout the 1600s, when such phenomena could not be otherwise ascribed to sensory illusions, melancholy, or popish impostures.

But this was not the end of matters. Despite the consensus of Protestant opinion, reports of the returning dead did not conform neatly to theological expectations. In part, this was because the idea that ghosts were either delusions or satanic tricks was unconvincing to many of those who encountered spirits at first hand. The bereaved daughters described by Henry Howard were, apparently, convinced that they had experienced visions of their father; and Sir Thomas Wise was initially unsure whether he had seen an angel or a devil. In two exceptionally well-documented hauntings from 1636 and 1650, those who witnessed the apparitions treated them not as demons but as the spirits of the dead.[27] Whatever the official position of the English church, it seems that belief in some kind of contact between the living and the dead was tenacious in these cases. It may well be, as Peter Marshall has suggested, that reformed teaching on ghosts "was simply too cruelly counter-intuitive ever fully to take root in the popular consciousness".[28]

The doctrine of divine providence was sufficiently elastic to contain the various tensions between reformed theology and traditional ghost beliefs. Since God bent the activities of evil spirits to suit His will – despite their malevolent intentions – it was possible to accommodate many long-established beliefs about apparitions within an orthodox framework. In practice, this allowed folkloric tropes concerning the returning dead to persist: the Lord permitted demons-as-ghosts to behave in the ways that such spirits were expected to. The association between ghosts and graveyards is a good example. If visions of the dead were actually demons, there was no compelling theological reason why they should haunt cemeteries. Indeed, Thomas Cranmer had dismissed the idea that spirits were attached to the physical remains of the dead.[29] The connection between ghosts and graveyards proved enduring, however. Preaching at York in 1594, John King remarked that "the common people deem that the spirits and ghosts of the dead walk at their graves and relics, and are most conversant in churchyards".[30] In the middle years of the seventeenth century, Henry More took the fact that spirits congregated in graveyards as one of the starting points for his discussion of ghosts.[31] By the same period, many orthodox writers on the subject had come to accept that both ghosts and evil spirits in general were common frequenters of graves.[32]

The pull of traditional expectations shaped many of the other attributes of early modern English ghosts. Typically, they appeared as the shades of men and women who had died in unusual circumstances, often leaving unfinished business on earth. Many were the victims of crime, apparently bent on retribution: in the words of the poet George Chapman in 1594, "ghosts whom vengeance holds from rest".[33] Such spirits often assisted the cause of human justice by exposing the perpetrators of murder or fraud. Alternatively, they offered guidance or warnings to those who had known them in life. These roles were so familiar that in 1659 Henry More used them to question the supposedly demonic nature of ghosts: why, he asked, were such creatures employed to serve apparently benevolent purposes?[34] The orthodox answer, of course, was the unsearchable wisdom of providence. Nonetheless, there was no strong reason in theology why evil spirits masquerading as ghosts should behave in this way: it appears that they did so because these roles were traditionally associated with the spirits of the dead.

The persistence of these tropes was illustrated in reports of ghosts during the violent upheavals of the mid-seventeenth century. During the Irish rising in November 1641, Catholic rebels killed approximately one hundred Protestant settlers on a bridge over the river Bann in Portadown. In his *Generall Martyrologie* (1651), the godly English minister Samuel Clarke described the supernatural sequel to this massacre:

These bloody persecutors themselves confessed that the ghosts of diverse of the Protestants which they had drowned at Portadown bridge were daily and nightly seen to walk upon the river, sometimes singing of psalms, sometimes brandishing naked swords, sometimes screeching in a most hideous and fearful manner; so that many of the popish Irish which dwelt near thereabouts, being affrighted herewith, were forced to remove their habitations further off into the country.

What exactly were these doleful apparitions? Clarke could not have understood them to be the souls of the dead, as these had passed irreversibly to their place of judgement. To interpret them as demons was hardly helpful to his purpose – though this was not inconsistent with divine providence. It was conceivable that they were angels disguised as slaughtered Christians. This was, perhaps, appropriate to the image of psalm-singing martyrs; but it jarred with the spirits' "hideous and fearful" screams.[35] Two things are clear from Clarke's account of the haunting at Portadown: the ghosts were pursuing their traditional role of calling for vengeance against the guilty, and the minister was prepared to relate their appearance without dwelling on the theological questions that it raised.

A similar ambiguity marked reports of the most spectacular apparition of the English civil wars: the appearance in January 1643 of ghostly armies above the battlefield at Edge Hill. According to one of the two pamphlets that described the event, the inhabitants of Kineton were troubled by doleful sounds in the night: the "groans of dying men were heard crying revenge, and some again to ease them of their pain by friendly killing them". These cries were joined by the din of trumpets and drums, "as if an enemy had entered in their town to put them to a sudden execution and plunder all their estates". Through their windows, some people saw troops of horsemen clashing outside, before departing into the air. On the following evening, a group assembled to watch for the spirits. They witnessed the return of the spectral armies, which again joined battle amid a cacophony of drums and gunshot. Then at daybreak they "in the twinkling of an eye did vanish".[36]

Like the apparitions at Portadown, the true nature of these spirits was uncertain. The pamphlets printed in January 1643 related them unambiguously to the battle at Edge Hill: they even named Sir Edmund Verney, the king's standard-bearer who had died in the field, among the spectral troops. The visions at Kineton were also framed as providential judgements on the slaughter: they expressed divine indignation at the sin and horror of civil war.[37] But were the phantom soldiers demons or ghosts? The author of *The New Yeares Wonder* (1642) implied both possibilities. It was the purpose of the apparitions, he wrote, "to terrify the living with dead souls". He also observed that, after the haunting, the people of Kineton had searched for unburied bodies on the battle site, presumably in order to lay their spirits to rest. In a brief epilogue to the pamphlet, however, the incorporeal armies were described as "fiends".[38] The second account of the wonder was less equivocal. It began with a discussion of the prevalence of evil spirits and the Devil's capacity to "condense the air into any shape he pleases". The character of the spectres themselves was not in doubt: despite their appearance as men, they were "infernal soldiers" and "hellish and prodigious enemies".[39]

Some later accounts of ghosts preserved their role as instruments of providence but blurred the question of their origin. This meant, in effect, that spectres resumed their traditional roles as avengers of wrongs and dispensers of otherworldly advice − though they did so as agents of the Lord. A deposition to an Essex magistrate in 1650 preserved a glimpse of this outlook. When a servant was haunted by the vengeful ghost of her former mistress, and appealed to the woman's son for help, she received a brutally providential reply: "this is a just judgement of God upon you, for if she walks she walks to you and to nobody else".[40] Occasionally, it even seemed that the divine hand released spirits from the grave to punish wrongdoers. According to the author of a pamphlet in 1690, God was so determined to pursue those guilty of homicide "that when witnesses are wanting of the fact, the very ghost of the murdered parties cannot rest quiet in their graves till they have made the detection themselves".[41] More often, reports of apparitions simply abstained from metaphysical speculations. A pamphlet in 1679 described an apparition as an "airy form" in the shape of a dead man, but made no comment on its provenance; many others presented apparent appearances of the dead without any gloss at all.[42]

There was no doubt, however, about the heavenly purpose behind spectral interventions. Indeed, true-life ghost stories were framed most often as special providences. In 1677 a man in Devon awoke to discover the ghost of a gentleman at his bedside. Some thirty years earlier, the spirit explained, he had been robbed and killed in the same house; now he asked his host to report the information to a magistrate. The man was understandably hesitant. But a few days later the spirit returned to renew its demand, and promised that "God will raise up witnesses" to support the claim. This proved to be true, though the case remained unresolved at the time of the story's publication.[43] A grisly tale from Lincolnshire in 1679 produced a more definite outcome. A man hired a gang of thieves to murder his brother to obtain his share of their father's estate. Subsequently, a bloody apparition was seen on the land around his house; and the spectre eventually appeared to his brother, with "fresh bleeding wounds" from his fatal assault. Overcome with fear, the man resorted to magic to lay the ghost: he employed a conjurer to summon the spirit and drive it away. This operation succeeded in part: "the image of the murdered youth appeared on horse-back just as he was slain", and it told the magician he could not depart until his killer came to justice. This led his brother to confess. By this awful providence, the pamphlet concluded, "we may see and admire the power and justice of an almighty God, who alone is dreadful and to be feared".[44]

The motifs of these stories suggest conventional expectations of ghostly manifestations. They happened most frequently at night, and especially at midnight. The people of Kineton assembled to see the spectral armies at this hour; and the Lincolnshire conjurer awaited the apparition in "midnight silence".[45] The spirits of the dead were almost invariably attached to particular places, most often the sites of their physical remains, but also the habitations of those they had known in life. In their appearance too, ghosts retained traces of their earthly existence. Often they wore the winding sheets that had wrapped their bodies in the grave; or they dressed in a manner familiar from their lives. Even though he had never met the spirit that visited his bedside in Devon in 1677, the man took him for a gentleman because of his embroidered clothes.[46] In a deposition to York assizes in 1690, a man explained that he recognised the ghost of his sister-in-law by the petticoat and white hood that she had habitually worn.[47]

Accounts of early modern ghosts also reveal something of the sensory experience of those who encountered them – though here the evidence is mixed. Some references to spirits stressed their apparently insubstantial nature. In 1594 Robert Holland noted this quality in his verses on the resurrection of Christ, which contrasted the flesh of the risen saviour to the flimsy stuff of apparitions. This allowed Jesus to prove to the disciples at Emmaus that he was not merely a ghost:

> And that no feigned shape he had,
> As ghosts or spirits have,
> To ease their fear, and make them glad,
> His hands and feet he gave
> That they should handle them and see
> That he had flesh and bone:
> And not as spirits wont to be,
> For they have neither none.[48]

The immaterial appearance of spirits was implied in other sources. According to a pamphlet in 1598, the survivors of a fire in Devon were so emaciated that they seemed "more like spirits and ghosts than living creatures".[49] The propensity of spectres to emerge at night also, perhaps, indicates their insubstantial qualities. It was a commonplace that the shadowy effects created by moonlight were sometimes mistaken for ghosts.[50]

These unearthly attributes were balanced, however, by the physicality that was sometimes ascribed to apparitions. Indeed, they were occasionally mistaken for mortals. In 1662 a couple from Yorkshire took the ghost of a young woman to be "some wandering person that might have come for lodging".[51] Spectres also communicated in direct speech, unlike the interior voices associated with demonic temptation or prayer. The most consistent sign of their otherworldly nature was their capacity to vanish. In some cases, it seems, this was the only indication that apparitions were not what they appeared to be. In 1690 a man saw the figure of a woman walking ahead of him as he went to fill a bucket from a pond; then she sat down on a small hill and he continued on his way. As he returned with the water he observed that she was still there; but as "soon as he had emptied his pail, he went into his yard and stood still to find whether he could see her again, but she had vanished".[52] Occasionally, witnesses described the process by which such spirits departed. Bedside apparitions could fade gradually into air, like the spectre that visited Sir Thomas Wise in the early 1600s.[53] More dramatically, the young woman initially mistaken for a wayfarer in 1662 vanished by "gliding away without any motion of steps".[54]

These motifs reveal the expectations that were conventionally attached to visions of the dead, and to this extent they suggest something of the experience of those that beheld them. Beyond this, it is difficult to speculate on the meaning of apparitions to individuals. The emotion most frequently associated with ghosts was fear. While the appearance of the dead could bring comfort to the recently bereaved, it was more common for such manifestations to produce anxiety and tribulation. This reflected, perhaps, the association between ghosts and social disruptions of various kinds: shocking or untimely deaths, fractured human relationships, and business left undone on earth. It is tempting to read the spectacular haunting that followed the battle of Edge Hill as a response to the traumas of civil war – though such interpretations are inevitably speculative. In this context, it is suggestive that Major George Wither reached for the metaphor of haunting to describe the psychological aftershock of the conflicts of the 1640s:

> What ghosts are they that haunt
> The chambers of my breast!
> And, when I sleep, or comfort want,
> Will give my heart no rest?
> Me thinks the sound of groans
> Are ever in mine ear:
> Deep graves, deaths heads, and charnel bones
> Before me still appear.
> And when asleep I fall,
> In hope to find some ease,
> My dreams, to me, are worst of all,
> And fright me more than these.[55]

Some scholars have sought the meaning of individual hauntings in the exploitation and betrayal that characterised some "disordered households". According to Laura Gowing, the apparition of Priscilla Beauty that in 1650 tormented her former servant, Susan Lay, manifested Lay's guilty and frustrated feelings towards her mistress: she had borne an illegitimate child by Priscilla's husband and entertained hopes of becoming his wife upon her death. For Gowing, Lay's vision "dramatised the intimate ties, fears and conflicts between servant and mistress, lover and wife".[56]

Ultimately, all interpretations of this kind risk the imposition of modern assumptions on the people of the past. Neither the residents of Kineton in 1643 nor Susan Lay in 1650 believed they had witnessed projections of their traumatised minds: they thought they had seen ghosts. As Brad Gregory has noted of historical reconstructions of the supernatural in general, the need to find naturalistic explanations, including psychological interpretations, belongs to modern commentators rather than those that originally witnessed the phenomena.[57] Nonetheless, the association that contemporaries made between ghosts and social dislocation reveals something of the experience of haunting in the early modern period: unlike the angels that they in some ways resembled, ghosts were frequently accompanied by anxiety and dread. It was for this reason that walking spirits were often named alongside the "bugs, goblins, fiery sights, and diverse terrible . . . shapes of things" that resided in the shadows of Tudor and Stuart England and which provide the subject of the next section.[58]

The reformation of the bugs

In 1584 the English demonologist Reginald Scot presented a marvellous catalogue of monsters that, he claimed, populated the tales that maidservants told to young children. These included witches, fairies and imps, as well as an array of exotic and extraordinary terrestrial spirits: "the man in the oak, the hellwain, the fire-drake, the puckle, Tom Thumb, Hobgoblin, Tom Tumbler, [and] Boneless". Scot also named the will-o'-the-wisp spirit "Kit with the Candlestick", the lascivious incubus demon, and "the mare", a creature that paralyzed and smothered sleepers in their beds. These terrors, he suggested, made such an impression on young minds that they lurked in the recesses of adult consciousness. They could make men tremble to walk at night, when spirits might appear as animals or be heard in the shrieks of owls.[59]

Scot's catalogue of "bugs" cannot be taken at face value. For a start, he included creatures from classical mythology that seem improbable visitors to English villages. He also borrowed the incubus demon from continental texts that featured prominently in his critique of contemporary demonology.[60] As Timothy Scott McGinnis has argued, Scot was primarily interested in entering a learned debate with other writers on witchcraft rather than addressing directly the religious ideas of ordinary people. Nor did he see himself as an archivist of the folk beliefs of his community.[61] Nonetheless, his compendium of monsters should be taken seriously for two reasons. First, the bugs he identified were not merely rhetorical, though he undoubtedly added some names to fatten the list. Creatures like the mare and the puckle were recorded in other contemporary texts, and appear to be authentic inhabitants of the popular world of spirits.[62] The activities of fairies, hobgoblins and imps, as well as roaming spirits such as Kit with the Candlestick, were also well attested in the sixteenth century. Thus Scot presents an interesting overview of the bogeys of the late Tudor imagination, though one that cannot be accepted uncritically.

Secondly, the fate of Scot's bugs indicates the wider effects of the Reformation. Scot presented his assembly of monsters as part of the larger argument of his book: that the fear of witchcraft was a delusion encouraged by Catholicism, and its remedy was the preaching of the unsullied Word of God. The presence of bugs in people's imagination was a marker of the success or failure of this project. Scot was generally optimistic that fear of such creatures had declined. In the preface to the *Discoverie*, he noted baldly that the hobgoblin Robin Goodfellow "ceaseth now to be much feared", and he hoped that one day most people would regard the fear of witches as equally foolish. Elsewhere he was less sanguine. He began his account of "how people have been brought to fear bugs" by stating that the causes have been only "partly reformed by the preaching of the gospel". Some groundless anxieties about goblins and walking spirits remained, and he hoped that "those illusions will in short time (by God's grace) be detected and vanish away".[63]

So what became of Scot's bugs? In broad terms, English Protestants discouraged belief in these creatures, but there was no campaign to abolish or reclassify them. Unlike the cult of saints, they had not played a central role in medieval Christianity; and unlike ghosts, they were not associated with the discredited doctrine of purgatory. Consequently, their expulsion from the supernatural world was a low priority for English churchmen. Official responses to the reported activity of these spirits emerged on an *ad hoc* basis, and depended largely on the attributes of the entities themselves and the circumstances in which they manifested themselves. As a consequence, many of the bugs of folklore survived at the margins of acceptable belief, only occasionally exciting the attention of the authorities.

The fate of the bugs is illustrated by the various spirits in Scot's list that can be classed as "fairies".[64] As well as fairies themselves, these included will-o'-the-wisps, hobgoblins and elves. These creatures appear only passingly in the written sources of the period: they belonged to an oral culture that could not, by its nature, be preserved in detail for future historians. The surviving records suggest considerable fluidity between various fairy forms. This was shown in the cluster of creatures known as "puckles" or "pucks". In one persistent tradition, pucks were believed to be spirits that led travellers astray at night, also known as will-o'-the-wisps or jack-o'-lanterns.[65] The hobgoblin Robin Goodfellow was usually included among them: he appeared in this role in William Tyndale's commentary on the first epistle of St John in 1531, and in tales circulating in the late sixteenth and early seventeenth centuries.[66] But Robin also entered houses to steal cream, like a domestic fairy. In the 1590s he provided the basis for Shakespeare's mischievous spirit named Puck in *A Midsummer Night's Dream*. In another context, "puckrils" were identified as malicious spirits in allegations of witchcraft.

Despite these overlapping identities, several broad characteristics were ascribed to English fairies. They lived at the margins of human habitation, usually on hilltops or in marshes and woods; they could interact with mortals, and possessed the power to heal sickness and locate hidden things; and they could enter homes to steal food or receive gifts from their inhabitants. They appeared in various forms, often as adult humans but also as animals or "walking fires". This reflected the pleasure they took in deception: in colloquial language, "fairy gold" was an illusion, and "fairy trappings" were decorations that tricked the eye. In their deeds fairies were unpredictable. They could help men and women, especially in domestic work, and took small gifts in return. But they also punished those to whom they took offence, particularly slovenly housekeepers. They could attack or torment unfortunate mortals, leaving them "fairy pinched" or "haunted with fairies". As will-o'-the-wisps, they guided the unwary into remote and treacherous places or abandoned them in bogs.

Numerous sources suggest a continued and lively interest in fairies throughout the early modern period. Indeed, Ronald Hutton has suggested that "fairy mythology was probably more prominent in British culture between 1560 and 1640 than at any time before or since".[67] For a start, there was a demand for medicines for the various afflictions that fairies were believed to cause. In his herbal *The Garden of Health* (1597), William Langham recommended bay oil soaked in a linen cloth as a treatment for fairy pinches, and advised parents to hang peony seeds around their children's necks to prevent "the haunting of fairies and goblins".[68] Charms derived from the devotions of the medieval church — sometimes retaining a markedly unreformed character — were also used to cure children tormented by fairies.[69] Richard Napier treated a patient troubled by the creatures in 1608.[70] More positively, Diane Purkiss has noted the strong association between fairies and buried treasure.[71] This led both scholarly magicians and village cunning folk to solicit their aid in uncovering riches; and it also created openings for fraud. In the early 1590s the scandalous career of Judith Phillips, who gulled and robbed a succession of people by claiming that the fairy queen could lead them to hidden gold, illustrated the allure of such arrangements.[72] Sightings of fairies of various kinds continued throughout the period and were preserved in the collections of proto-folklorists such as John Aubrey in the late seventeenth century. Aubrey himself recalled that as a schoolboy in 1634 he searched for fairies on the Wiltshire downs, after hearing that his curate had been enchanted and pinched by a troop of the dancing spirits.[73]

How did the Reformation affect these beliefs? In many cases, it seems, they were left quietly alone. Unless they attracted the attention of religious or legal authorities, there was little need to explain or reclassify the spirits concerned. The belief in will-o'-the-wisps provides a good example. As "false lights" that led the unwary from the true path, these creatures were comparable to the Devil; and this likeness was often exploited in literature. In *Paradise Lost* (1667), John Milton compared Satan to "a wandering fire" that "misleads th'amazed night wanderer from his way / to bogs and mires".[74] Outside such figurative contexts, however, very little was written on such apparitions. In the English translation of his treatise on spirits in 1572, Ludwig Lavater explained them largely as natural phenomena, though he noted that they might sometimes be demons.[75] Robert Burton classed them as "walking devils" in 1621.[76] Towards the end of the seventeenth century, will-o'-the-wisps were mentioned as curiosities in compendia of natural history, where they were explained variously as luminous insects or vapours produced by marshy ground.[77]

In the absence of a campaign to discredit their existence, or any official context that required their explanation, will-o'-the-wisps were untouched by the religious reforms of the Tudor and Stuart period. At the same time, the related character of Robin Goodfellow appears to have migrated from popular belief into the pages of jocular fiction. A pamphlet in 1588 noted that Robin was "famous in every old wives' chronicle for his mad merry pranks".[78] Several of these were printed in a jestbook in 1628; and Robin also appeared in a number of comic ballads in the early 1600s. In these texts he was a mischievous but good-hearted spirit, addicted to deception but always willing to "help those that suffered wrong".[79] In this capacity, he assisted two lovers whose union was prevented by a lecherous uncle, and he punished a publican who defrauded his customers; and in a ballad in 1648 he disguised himself as a mare to teach a lesson to horse thieves, whom he rode through filthy "water, earth and mire" when they attempted to steal him.[80] These comic turns appeared to coincide with his decline as a figure in English folk belief, which Reginald Scot had already observed in 1584.

While some fairy beliefs were ignored by the authorities, or receded into popular entertainment, others provoked more serious concern. This was sporadic, however. Cunning folk were occasionally examined by the courts in connection to magical practices involving fairies. This was the case with the Dorset magician John Walsh, who admitted in 1566 to consulting with fairies to discover the victims of bewitchment. A Leicestershire cunning woman, Joan Willimot, employed a fairy for the same purpose according to a pamphlet published in 1619.[81] The Cornish maidservant Ann Jeffries was examined by clergy and magistrates in 1645 when she claimed to cure the sick through the ministration of fairies.[82] A similar medical scandal was recorded by the demonologist John Webster in *The Displaying of Supposed Witchcraft* (1677). This involved a magician who cured illnesses with a white powder that he claimed to have acquired from the queen of the fairies, who entertained him in a great hall concealed within a hillside. Webster believed that the powder did, indeed, possess medicinal qualities, but he concluded that the man had obtained it from a travelling chemist rather than fairyland.[83]

These cases attracted official attention for various reasons. Joan Willimot was questioned in connection with allegations of murder by witchcraft in the neighbouring county of Lincolnshire; these were driven by Francis Manners, the Earl of

Rutland, who believed that his sons had been killed by the *maleficium* of Margaret and Phillip Flower. Willimot was apparently drawn into the investigation to testify against Margaret Flower, and mentioned her own dealings with a fairy under examination.[84] Both Ann Jeffries and the healer mentioned by Webster attracted large numbers of patients and freely proclaimed their involvement with fairies. This raised suspicions about the true nature of the spirits they served. In Jeffries' case, this was compounded by the political message attached to her activities: she was vocally loyal to the king in the civil war, and encouraged people to use the Book of Common Prayer in the years immediately following its suppression by the parliament.[85] In less ostentatious circumstances, it is doubtful that magic involving fairies would have provoked legal interventions: it was far more common for harmful sorcery, rather than magical cures, to provoke allegations to the courts.

The same was true of the operations of scholarly magicians, which sometimes involved fairies. In the second half of the seventeenth century, the antiquarian and amateur sorcerer Elias Ashmole wrote out a series of spells for conjuring and binding these creatures. These texts involved considerable knowledge of the kingdom of fairies, which suggests that Ashmole had immersed himself in practical research: for instance, each spirit had to be conjured by name, and some spells depended on a detailed understanding of the geography of spirits. The recipe for an unguent to be anointed on the eyes required thyme "gathered near the side of a hill where fairies use to be, and the grass of a fairy throne". Ashmole addressed by name the fairies that he sought to bind: these included "Elabigathen", whom he commanded to give "true obedience" in a long and carefully contractual conjuration. He also acknowledged that fairies were employed by other magicians: indeed, he noted that attempts to call and subjugate such spirits would work only if they were "not already bound".[86]

The activities of another class of spirits aroused wider attention and received more frequent scrutiny from churchmen and lawyers. These were the noxious creatures allegedly employed by witches to torment their neighbours. Such bugs appeared in early accounts of English witchcraft in the 1560s and retained a prominent role in allegations throughout the seventeenth century. Their origins and identity are unclear. Those Protestant writers that accepted their existence classed them as "familiar spirits" or demons – though they were careful to point out that their behaviour did not conform to the biblical account of Satan. Villagers fearful of witches' spirits may have understood them as a species of malicious fairy or imp.[87] The Essex minister George Gifford referred to a witch's spirit as a "puckril" in a treatise in 1587.[88] Six years later, a character in his *Dialogue Concerning Witches and Witchcraftes* described an old woman who kept "three or four imps", and noted that "some call them puckrils".[89] In Ben Jonson's unfinished play *The Sad Shepherd*, a familiar spirit is also named "Puck Hairy". The creature reveals its true nature in a soliloquy: it is a demon that both deceives and protects its mistress, and sometimes dances "about the forest . . . like a goblin".[90] The terms "puckril" and "imp" were used rarely in the judicial records of English witchcraft before 1645, but in that year the depositions of several witches apprehended in Suffolk referred to harmful spirits as imps.[91] Whatever they were, it is clear that these creatures had several qualities that set them apart from ordinary fairies: they normally took the form of small animals, suckled from teats concealed on their owners' bodies, and obeyed their commands. Most pertinently for those that encountered them, they were always malevolent.

These malignant creatures remained a tenacious, if somewhat anomalous, presence throughout the early modern period. Many educated writers followed Scot in dismissing them as figments of the superstitious imagination; others, more cautiously, retained the possibility that demons might masquerade as small animals to prosecute their designs – though this interpretation required some ingenuity. George Gifford viewed the involvement of imps in allegations of harmful sorcery as evidence of popular folly: he mocked the belief "that the Devil lies in a pot of wool, soft and warm, and stirs not but when he is hired and sent".[92] Nonetheless, he acknowledged that evil spirits could assume bodily shapes in order to deceive the unwary.[93] In 1627 Richard Bernard, the godly minister of Batcombe in Somerset, attempted to combine continental demonology with reports of witches' imps. He argued that the teat at which witches suckled their spirits was the Devil's mark, by which he sealed a formal compact with his servants.[94] Such ideas allowed some churchmen to accept the activity of imps within the framework of satanic witchcraft. But they remained problematic. In 1646, for example, the Cambridgeshire minister John Gaule listed testimony concerning imps among the factors that made witch trials an uncertain and dangerous business.[95]

Witches' imps were related to another of Reginald Scot's bugs: the cluster of night terrors known collectively as "the hag" or "the mare". Typically, the victims of this phenomenon experienced a kind of waking dream attended by feelings of dread and sometimes by frightening visions as well; they also suffered paralysis and a sense of suffocating pressure on their chests. Scot himself explained the condition in medical terms, though he noted that others believed it had supernatural origins. Consequently, he observed that its victims sometimes slept with protective charms above their beds.[96] It appears that the mare was sometimes attributed to night-coming fairies. The Robin Goodfellow jestbook in 1628 featured a fairy named Gull that ventured out "when mortals keep their beds" and that delighted in causing nocturnal distress. "Many times", the creature boasts, "I get on men and women, and so lie on their stomachs that I cause . . . great pain, for which they call me by the name of hag, or night mare".[97]

More often, however, attacks of this kind were associated with witchcraft. In these cases the spirits involved did not act independently but at the behest of human associates. In 1579 Richard Galis of Windsor ascribed a series of night terrors to the activity of local witches. The first of these episodes was especially dramatic:

Suddenly about twelve o' clock in the night a shadow of a huge and mighty black cat appeared in my chamber, which the more as she approached near my bedside, so much the more began my hair to stand upright, my heart to faint, and my pains more and more to increase.

The creature menaced Galis so often that he took to lying awake in prayer with a dagger by his side.[98] Another monstrous cat was described in 1599 in the deposition of Olive Barthram, who was tormented by a witch in the Suffolk village of Stradbroke. This spirit awoke its victim in bed and then "pressed her so sore that she could not speak, [and] at other times he held her hands that she could not stir, and restrained her voice that she could not answer".[99] An anonymous manuscript from the reign of Charles I reiterated the connection between witchcraft and the mare. This described how the victim of a night spirit took magical revenge on his attacker. He rose early in the morning and urinated into a chamber pot, and then he worked a charm over its contents. This caused the witch responsible to visit him and complain of a "grief in her bladder, and that she could not piss".[100]

As Owen Davies has observed, the symptoms of "the mare" are recognised today in the medical condition known as "sleep paralysis disorder". Indeed, some readers of this book will have experienced sensations very similar to those recorded in the early modern period. The physical effects of the syndrome have remained constant across time and cultures, but their interpretation has reflected the assumptions of sufferers and the communities to which they belonged.[101] Even in Tudor and Stuart England, multiple explanations were available. Some shared Scot's belief that the mare was a natural malady, while others viewed it as the work of fairies or witches. When bewitchment was suspected, the attacks were normally attributed to witches' imps; but in some cases these creatures were believed to be wicked angels in disguise. Richard Galis, for example, believed that the thing that attacked him was "the Devil himself in a cat's likeness" – a view consistent with his self-image as a Christian assailed by the satanic enemy.[102] The experience of the mare, therefore, indicates the various interpretative models available to early modern people: it could be perceived as a fairy, a witches' imp, a satanic incursion or a physical illness.

Other creatures in Scot's collection of bugs made fleeting appearances in the records of early modern England. The "man in the oak" may be related to the spirit that lived in a hollow tree in George Gifford's dialogue on witchcraft in 1593. This entity was introduced by the character Daniel, who represented in the text the opinions of an untutored countryman. Daniel bestowed on the creature the role and powers of a witch's imp. It spoke to its mistress from the tree and menaced her neighbours at her command: "when she was offended with any, she went to that tree and sent him to kill their cattle". These claims produced a memorably withering response from Gifford's spokesman in the dialogue. The voice from the tree was either a delusion or a demon; and if the latter was true, it involved a signal diminution of the prince of darkness: "Do you think Satan lodges in a hollow tree? Is he become so idle and lazy? Has he left off to be as a roaring lion, seeking whom he may devour?"[103] Whatever the provenance of this creature, tree-spirits of this kind do not appear to have featured prominently in later accounts of English witchcraft.

Another of Scot's monsters, the "firedrake", maintained a presence in the seventeenth century. The firedrake was originally a kind of fire-breathing serpent but could also appear as "a burning fire in the air". In *The Historie of Serpents* (1608), Edward Topsell described a sighting of such a fireball by fishermen on the Cornish coast, reported to him some twelve years earlier. While Topsell regarded the moving flame as a natural phenomenon, it was clearly assigned otherworldly significance by the ship's master:

> There came by them a firedrake, at the sight whereof the old man began to be much troubled and afraid, telling his servants that those sights seldom pretended any good, and therefore prayed God to turn away all evil from them, and withal willed his servants to take up their nets, lest they did all repent it afterward; for he said he had known much evil follow such apparitions.

This apprehension proved to be well founded, as shortly afterwards the master was robbed and murdered by his crew.[104] Writing in the 1630s, the pious lawyer William Austin took a more naturalistic view of firedrakes. Like will-o'-the-wisps, he observed, they were mere "exuberances of nature".[105] In his dictionary of 1658, Edward Phillips echoed this scientific interpretation by defining a firedrake as "a fiery meteor, engendered of a hot exhalation inflamed between two clouds".[106]

The firedrake, like the other monsters in Scot's compendium, appears to have persisted quietly in the hinterland of early modern belief. In many ways the fate of such creatures resembled that of the grotesque carvings in English parish churches: they were a marginal presence before the Reformation, and remained generally too obscure or unimportant to feel the destructive force of the new orthodoxy. Mostly ignored and unreformed by Protestant authorities – except when they intruded on public affairs in cases of witchcraft – they remained an anomalous but largely uncontroversial presence in English culture. Whether they lost their power to unnerve the unwary visitor to marshlands, forests and remote hills remains an open question. It may be that the goblins, pucks and imps of traditional belief continued to skitter in the dark places, and nightmares, of English communities long into the Age of Reason.

Notes

1 Bodleian Library, Ashmole 1790, 108r, 109r.
2 Richard Baxter, *The Certainty of the Worlds of Spirits* (1691), 159.

3 Thomas Cooper, *Certaine Sermons Wherin Is Contained the Defense of the Gospell* (1580), 81.

4 This gloss is attached to the June segment of Spenser's poem, expanding on his reference to "friendly fairies" in line 25. A facsimile of this edition is included in Edmund Spenser, *The Shorter Poems*, ed. Richard A. McCabe (Penguin: 1999).

5 For the occasional intersection of fairies and the medieval English church, see Ronald C. Finucane, *Miracles and Pilgrims: Popular Beliefs in Medieval England* (Macmillan: 1995), 72.

6 Thomas Cranmer, *Miscellaneous Writings and Letters of Thomas Cranmer, Archbishop of Canterbury*, ed. John Edmund Cox (Cambridge: 1846), 44. The biblical text is Wisdom 3:1.

7 Peter Marshall, *Beliefs and the Dead in Reformation England* (Oxford University Press: 2002), 264.

8 This tale is reproduced in David Englander, *et al*, eds., *Culture and Belief in Europe, 1450–1600* (Blackwell: 1990), 16–7.

9 William James, *A Sermon Preached before the Queenes Maiestie* (1578), Br.

10 Edwin Sandys, *Sermons Made by the Most Reuerende Father in God, Edwin, Archbishop of Yorke* (1585), 10.

11 Robert Horne, *Of the Rich Man and Lazarus* (1619), 135.

12 See Francis Young, *English Catholics and the Supernatural, 1553–1829* (Ashgate: 2013), 21, 82–9, 95.

13 For Allen's work see Young, 83–4, and Marshall, *Beliefs*, 125, 242.

14 James VI, *Daemonologie* (1597), 59.

15 Sir Thomas Browne, *The Major Works*, ed. C. A Patrides (Penguin: 1977), 98, 108.

16 Bodleian Library, MS Rawlinson, D 47, 43*v*.

17 *The Wonder of Wonders* (1659), 2–3.

18 Ludwig Lavater, *Of Ghostes and Spirites Walking by Nyght* (1572), preface by Robert Harrison.

19 See Laura Gowing, "The Haunting of Susan Lay: Servants and Mistresses in Seventeenth-Century England", *Gender & History*, Vol. 14, No. 2 (2002), 183–201; Marshall, *Beliefs*, 251–2; Peter Marshall, *Mother Leakey and the Bishop* (Oxford University Press: 2007).

20 Henry More, *The Immortality of the Soul* (1659), 286.

21 Lavater, *Of Ghostes*, 19.

22 Robert Burton, *The Anatomy of Melancholy* (1621), "The Author's Abstract of Melancholy".

23 Cranmer, *Miscellaneous Writings*, 44.

24 Henry Smith, *The Sermons of Master Henrie Smith* (1592), 537–8, 540.

25 Henry Howard, *A Defensative Against the Poison of Supposed Prophecies* (1583), Bb2r.

26 Marshall, *Beliefs*, 251–2.

27 Marshall, *Mother Leakey*, 50–1; Gowing, "Haunting", 185–6.

28 Marshall, *Beliefs*, 263.

29 Cranmer, *Miscellaneous Writings*, 43.

30 John King, Lectures upon Jonas Delivered at Yorke (1599), 109.

31 More, *Immortality*, 289–90.

32 Sir Thomas Browne noted in 1645 that "those phantasms . . . do frequent cemeteries, charnel houses and graves"; and in 1658 the Glasgow minister James Durham echoed this point in his commentary on the Book of Revelation. Browne, *Religio Medici*, 108; James Durham, *A Commentary upon the Book of the Revelation* (1658), 679.

33 George Chapman, *The Shadow of Night: Containing Two Poetical Hymnes* (1594), B3*v*.

34 More argued, unconventionally, that ghosts were truly apparitions of the dead. This was because their benevolent acts contravened the normal behaviour of demons, and it was unlikely that angels would appear falsely in the form of the dead. More, *Immortality*, 295–6.

35 The dreadful screeching of the spirits alludes, perhaps, to the Irish tradition of the banshee. A little later in his text, Clarke describes the same spirits standing breast high in the water and screaming for vengeance. Samuel Clarke, *A Generall Martyrologie* (1651), 360, 362.

36 *The New Yeares Wonder* (1642), 6–8.

37 Both pamphlets read the apparition as a judgement on the war, but they apportioned responsibility rather differently. The author of *The New Yeares Wonder* hoped that God would cause the king to dispose of his evil counsellors, while *A Great Wonder in Heaven* emphasised the need for mutual reconciliation. *New Yeares Wonder*, 8; *A Great Wonder in Heaven* (1642), 7.

38 *New Yeares Wonder*, 5, 8.

39 *Great Wonder*, 3–4, 5, 6.

40 Gowing, "Haunting", 183.

41 *A Full and True Relation of the Examination and Confession of W. Barwick and E. Mangall* (1690), 1.

42 *Strange and Wonderful News from Linconshire* (1679), 3.

43 *The Wonder of this Age: or God's Miraculous Revenge Against Murder* (1677), 3.

44 *Strange and Wonderful*, 3–4.

45 *New Yeares Wonder*, 7; *Strange and Wonderful*, 4.

46 *Wonder of this Age*, 2.

47 *Full and True Relation*, 3.

48 Robert Holland, *The Holie Historie of our Lord and Saviour* (1594), 321.

49 *The True Lamentable Discourse of the Burning of Teverton in Devon-shire* (1598), B2r.

50 Lavater, *Of Ghostes*, 20.

51 *A Strange and Wonderfull Discovery* (1662), 3.

52 *Full and True Relation*, 2.

53 Marshall, *Beliefs*, 251.

54 *Strange and Wonderfull*, 4.

55 George Wither, *Campo-Musae: or The Field-Musings of Major George Wither*, 18. I am grateful to Erin Peters for alerting me to this text.

56 Gowing, "Haunting", 194.

57 See my discussion of Gregory in the introduction.

58 John Nicholls, *Pilgrimage, Wherin Is Displayed the Lives of the Proude Popes* (1581), C5*v*.

59 Reginald Scot, *The Discoverie of Witchcraft* (1584), book 7, chapter 15.

60 Diane Purkiss makes these points in her analysis of Scot in *Fairies and Fairy Stories: A History* (Allen Lane: 2000), 172–6.

61 Timothy Scott McGinnis, *George Gifford and the Reformation of the Common Sort* (Truman State University Press: 2004), 122–7.

62 For the mare, see Owen Davies, "The Nightmare Experience, Sleep Paralysis, and Witchcraft Accusations", *Folklore*, 114 (2003); for "puckles", see below.

63 Reginald Scot, *The Discoverie of Witchcraft* (1584), book 7, chapter 15.

64 The historical literature on fairies is relatively small. For valuable general studies, see Minor White Latham, *The Elizabethan Fairies* (Columbia University Press: 1930);

Katherine Briggs, *The Anatomy of Puck: An Examination of Fairy Beliefs among Shake-speare's Contemporaries and Successors* (Routledge: 2003; 1st ed. 1959); Diane Purkiss, *Fairies and Fairy Stories: A History* (Penguin: 2000); and Peter Marshall, "Protestants and Fairies in Early Modern England", in C. Scott Dixon, Dagmar Freist and Mark Greengrass, eds., *Living with Religious Diversity in Early Modern Europe* (Ashgate: 2009).

65 In his discussion of these spirits in *The Anatomy of Melancholy* (1621), Robert Burton noted that "we commonly call them pucks". Burton, *Anatomy*, part 1, sec. 2, mem. 1, sub. 2.

66 William Tyndale, *The Exposition of the Fyrste Epistle of Seynt John* (1531), prologue; *Robin Goodfellow his Mad Merry Pranks* (1628), 21–2; *The Mad Merry Pranks of Robin Good-fellow* (c 1640).

67 Hutton argues that popular traditions about fairies were systematized in late medieval literature, and this literature subsequently interacted with wider culture in the early modern period. Ronald Hutton, "The Making of the Early Modern British Fairy Tradition", *Historical Journal*, Vol. 57, No. 4 (2014); quotation, 1147.

68 William Langham, *The Garden of Health* (1597), 47, 483.

69 One magical cure, involving the recital of "five Aves in the worship of the five joys of our Lady", was recorded at Ely in 1566. This was apparently unchanged from a formulation used in the fifteenth century. See Keith Thomas, *Religion and the Decline of Magic* (Weidenfeld & Nicolson: 1971), 217.

70 Bodleian Library, Ashmole 1790, 104r.

71 Purkiss, *Fairies*, 127–43.

72 *The Brideling, Sadling and Ryding, of a Rich Churle in Hampshire* (1594).

73 Aubrey's account is reproduced in Briggs, *Anatomy*, 33–4.

74 John Milton, *Paradise Lost* (1667), book 9, 639–41.

75 Ludwig Lavater, *Of Ghostes and Spirites Walking by Nyght* (1572), 51.

76 Burton, *Anatomy*, part 1, sec. 2, member 1, sub. 2.

77 See, for example, Thomas Blount, *A Natural History: Containing Many not Common Observations* (1696), 306; and *The Sheepherd's New Kalender* (1700), 37–8.

78 *Tarltons Newes out of Purgatorie* (1588), A3.

79 *Robin Goodfellow, His Mad Merry Pranks* (1628), 21.

80 *Robin Goodfellow*, 12–5, 29–31; *The Fairy Queene* (1648).

81 The texts containing the examinations of Walsh and Willimot are available, with commentary, in Marion Gibson, ed., *Early Modern Witches: Witchcraft Cases in Contemporary Writing* (Routledge: 2000), 29, 291–2.

82 See Peter Marshall, "Ann Jeffries and the Fairies: Folk belief and the War on Scepticism in Later Stuart England", in Angela McShane and Garthine Walker, eds., *The Extraordinary and the Everyday in Early Modern England* (Palgrave Macmillan: 2010).

83 Webster, *The Displaying of Supposed Witchcraft* (1677), 300–2.

84 For the background to this case and a reconstruction of the sequence of events, see Gibson, *Early Modern Witches*, 276–9.

85 For the political aspect of Jeffries' activities, see Marshall, "Ann Jeffries", 130–1. Jeffries also attracted suspicion at a time of exceptional anxiety about witchcraft occasioned by the East Anglian witch trials in 1645. See Malcolm Gaskill, *Witchfinders* (John Murray: 2005), 167.

86 Bodleian Library, MS Ashmole 1406, 50v, 51r, 53r. One of these spells is reproduced in Purkiss, *Fairies*, 141. See chapter 7 of this book for the magical context of Ashmole's dealings with fairies.

87 James Sharpe has advanced this possibility. He suggests that the belief in good fairies that assisted cunning folk may have been "paralleled by beliefs about malevolent spirits who helped malefic witches". James Sharpe, "The Witch's Familiar in Elizabethan England", in G. W. Bernard and S. J. Gunn, eds., *Authority and Consent in Tudor England* (Ashgate: 2002), 228.

88 George Gifford, *A Discourse of the Subtill Practises of Devilles by Witches* (1587), G3r.

89 *A Dialogue Concerning Witches and Witchcraftes* (1593), Br.

90 Jonson's *The Sad Shepherd: or A Tale of Robin-Hood* was published posthumously in 1641. Puck Hairy's soliloquy comprises the first scene of act three.

91 These depositions were reproduced in C. L'Estrange Ewen, *Witch Hunting and Witch Trials* (Dial Press: 1929), 291–313.

92 Gifford, *Dialogue*, C4v.

93 Gifford, *Discourse*, Cr.

94 Richard Bernard, *A Guide to Grand-Jury Men* (1627), 218.

95 John Gaule, *Select Cases of Conscience* (1646), 106–7.

96 Reginald Scot, *Discoverie*, book 4, chapter 11.

97 *Robin Goodfellow*, 42.

98 Gibson, *Early Modern Witches*, 53, 63.

99 C. L'Estrange Ewen, *Witchcraft and Demonism* (Heath Cranton: 1933), 188.

100 Bodleian Library, Oxford, MS Ashmole 1417, V, 1v.

101 For the physiology of the condition, and its manifestation in diverse cultural settings, see Davies, "The Nightmare Experience".

102 Marion Gibson suggests that Galis' account contains elements of spiritual autobiography and "presents him as a godly hero, combatting the Devil". Gibson, *Early Modern Witches*, 51, 63.

103 Gifford, *Dialogue*, J4v-Kr.

104 Edward Topsell, *The Historie of Serpents* (1608), 170.

105 William Austin, *Devotionis Augustinianæ Flamma, or Certayne Devout, Godly, and Learned Meditations* (1635), 61.

106 Edward Phillips, *The New World of English Words* (1658), P2r.

7

HUMAN INTERVENTIONS

Harnessing the unseen world

The acceptance of occult powers and invisible spirits in early modern England
had one practical, and often disreputable and controversial, consequence. This
was the prospect that men and women might manipulate these forces for their
own ends. The idea of human interventions in the supernatural was riddled with
problems – and these were magnified by the Protestant Reformation. Not only
were dealings with spirits potentially hazardous, but they also contravened a basic
tenet of reformed theology: that men and women should not seek to command
the residents of the unseen world. Indeed, the repudiation of the Catholic Mass
was based on the belief that priests were tempting God to deliver miracles at
their behest, instead of humbly accepting God's grace. The practice of "natural
magic", which exploited the occult properties of nature without trafficking with
spirits, was less problematic; but such operations could still excite controversy
and unease. Even the most respectable branch of natural magic, astrology, aroused
suspicion when it was used to predict future events, as this implied that earthly
affairs were governed by the movement of heavenly bodies rather than the sovereign will of God.[1]

Nonetheless, the desire to harness occult forces remained remarkably strong. In
part, this reflected the incomplete absorption of Protestant ideas by the English
population; the doctrine of human powerlessness before an unbiddable God was
taken seriously, and applied consistently, only by a devout minority. The insecuri-
ties of daily life meant that human interventions in the supernatural world were
hard to resist: to prevent hardship, to bring about cures for disease or to gain some
knowledge and control of an uncertain future. For more ambitious or unscrupulous
individuals, the manipulation of invisible powers was a potential source of insight

or wealth. The advent of print meant that magical texts were more widely available in the sixteenth and seventeenth centuries than ever before: knowledge once preserved in isolated manuscripts was increasingly accessible to a wide audience.[2] This probably broadened the appeal of learned magic as well as spread news – both real and fantastical – about the activity of sorcerers and witches.

Contemporaries used the word "magic" to describe the various attempts to understand and direct the unseen powers of the cosmos that are examined in this chapter. The definition of magic is famously fuzzy. Here I have adopted, loosely, a definition that was recognised in the period and has been appropriated by scholars ever since: the manipulation and exploitation of occult forces for human purposes.[3] The people of Tudor and Stuart England distinguished between particular kinds of magical activity, including witchcraft and certain varieties of "natural philosophy"; and these broad categories are observed in the pages that follow. The first section considers the spectrum of magical activities that were practiced in the period, and it surveys the sometimes grubby and deceitful social environment in which they took place. The second section focuses on witchcraft, an area of magic that was explicitly prohibited and intermittently punished under English law. The chapter concludes with an examination of the relationship between magic and natural philosophy, and it considers the contribution of supernatural beliefs to the "scientific revolution" of the late seventeenth and early eighteenth centuries.

Varieties of magic

The magic of early modern England was often associated with deception and fraud. This spotty reputation will not surprise modern readers, for whom magic exists mainly as a form of entertainment based on ingenious illusions. The intellectual context of Tudor and Stuart magic was, of course, very different: few people doubted that the effects created by magicians were potentially possible, and hardly any questioned the supernatural assumptions that underpinned them. Nor, however, were people blind to the existence of chicanery. Indeed, the very fact that magic sometimes worked created a lucrative environment for fraud. As Alec Ryrie observed in his study of the cozening magicians of Tudor London, the fact that people believed in the supernatural encouraged all manner of scams.[4] These gave rise to a lively popular literature of fake magic. In 1613 the larcenies of John and Alice West provided one entry in the genre. The couple apparently masqueraded as the king and queen of fairies in order to relieve their victims of gifts in return for the promise of gold. They were eventually apprehended and pilloried, and their sensational tale provided a warning to other charlatans and their potential victims.[5] Beyond such specific cases, the idea of magic carried the taint of illusion. Preaching at St Paul's Cross in 1637, for example, Thomas Drant described the false pleasures of the world as "but alchemy and daubing".[6]

The disreputable nature of magic was illustrated gaudily in the memoir of the seventeenth-century astrologer William Lilly. In his own career, Lilly sought to dispel the less savoury aspects of his craft; but as a young man in London, he learned his trade from a decidedly seamy mentor. Around 1632 Lilly sought out an "excellent wise man" named Evans in Gunpowder Alley. Their first meeting established the magician's character:

> He having been drunk the night before was upon his bed, if it be lawful to call that a bed wheron he then lay. He roused up himself, and after some compliments, he was content to instruct me in astrology. . . . [He] was much addicted to debauchery, and then very abusive and quarrelsome, seldom without a black eye, or one mischief or other.

Lilly's account of his tutor conveyed the mixture of deceitfulness and genuine power that characterised many magicians. He was, Lilly observed, an acute judge of astrological signs and a skilled conjurer of good and wicked spirits. On one occasion he was carried through the air by a demon summoned in a ritual. But these abilities were combined with a dishonest nature. Lilly noted that Evans was exceptionally good at identifying thieves through magical techniques – "yet for money he would willingly give contrary judgements".[7]

Evans' career demonstrated another quality of early modern magic: its appeal to individuals in all ranks of society. The dissolute magician counted among his clients the courtier Sir Kenelm Digby and the nobleman Lord Bothwell. These men employed him to conjure the spirit that propelled him through the sky, apparently after a bungled incantation. The interest in magic among members of the elite made sorcery a path to social advancement for ambitious and edu-cated men: the Tudor magicians Gregory Wisdom and John Dee both moved in elevated circles, and William Lilly benefited from loyal and powerful patrons in the seventeenth century.[8] The wide circulation of magical beliefs resulted, in part, from the remarkable variegation and fluidity of the subject. The most sophisti-cated practitioners drew upon arcane and supposedly ancient texts such as the *Corpus Hermeticum* (attributed to the Egyptian magus Hermes Trismegistus) and the *Clavicula Salomonis* (which purported to contain the occult wisdom of King Solomon). Command of these texts could impress (and beguile) well-educated clients. The "cunning folk" who served ordinary people, in contrast, employed an array of traditional charms and rites, often derived loosely from medieval Chris-tianity. These less esoteric methods also fattened the repertoire of self-consciously "learned" magicians such as Richard Napier and Elias Ashmole, who collected spells from both high and low culture.

The broad appeal of magic also reflected the diversity of its applications. Almost every aspect of life was, potentially, the subject of magical speculations. This quality is evident in the copious notebooks of Simon Forman, a London magician who worked with Richard Napier and inspired William Lilly. From the early 1580s until his death in 1611, Forman offered a range of magical services from his home in Westminster.[9] Many of these involved astrological readings to obtain hidden information, concerning both property and human relationships. His journals contain systematic procedures for identifying thieves and finding stolen property, and they also address a host of interpersonal questions: these include "whether a servant be true and trusty to his master or no", and "whether one's wife be honest or not". The magician also dealt with anxieties about sexual fidelity: one reading, dated 1584, sought to know "whether a woman had any man lay with her [on] such a night or no". Poignantly, Forman composed around 1609 a brief treatise "Of the Absent", followed by individual readings for missing persons.[10] The magician's concern for such intimate matters was combined with a larger interest in medicine. Having survived the plague in London in 1583, he developed an astrological theory of the causes of the disease and the natural signs that betokened it. These included the appearance of monsters in the sea and mass spawnings of frogs and toads.[11]

The methods used to obtain magical effects were equally diverse. At their simplest, and least controversial, they involved the observation of nature to assist in medicine or obtain knowledge. Medical practitioners required at least a basic understanding of astrology, as the cropping and consumption of healing plants could depend on the phases of the planets. The scrutiny of human bodies could yield more surprising information. Among Forman's papers is a note on the significance of facial moles: this advises men with moles on their eyebrows not to marry, and observes that "a mole on the nose of a man, somewhat ruddy, and having another in his privy place, doth show that such a person is given over much to venery".[12] Simple experiments could disclose other helpful knowledge. According to one seventeenth-century text, the milk of expectant mothers could be used to determine the sex of their offspring: a drop of milk on a marble stone "would hang together if it is a boy, [and] if it spread abroad it is a girl".[13] Such operations sought merely to exploit the hidden properties of the physical world, and elided into the study of nature more generally.

The art of "horary astrology" also attempted to elicit knowledge from natural events. Its adepts assumed that scrutiny of the heavens, combined with an understanding of the astrological qualities of individuals, could yield answers to specific questions. This was the method that Simon Forman used to discover information about "the absent" and that Richard Napier applied to the medical problems of his patients. In 1647 William Lilly published the first book on the art in English, introducing a general audience to the "heavenly knowledge of the stars".[14] The papers of Elias Ashmole, Lilly's patron and student, indicate the practical application of his techniques. In 1673 Ashmole sought guidance from the planets on the vagaries of finance: "I have a considerable sum of money [that] lies at interest in the excise office", he wrote, and asked "whether I had best let it lie so still, or turn it into gold and keep it by me". His horary calculations produced a prudent conclusion: "if it were in your own hands, you would either squander it away or convert it to less purpose than it is now".[15]

For those who lacked the time or expertise to make such prognostications, the future was revealed in more-general terms in printed almanacs.[16] These offered day-by-day predictions of the year ahead. The earliest English almanacs were published in the mid-1500s: their authors presented divinations on medical matters and the weather, issues of practical concern that attracted a large audience. The devotion of this audience was noted in 1596 by Thomas Nashe, who observed that almanacs provided "readier money than ale and cakes".[17] The market grew substantially in the seventeenth century, and particularly during the violent and uncertain decades after 1640, when knowledge of the future was uncommonly precious. It is striking that the genre flourished alongside the widespread interest in divine providence, which offered another kind of security in fragile times. Almanacs were about more than divination, however. As the form developed, it incorporated other kinds of (securely predictable) information: the dates of fairs and anniversaries, road directions, and miscellaneous historical and medical knowledge. Almanacs also included blank pages for readers to annotate, creating a kind of notebook. These non-magical features undoubtedly contributed to the success of the genre; they also integrated judicial astrology into the pattern of everyday life.

If astrology sought knowledge and guidance from nature, other forms of magic tried to intervene directly in the world. One of these was the use of charms. Many Protestants viewed this practice with suspicion, not least because it relied on the occult power of language.[18] The Catholic Mass was routinely condemned as a kind of idolatrous incantation, and popular charms were often corrupted versions of the discredited medieval liturgy. Nonetheless, the use of both spoken and written charms was widespread: they were employed to cure and prevent disease, to protect property, to deflect witchcraft and to ward off harmful spirits.[19] In the late sixteenth century, William Perkins observed dismissively that there were "charms for all conditions and ages of men, for diverse kinds of creatures, yea for every disease".[20] One curious example, preserved among Elias Ashmole's collection of magical texts, was a medical spell designed to expel parasitic worms. With solemn precision, this addressed the various kinds of invertebrate to be expunged:

> for liver worm, for lung worm, for tooth worm, for tongue worm, for bone worm, for flesh worm, for canker worm, for fester worm . . . for day worm, for night worm, for he-worm, for she-worm, and for all the worms that ever made was since the time my Lord Jesus born was, I conjure thee by more and less, by all the virtues of the mass, with Job and Joseph, and Saint John Baptist and with the holy crown of thorns that was put on Jesus' head for scorn.[21]

The cadences and internal rhymes signal the incantatory power of the text, while its comprehensiveness implies a legalistic desire not to exclude any worms from its influence. The references to the Mass and the saints indicate a medieval origin, though the charm may well have been used in the sixteenth century: similar texts were copied out by Richard Napier and others.

Another charm, which was certainly in wide circulation, illustrates the endurance and flexibility of these verbal formulae. In this case, the words were recited to deflect bewitchment. One version of the text, recorded in a statement taken during the Lancashire witch trials in 1612, reads as follows:

> Three biters hast thou bitten,
> The heart, ill eye, ill tongue:
> Three bitter shall be thy boot,
> Father, Son, and Holy Ghost,
> A God's name.
> Five Pater Nosters, five Aves,
> And a creed,
> In worship of five wounds
> Of our Lord.[22]

The words make more sense to modern readers if "bitter" in the third line is replaced with "better" and if "boot" is understood in the archaic sense of "help". Thus the opening passage may be paraphrased as follows: three things have harmed you – an evil heart, evil eye and evil tongue – but three better will bring you aid. These are the Holy Trinity. The rest of the text promises release from suffering through the devotions of the pre-Reformation church: the recital of five *Pater Nosters* and *Ave Marias*, and the words of the Creed. The last two lines recall another commonplace of medieval piety: devotion to the wounds of Christ.[23] This reading indicates the roots of the charm in the religious culture of the Middle Ages, and testifies to its longevity. But to decipher the text is, perhaps, to misconstrue its purpose: the words of the formula were important, but only insofar as they were able to produce the desired supernatural effects.

This becomes clear when one considers the ways in which the charm was used. The correct performance of the verse was essential: for example, some surviving copies stipulate that it should be recited three times. The text of the charm suggests that it was intended originally to cure individuals afflicted with curses; and it was often employed in this way. In 1622 Robert Booker, a London empiric, diagnosed bewitchment in one of his patients and recited the charm as part of his treatment.[24] One surviving copy of the text describes it as a remedy for both bewitchment and "falling sickness", a condition now viewed as a form of epilepsy.[25] But the charm was also addressed to inanimate things. In the testimony from Lancashire in 1612, it was used to improve beer that was badly fermented as the result of a curse. In 1634 a cunning man from the same county performed a version of the charm to cure sickly cattle. This involved singing the words in a style that he had learned from his father. In an intriguing detail, the healer claimed that the sickness afflicting the beasts passed into his own body for the duration of the song.[26]

The recital of verbal formulae could also charge objects with occult powers. Some forms of love magic exploited this effect. One seventeenth-century spell required the practitioner to kneel beside a wild plant and utter words of enchantment: "*In nomine patri*, I sought thee; *In nomine fili*, I have found thee: *in nomine spiritus sancti*, I conjure thee, that thou man or woman love me that I touch with thee". The plant could then be gathered and used to induce passion in its target.[27] Other objects, similarly enchanted, could be used to discover treasure. A branch from a hazel tree, cut at midnight on Good Friday, could be charmed in the name of the Holy Trinity "to find silver and gold".[28] The Christian elements in these operations suggest their origins: they were appropriations of the power of the medieval church to bless physical things. Their persistence in Tudor and Stuart England indicates the continued appeal of such manipulations, not least for the practical benefits they promised. This is illustrated by another form of verbal enchantment: spells cast on property to prevent their theft. One seventeenth-century charm sought to bind burglars magically to the places they attempted to rob: "stand thieves, stand thieves, in the name of the Holy Trinity, that you have no power to go, nor part away, but bind them so sore as St Bartholomew bound the foul fiend with the hair of his beard".[29]

Through the use of sacramental language, spells of this kind relied implicitly on the power of God. Other forms of magic sought expressly to summon and direct lesser spirits. This art was well documented in the period: it was used by the fraudulent magus Gregory Wisdom in the 1540s and by the devout Elizabethan sorcerer John Dee; the magician who taught William Lilly in the 1620s was famed for his skill at calling and commanding spirits; and Lilly's patron and friend, Elias Ashmole, later attempted his own experiments in this field. The techniques of conjuration were diverse, but two methods were often favoured. The art of crystallomancy involved the appearance of spirits on polished surfaces such as crystals and stones; sometimes the magician deciphered these manifestations directly, and sometimes a spiritually gifted assistant, or "scryer", was employed for this task. William Wycherley used this technique in the reign of Edward VI, and it was later practiced by John Dee and his scryer Edward Kelly.[30] Another method, derived from the magical writings attributed to King Solomon, was to invoke spirits from within a protective circle. Once summoned in either way, it was believed that a spirit could be bound to its master and required to appear on demand. One conjuration, possibly written out by Richard Napier in the early seventeenth century, claimed that the spirit would return "after his first appearance in any secret place as you shall be, either in field or town, especially under trees or in some wood".[31]

What creatures could these operations raise? The surviving evidence suggests that a diversity of occult beings were responsive to the magicians' call. Gregory Wisdom proposed to summon the ghost of Orpheus for his patron, Lord Neville. Dee and Kelly communicated with angels; and Lilly's dissolute tutor also conjured celestial spirits − though he appears to have dealt with demons as well. In 1590 an attempt to conjure the Devil himself in a field in Middlesex was foiled. A slaughtered cockerel was found beside a crystal stone inscribed with the name "Satan", alongside magical circles and objects apparently intended to protect the sorcerers from the subject of their invocations.[32] Less ambitiously, Elias Ashmole tried to summon fairies. The motives of conjurers were similarly diverse. Wisdom promised his aristocratic client (and dupe) that Orpheus, in the guise of a small boy, would confer upon him the skills of an expert musician. The spirits conjured by Lilly's tutor satisfied the curiosity of his patrons, and were also sent on errands such as the recovery of lost goods. It appears that Ashmole was motivated by the power that his fairy companion would give him: in the exhaustive contract to which he bound the creature, he required it to attend him in "true obedience" and enact all his wishes.[33] It seems that others called on spirits for more elevated reasons. John Dee, for one, believed that the angels reflected in his glass had revealed the secret language of God, through which he could probe the mysteries of religion and science.

Inevitably, the practice of magic was often in tension with the orthodoxies of early modern Christianity. Here it is important to distinguish between varieties of magic and the particular issues they raised. Predictive astrology was condemned by leading figures in the Protestant Reformation, including Calvin and Beza, on the grounds that it attributed power to the stars that belonged rightly to God. William Perkins devoted a section of his much-reprinted work of popular theology, *A Golden Chaine* (1591), to discrediting the "counterfeit art".[34] But for many English Protestants, it seems, astrological divinations were compatible with religious faith. Godly men and women certainly owned almanacs; and in some cases, such as the seventeenth-century preacher John Booker, they even published in the genre. William Lilly insisted in *Christian Astrology* (1647) that his art complemented human understanding of divine providence; and this view was apparently accepted by the parliamentarian generals who sought astrological guidance on their battle plans. As Alison Chapman has observed, such zealous Protestants found in astrology one explanation "of the ways in which God's divine will was enacted on earth".[35]

It was harder to apply such thinking to forms of operative magic such as charming or to the conjuration of spirits. The former was easily construed as "superstition", not least because charms often employed the language of the unreformed church. The use of charms was frequently condemned in English discussions of witchcraft, which are considered later in this chapter. The raising of spirits was even more problematic: several passages of scripture appeared to prohibit the practice, and the propensity of demons to appear in disguise made conjurations potentially hazardous.[36] Occasionally, anxieties about the propriety of calling on spirits surfaced in magical texts. The unknown author of a sixteenth-century account of a spell to disable thieves expressed misgivings about the summoning of angels that the process involved: to make offerings to spirits, the writer suggested, was a "grievous sin" because it implied "an adoration which is proper to God alone". The magician tested the spell without invoking angelic assistance and found that it worked just as well. He thereby avoided the "diabolical labyrinth of superstition and impious idolatry" which, he noted darkly, had trapped the souls of less cautious practitioners.[37]

Others reconciled their faith with the conjuration of spirits. The Elizabethan magician John Dee provides a particularly well-documented example. According to one recent study, Dee not only was a devout Christian but also brought a notably Protestant sensibility to his dealings with the unseen world.[38] In the early 1580s Dee used the art of crystallomancy to make contact with angels; these presented him and his scryer, Edward Kelly, with a series of revelations that promised great earthly power and appeared to presage the return of Christ. Dee was aware of the dangers of satanic dissimulation but placed trust in providence. In a spiritual strategy that resembled the self-examination of godly Christians for signs of election, he persuaded himself that his celestial experiments were an expression of God's will. The religious context of conjuration was evident in the written invocations of other ritual magicians: while these reveal little of their personal faith, they indicate the Christian framework on which they relied. Spirits were summoned in the name of the Trinity and commanded "by the virtue and divine power of God".[39] Such formulae were applied to spirits of all kinds: indeed, they were especially important for the binding of demons – a practice derived from the rite of exorcism. It appears that conjurors accepted the facts of the Christian cosmos even when they tried to exploit them. Elias Ashmole, for instance, commanded a fairy to appear by the power of "all angels and archangels, and all the holy company of heaven worshipping the omnipotent God". He even addressed the creature as a fellow Christian, whose fate was bound up in the unfolding scheme of salvation. It would face "the Lord of hosts at the dreadful Day of Judgement, before whose glorious presence both thou and I and all other Christian creatures must and shall appear".[40]

The tangle of problems, confusion and compromise that surrounded sorcery in the English Reformation was illustrated in the most public manifestation of the dangers of magic: the crime of witchcraft. For those Protestants that accepted that the threat of witchcraft was real, the activity demanded a careful examination of the nature and effects of human interventions in the supernatural and of their relationship to divine providence. More broadly, allegations of bewitchment provide evidence of the economy of magical beliefs in early modern communities. The attention that contemporaries paid to the crime opens a window on the larger experience of men and women who inhabited a world apparently penetrated by occult powers.

Witchcraft

In England, as elsewhere, allegations of witchcraft began in small communities and seldom moved far beyond them. For the great majority of people, the crime was a kind of magical assault: the use of occult means to harm the health or property of its victims. This understanding was acknowledged in English law, which defined witchcraft primarily as a crime against the person.[41] As an offence committed in secret, it was extremely hard to prove; and consequently prosecutions were uncommon in normal circumstances, and often unsuccessful. Most of those accused at the Essex Assizes, for example, either were acquitted or had their cases dismissed at the preliminary stage.[42] Accusations of destructive magic – or *maleficium* – were rooted in interpersonal relationships: the suspects were usually known to their supposed victims and believed to bear them ill feelings, and also to possess the occult skills required to cause them harm. Reputations for witchcraft were built over time. It is striking that many witnesses in witch trials referred to offences committed many years, and sometimes decades, before the incident that occasioned the prosecution. This implies, in turn, that most cases of bewitchment were dealt with informally, or merely nurtured as suspicions within the community, without reaching the attention of the courts.

This impression is confirmed by the cases of witchcraft reported to Richard Napier and his nephew (and namesake) in the early seventeenth century.[43] In 1635 the younger Richard dealt with a sixty-five-year-old gentlewoman named Joan Prescott, from the village of Kimbolton in Huntingdonshire, who believed she was bewitched. He recorded her symptoms in unusual detail:

> This gentlewoman is not sick but tormented in her body, both inwardly in her bowels by pricking and pulling . . . and pricking at her heart, and sometimes outwardly all over her body, sometimes in her head and then in her eyes, shoulders, arms, hands, thighs, knees, legs, and no place free. . . . Sometimes [she is] reasonable well, and then [it] comes again. And thus she hath been this few weeks or thereabouts. She hath taken physic and hath wrought reasonable with that, but yet these maladies aforesaid [are] not redressed.[44]

During a series of consultations, Prescott disclosed her fear that two women in the village were responsible for her distress. Her suspicion fell with particular force on Ann Hart, a woman whose conduct and reputation made her a convincing witch. She had a "bad conversation" and relished swearing and cursing; and some of her neighbours had previously blamed her for "the loss of their several goods, as horses, cows, calves, pigs, and their ducks".[45]

Prescott's account of her affliction illustrates the assumptions underlying the experience of bewitchment. She noted the seemingly unnatural character of her disease and its failure to respond to treatment. Indeed, she told Napier that his medicines only made her feel worse. She identified another woman as her likely tormenter, and was at pains to establish her wicked reputation and propensity to harm. It appears that she regarded the *maleficium*, or "ill favour", of people like Ann Hart as a weapon that was sometimes unleashed in disputes. Tellingly, she asserted that Hart had acted "without any just cause given on her part".[46] Consciously or otherwise, Napier's patient created a narrative that contained the expected ingredients of a witchcraft allegation and might appear convincing as a result.[47] It seems that the physician was unimpressed. He noted prosaically that her ailments were caused by a combination of wind and "melancholy blood".[48]

The remedies available to witchcraft victims were diverse. Some, such as Joan Prescott, apparently submitted to natural treatments. Others pursued occult therapies or practiced counter-magic to relieve their sickness or misfortune. The elder Richard Napier occasionally gave his patients astrological sigils to wear around their necks; these could apparently remove the symptoms of bewitchment. In 1637 his nephew was consulted by Margaret Franklin of Marston in Bedfordshire, who believed she had been cursed by a woman in a nearby village. He noted that she "had something to wear about her neck of my uncle, which did her good. So long as she wore that she [was] very well, and since she hath lost it she hath been ill again".[49] Such elaborate devices were beyond the means of many villagers, who resorted instead to the counter-magical rituals offered by cunning folk or prescribed by tradition. These often involved some kind of contact with the witch. Items from the suspect's body, such as a lock of hair, could be burned to break a spell. Afflictions could also be lifted by scratching the witch's face to draw blood.[50] According to a pamphlet in 1579, an ostler from Windsor applied this brutal remedy with success: as blood spattered the witch's face, "his pain went away, so that he hath been no more grieved since".[51]

This nexus of magical beliefs was remote from Protestant orthodoxy. Indeed, the idea of witchcraft appeared to challenge one of the central themes of reformed religion: the doctrine of divine providence. Instead of explaining suffering as the corrections of a loving God, and enjoining the afflicted to respond with prayerful self-examination, it attributed all kinds of misfortune to the occult power of individuals that could be defeated by counter-magic. Unsurprisingly, English demonologists condemned these beliefs. Tudor and Stuart writers on witchcraft were united in their commitment to providence and forthright about its implications. The sceptical Reginald Scot affirmed that nothing attributed to witchcraft happened without divine permission. Indeed, disease and hardship would continue unrelieved if every witch in the kingdom were hanged.[52] Despite their profound disagreements with Scot on other matters, later writers such as William Perkins and Richard Bernard concurred. Perkins affirmed that witches could do nothing beyond what "God shall in justice permit"; and Bernard observed that the supposed effects of witchcraft were "strictly limited" by God's will.[53] English theologians were equally opposed to magical cures for bewitchment. It was this conviction that led Perkins to denounce the cunning folk who tried to repel *maleficium* as worse than the witches themselves.[54]

The providential character of English demonology had important effects. Most notably, it led the experts on witchcraft to criticize those who blamed their hardships on *maleficium*. The sufferings attributed to witches were, in reality, chastisements delivered by God; and the appropriate response of the victim was prayer and self-amendment rather than any attempt to deal with the witch. In 1587 the Essex minister George Gifford made this point with particular force. He noted the regrettable belief "of the multitude" that witches possessed great power, and he observed that this misconception bred "innumerable sins". The worst of these was the tendency to ignore the works of God. Instead of acknowledging God's power in times of tribulation, people focused on the activities of deluded old women. They believed that "all would be well, and safe from harms, if they were rooted out". This providential analysis could encourage caution towards witch trials, as these were overwhelmingly based on the perceived harm done by the accused and the need to remove this harm. In Gifford's case this caution was clear. He warned that the prosecution of witches was normally misconceived, and he urged those people that had to "deal in such matters" to exercise "wisdom, discretion and wariness".[55]

The providential understanding of witchcraft did not, however, exclude entirely the prosecution of those suspected of the crime. This was because witchcraft involved not only malicious magic but also consorting with spirits. All learned writers on the subject acknowledged the involvement of the Devil; and the allegations of ordinary people frequently mentioned the evil spirits, or "puckrils" or "imps", that witches employed to torment their neighbours.[56] English demonologists agreed that Satan directed the activity of witches, either directly or at a distance; and most of them also accepted that demons could masquerade as small creatures that pretended to serve human masters. Accordingly, witches could be guilty of dealing with wicked spirits and breaking the numerous biblical injunctions against this practice. George Gifford acknowledged that it was right to condemn witches for this reason: indeed, their prosecution on this basis was "much to be commended". But he immediately pointed out that cases were seldom, if ever, pursued with such pious motives.[57] Others were less reserved. William Perkins argued that all witches were guilty of a compact with the Devil and deserved severe punishment for this crime.[58] In the seventeenth century, similar arguments were advanced, with varying degrees of subtlety, by the churchmen Thomas Cooper and Richard Bernard, as well as the self-appointed "witchfinder" Matthew Hopkins.[59]

The presence of tormenting spirits in allegations of witchcraft elicited various responses from Protestant writers. The creatures described by the victims of *maleficium* bore little resemblance to the orthodox understanding of demons. In the earliest detailed account of these supernatural assailants, the spirit concerned appeared first as a cat and then as "an evil favoured dog with horns on his head".[60]

In later testimonies the spirits were normally small animals. For Scot and Gifford in the 1580s, the involvement of these beings merely reinforced the superstitious nature of witch beliefs – though the latter admitted that Satan could deceive mortals by appearing in disguise. In 1590, however, the Cambridgeshire divine Henry Holland noted the existence of "certain familiar spirits, which whisper with their witches".[61] Holland took his examples from the Bible and continental sources, but his belief that witches worked with "familiar spirits" could be transferred to a contemporary English context. The fact that ordinary people already believed puckrils and imps to be agents of supernatural harm made it possible to yoke them, somewhat awkwardly, to the idea that witches entered pacts with demons in order to afflict their neighbours. In 1627 Richard Bernard published the most complete surviving integration of these concepts. For Bernard, the malicious creatures involved in witchcraft were akin to the familiar spirits described in scripture. It was plain that "witches have devils and familiar spirits, as is evident from the confession of a multitude of witches".[62]

It was no accident that Bernard presented his discussion of witches' familiars in a guide for members of grand juries dealing with allegations of witchcraft. These men were required to decide whether the accusations were sufficiently convincing to merit a full trial. As witchcraft was a secret crime involving occult practices, it was hard to secure the evidence required. The activity of evil spirits provided potential corroboration for accusations of bewitchment. The popular belief that witches suckled their imps from teats concealed on their bodies meant that the discovery of such excrescences might lend weight to an allegation – though whether such marks were "unnatural" remained a matter of judgement. In the earliest surviving record of its kind, a leet jury in Southampton requested the search of an alleged witch for incriminating physical marks in 1579.[63] Three years later, a similar search was made of a woman in St Osyth in Essex.[64] In the mid-1590s a list of "presumptions against witches" for the use of Yorkshire JPs noted that they were "seldom without some strange mark" on their body.[65] It appears that the search for such marks was a common feature of the investigation of witchcraft by the 1620s, when Bernard claimed that the teats that witches used to feed their imps were tangible signs of a demonic pact.[66]

It is easy for modern readers to dismiss the desire of magistrates and jurors for physical signs of witchcraft. The discovery of "unnatural" marks on a suspect's body could and sometimes did incriminate the innocent. But the desire for tangible evidence in cases of supposed bewitchment also reflected the awareness of contemporaries that proof was elusive, and reflected their reluctance to pursue allegations without sufficient justification.[67] Indeed, the number of convictions fell steeply in Essex in the period after 1620, at the same time that Bernard was formulating his theory of the Devil's mark.[68] The conventions and procedures of English law generally impeded the overzealous collection of evidence in witch trials. The prohibition of torture, in particular, prevented the abuse of suspects in pursuit of the most valuable kind of proof: confessions to the crime. In comparison, the physical traces of supposed supernatural activities were at best only "presumptive" evidence against a suspect, and normally insufficient to secure a conviction.[69]

The importance of these restrictions became tragically apparent in 1645. The East Anglian witch trials of that year were by far the most extensive, and lethal, in English history: around a hundred people were hanged in the space of a few months.[70] These trials were the product of a unique configuration of circumstances that released the destructive potential of witchcraft beliefs. The most important of these was the lapse of normal judicial procedures during the civil war. This was combined with the activities of two minor gentlemen, Matthew Hopkins and John Stearne, who took it upon themselves to examine and bring to trial those suspected of *maleficium* across several counties. The methods employed by Hopkins and Stearne included "watching" the accused for signs of witchcraft, during which time they were denied sleep and encouraged to confess. This process produced lurid and dreadful testimonies. As well as afflicting their neighbours, the East Anglian witches admitted to entering pacts with the Devil and copulating with evil spirits. These satanic activities were described by Stearne in 1648, when he observed that "witches worship devils, they invoke them, crave help of them, work by them, and do them homage".[71]

For many years the peculiarities of the Hopkins trials led historians to treat them as a grotesque aberration. This was explained by the actions of the self-appointed "witchfinders" and by their appropriation of continental theories of diabolism. The circumstances and scale of the East Anglian persecutions were indeed unprecedented. But it should also be noted that the accusations of ordinary villagers, and the confessions of the witches themselves, conformed largely to patterns established much earlier. Indeed, many of the harmful deeds recorded in the testimonies had taken place years, and in some cases even decades, before. The evil spirits, or imps, that figured prominently in the trials were familiar to English communities, and resembled those described by George Gifford in the 1580s. The confession of Joyce Boanes, taken in Essex in May 1645, provides an illustration:

> About thirteen years since, she had two imps which came into the bed to her in the likeness of mice, and they sucked on this examinant's body; and afterwards this examinant employed and sent the said imps to a farm house in St Osyth . . . where one Richard Welth then lived, where the said imps killed ten or twelve lambs of the said Richard's. And this examinant says further that a little while after she sent her said two imps to the house of one Thomas Clynch, where they killed a calf, a sheep and a lamb.[72]

The diabolical aspects of the trials were also based on older ideas. Richard Bernard had conflated the witch's hidden teat with the Devil's mark in the 1620s. When Satan himself appeared in the confessions, he assumed forms that were familiar in popular culture; and sometimes he simply merged with the witches' imps.[73] It appears that Hopkins and Stearne did not bring a new set of beliefs to the prosecution of English witches; rather, they exploited existing ideas with appalling results.

The witchfinders also mobilized long-standing fears in the communities they visited. Their progress was made possible by the anxieties and allegations of ordinary parishioners, often accumulated over many years without recourse to the formal apparatus of the law. Hopkins and Stearne were, in Malcolm Gaskill's words, "catalysts who gave accusers confidence by confirming their suspicions and beliefs".[74] In 1646 Hopkins stopped at Kimbolton in Huntingtonshire. A decade earlier, Joan Prescott had feared the malevolent attention of a group of women already reputed as witches, and she had taken her concerns to the physician Richard Napier. The outcome of Hopkins' visit is unknown; but it may well have removed Prescott's supposed tormenters for good.[75]

Science and the supernatural

The world of witchcraft and magic seems remote from the concerns of modern science, and the prevalence of occult beliefs in Tudor and Stuart England appears to indicate the limitations of "the scientific revolution". The once fashionable view that the Protestant Reformation engendered an age of objective scientific enquiry is hard to sustain. There were, however, trends within reformed Christianity that encouraged a view of the world that was at least consistent with later developments in the study of nature. The doctrine of providence encouraged scepticism about magic, and made space for a naturalistic understanding of earthly events; and distain for "superstition" often promoted this-worldly explanations for phenomena once attributed to spirits. At the same time – and perhaps surprisingly – the recognition and investigation of occult forces underpinned the development of new forms of physical science in the late seventeenth century.

The relationship between providence and natural science was multilayered. At one level, the doctrine encouraged scepticism about operative magic. This was expressed with particular clarity in the demonology of Reginald Scot. For Scot, there was simply no room for sorcery in the cosmos of a sovereign God, whose will alone determined all events. In the opening pages of *The Discoverie of Witchcraft* (1584), he observed that "if all the old women in the world were witches, and all the priests conjurers, we should not have a drop of rain, nor a blast of wind the more or the less for them".[76] Later writers also looked to providence to discredit magical beliefs. In 1655 the physician Thomas Ady noted that God was the sole author of disturbances in the weather, such as electrical storms, though some people mistakenly attributed them to sorcery.[77] Another physician, John Webster, echoed this view in 1677: he observed that belief in magic denied "the wisdom and power of God in His government of the world by divine providence".[78]

Arguments of this kind flowed easily in the currents of English Protestantism. They built on the central assertions of the reformed faith: the supreme power of God and the priority of scripture. Thomas Ady cited the Book of Job to demonstrate the Lord's command of the elements: He "scattereth the east wind" and caused "the overflowing of waters . . . [and] the lightning of thunder" (Job 38:24–5). The Bible testified to the sovereignty of God, and this sovereignty left no space for magicians. The repudiation of magic did not, in itself, imply an entirely naturalistic view of the world. As the author of nature, the Lord could still disturb its normal flow to produce miracles and wonders: such events were also vouchsafed by the scriptures, and were prominent among the "special providences" that proliferated in Elizabethan and early Stuart England.

The doctrine of providence could also foster a kind of Christian naturalism, however. It was possible to argue that God ruled at a distance through perfect natural laws. This less common opinion was also expressed by Reginald Scot.[79] Scot held that nature moved "according to the appointment and will of God, and according to the constitution of the elements and the course of the planets, wherein God hath set a perfect and perpetual order".[80] This view of providence implied a more remote Creator, as Scot's "perfect and perpetual order" did not need constant maintenance. It was possible, of course, for more secular writers to exploit similar ideas. In *Leviathan* (1651) the philosopher Thomas Hobbes observed that providence extended not only to humankind "but also to beasts and plants, and bodies inanimate".[81] The social and physical world was bound by "laws of nature". Unsurprisingly, Hobbes was sceptical of supernatural interventions of all kinds.[82]

While the doctrine of providence could support a non-magical and orderly vision of the cosmos, the reformation of spirits undermined traditional beliefs about the unseen world. The established church denounced the appearance of saints; and reports of other supernatural creatures, such as ghosts and fairies, were routinely met with scepticism. Both natural and otherworldly explanations could account for the persistence of such reports, but the former were generally favoured. The English edition of Ludwig Lavater's treatise *Of Ghostes and Spirits* (1572) illustrates this well. The first part of Lavater's text dealt entirely with natural explanations for supposedly spectral phenomena. Physical impairments accounted for many experiences, as "men which are dull of seeing and hearing imagine things which . . . are not so". Mental disturbance was another factor: individuals consumed with fear, as well as "melancholic persons and madmen", were prone to hallucinations. The physically and mentally fit could also be deceived. It was common for the nocturnal cries of wild animals – such as pine martens, weasels and rats – to be taken for spirits. Finally, Lavater warned his readers against deliberate counterfeits. He devoted several chapters to the exploits of human tricksters who masqueraded as ghosts, saints or angels. Somewhat improbably, these were mostly Catholic priests who "bewitched foolish men" in order to foster false religion.[83]

The attack on "superstition" encouraged innumerable small revisions to traditional lore about the natural world. In one semi-comical vignette, the minister and naturalist Edward Topsell exposed the mistaken belief that birch trees sometimes retained their leaves in winter through the intercession of the Virgin. It was not the Queen of Heaven that preserved the trees' foliage, but the migration of small lizards into the earth around their roots:

> By reason of their multitude gathered together at the root of this tree, it falleth out that their breath heateth the same, and so preserveth the leaves of it from falling off. Wherefore in ancient time the ignorant multitude, seeing a birch tree with green leaves in the winter, did call it Our Lady's Tree, or a holy tree, attributing that greenness to [a] miracle.[84]

Like Lavater's tales of priests disguised as ghosts, Topsell's enchanting theory shows that Protestant naturalism was not necessarily based on empirical observation.[85] Rather, the *a priori* rejection of certain kinds of explanation – such as the return of the dead from purgatory or the saintly preservation of trees – cleared the way for alternative theories about the natural world. These were normally based on (supposedly) natural causes. It remained possible, of course, to explain unusual phenomena in supernatural terms – as the work of God, angels or demons. But this was seldom the first resort.

While these tendencies within reformed religion encouraged natural interpretations of some phenomena, it should also be noted that the supernatural assumptions of early modern culture were not necessarily in conflict with the development of "science". This can be demonstrated by the fact that many English natural philosophers later regarded as scientific pioneers – such as William Harvey, Robert Boyle, and Isaac Newton – were steeped in the supernatural beliefs of their day. Harvey was committed to the theory of correspondences, whereby everything in the cosmos was linked by a nexus of occult relationships. Accordingly, he was keen to explain the invisible sympathies between human anatomy and other products of nature: the kidneys were akin to beans, and the spleen to the tongue of an ox.[86] Robert Boyle accepted many of the principles and experimental methods of alchemy.[87] So too did Isaac Newton, who also speculated extensively on the existence and properties of angels. In a commentary on the twentieth chapter of the Book of Revelation in the 1680s, he surmised that the heavens contained "beings whose nature we do not understand", and these celestial entities might have "a sufficient power of self-motion [to] move whether they will".[88]

Crucially, these occult interests were not merely supplementary to the work of English scientists; nor were they lingering survivals of a fading world view. On the contrary, they were often integral to scientific investigation and discovery. Thomas Wright has argued that Harvey's theory of the circulation of blood was inspired by his belief that natural forces moved in perfect circles; and he may have borrowed this idea from his friend and associate, the alchemist Robert Fludd.[89] The anatomist also assumed that an animating spirit, akin to the soul, was present in living blood.[90] Boyle's chemical experiments were influenced strongly by Johan Van Helmont, a Flemish disciple of the magician Paracelsus; and in the 1650s he collaborated with the American alchemist George Starkey.[91] Most dramatically, Newton's hypothesis of universal gravitation confirmed one of the central ideas of natural magic: the ability of objects to act invisibly on one another at a distance.

To twenty-first-century observers, the temptation to sift the real (and "scientific") content from the bogus (and "magical") speculations of early modern natural philosophy is almost impossible to overcome. Hindsight can be blinding. It should be recognised, however, that the various forms of natural magic practiced in sixteenth- and seventeenth-century England involved an assumption that was essential to any understanding of the physical world: the operation of unseen forces. Scholars distinguished between the "manifest" and "subtle" properties of nature: while the former could be observed directly, the latter were known only by their effects. The qualities that made some plants poisonous were invisible but real; so too were the interior forces that caused an egg to produce a chicken, or a tadpole to grow into a frog. It was appropriate for thinkers to explore such concealed – or "occult" – phenomena within the context of magic. In the words of Cornelius Agrippa in the 1530s, the magician's goal was to understand "those immaterial substances which regulate and administer all things".[92] The subsequent incorporation of some of these forces into Enlightenment science relegated others to the status of magic.[93] But the natural philosophers of Tudor and Stuart England were free to speculate on a wide range of "subtle" processes: Richard Napier the elder, for example, recorded observations on the medical properties of plants, the influence of astral bodies, and the "weapon salve" – a technique for curing flesh wounds at a distance by applying an ointment to the blade that caused them.[94]

In this context, it is interesting to consider the impact of new technologies that made parts of the invisible world available to human observation. The invention of microscopes entailed a series of adjustments to the understanding of the occult. Catherine Wilson has argued that the ability to magnify very small objects lent support to the corpuscular theory of matter, which held that the world was composed of minute particles. But this theory was not necessarily incompatible with magical beliefs. For example, the existence of invisible particles was used to explain the operation of the weapon salve. At the same time, the discovery of previously unseen phenomena – such as the pattern of ice crystals or the hairs on the legs of flies – brought aspects of the occult into the realm of observable science. Things seen through the microscope "had the intractability of fact", and they consequently narrowed the range of credible explanations for the subtle processes of nature.[95]

Robert Hooke's celebrated treatise on the unseen world, *Micrographia* (1665), illustrates the power of microscopic images to penetrate the occult. In a series of pictures of magnified objects, Hooke revealed a kingdom of strange precision and beauty beneath the normal range of human perception. The familiarity of his objects – the point of a needle, grains of sand, burnt vegetables and the wings of insects – enhanced the sense of a realm of hidden knowledge below the normal surface of things. For Hooke himself, this encouraged speculation about still deeper mysteries. As he observed the transformation of larvae into gnats in a pool of water, he imagined that the larvae themselves had spawned from eggs so small they were beyond the reach of his lens. Hooke's microscope also confirmed the apparent nexus of "correspondences" within the created world. The minute examination of a moth's wing, for example, exposed patterns similar to "the branched backbone of a herring" or the feathers on a peacock's tail. Evidence of design also seemed to saturate the miniature world. The tiny hemispheres – or "pearls" – that composed the eye of a fly were arranged to maximize their number within the smallest possible space. Discoveries of this kind led the author of *Micrographia*, and his many readers, to an enhanced appreciation of the power of divine providence in nature. As Hooke remarked in his description of gnat larvae, such small marvels indicated "the goodness and providence of the infinitely wise creator".[96]

The exploration of previously invisible things contributed to the idea of a regular, minutely patterned and orderly cosmos. For some, this implied an essentially mechanical account of natural processes. Here the concept of God's design and oversight of the universe – or "general providence" – appeared to correspond with the physical evidence. English theologians such as John Wilkins had already likened the creation to an intricate clock, with tiny wheels acting upon still tinier ones in a pattern of sublime precision.[97] Such a model was not necessarily inconsistent with direct acts of divine intervention: the clockmaker could still adjust, or suspend, His mechanism if He wished. As Jane Shaw has argued, miracles were still widely reported during the English Enlightenment: indeed, accounts of miraculous healing proliferated in the later seventeenth century. These accounts were increasingly subjected to empirical scrutiny; but the result of such scrutiny was often the validation rather than the dismissal of the healers' claims.[98]

Nor did the "mechanical philosophy" remove the need for occult explanations of natural phenomena. The idea of a clock-like cosmos was most compelling when it was applied to the movement of physical things, like the flow of rivers or the orbit of planets around the sun. Mechanical explanations were less satisfactory within the living world. It was possible, for instance, to observe the development of animal embryos through the various stages leading to birth, as William Harvey did in a series of bloody experiments on deer in the 1640s. But such unpleasant research only confirmed the "subtle" nature of the process involved. The force that shaped an undifferentiated foetus into an infant creature could not be understood in mechanical terms, although some thinkers tried to evade the problem by claiming that the ovaries (or sperm) already contained miniature embryos.[99] If empirical observation appeared to close down some areas of occult speculation, it also undermined some purely physical theories about the natural world: for instance, the work of Robert Hooke and later microscopists challenged the ancient belief that life could produce itself by spontaneous generation.[100] Ultimately, the developments in science in the late seventeenth century served to refine and consolidate the providential world view of English Protestantism, while the occult remained an important presence in intellectual life.

Notes

1 Contemporaries distinguished between "judicial astrology", which sought to divine the future, and the use of astrology in areas such as medicine. For the controversy over the former, see Patrick Curry, *Prophecy and Power: Astrology in Early Modern England* (Polity Press: 1989); and Ann Geneva, *Astrology and the Seventeenth-Century Mind: William Lilly and the Language of the Stars* (Manchester University Press: 1995).

2 On the expansion of the market for printed magical texts, see Owen Davies, *Grimoires: A History of Magic Books* (Oxford University Press: 2010).

3 In using this definition, I am not asserting a sharp distinction between magic and religion. Some practices normally viewed as religious appear to involve the manipulation of supernatural powers, or can at least be interpreted in this way: the use of holy relics to cure diseases, for example, or the expulsion of demons. There was much dispute in early modern England about the allegedly "magical" nature of such things. For reasons of economy, I have excluded from my discussion the various forms of "magic" that might be found in conventionally religious contexts.

4 Ryrie notes that the victims of such scams were deceived not "because they were exceptionally stupid, but because the lies which were spun to them were alarmingly plausible". Alec Ryrie, *The Sorcerer's Tale* (Oxford University Press: 2008), 108.

5 *The Severall Notorious and Lewd Cousenages of John West and Alice West* (1613).

6 Thomas Drant, *The Divine Lanthorne* (1637), 15–6.

7 Lilly composed his memoir for his friend Elias Ashmole in 1668, and it was eventually published in 1715 as *Mr William Lilly's History of His Life and Times*. See pp. 21–3 for the account of Evans; quotations p. 21.

8 In the 1540s Wisdom was employed by Henry, Lord Neville, whom he subsequently defrauded. Dee acted as an occasional advisor to Elizabeth I and was consulted on the most propitious date for her coronation. For Wisdom, see Ryrie, *Sorcerer's Tale*; for Dee and his circle, see Glyn Parry, *The Arch Conjuror of England* (Yale University Press: 2011), and "John Dee, Alchemy and Authority in Elizabethan England" in Marcus Harmes and Victoria Bladen, *Supernatural and Secular Power in Early Modern England* (Ashgate: 2015).

9 For Forman's busy career, see Lauren Kassell, *Medicine and Magic in Elizabethan London* (Oxford University Press: 2005).

10 Bodleian Library, Oxford, MS Ashmole 205, 150r, 198r, 202r; "Of the Absent" begins at 246r and is erratically paginated thereafter.

11 An ominous marginal note sits beside this observation: "23 Feb 1611, at the pond I heard the toads and frogs croak mightily". Bodleian Library, Oxford, MS Ashmole 1436, 40r.

12 Bodleian, MS Ash. 205, 242*v*.
13 Bodleian Library, Oxford, MS Ashmole 1447, XI, 20, 67.
14 William Lilly, *Christian Astrology Modestly Treated of in Three Books* (1647), "Epistle to the Student".
15 Bodleian Library, Oxford, MS Ashmole 1790, 133*r*.
16 The best general study of the genre remains Bernard Capp, *Astrology and the Popular Press: English Almanacs, 1500–1800* (Faber: 1979). For the cultural context of almanacs, see Alison Chapman, "Marking Time: Astrology Almanacs, and English Protestantism", *Renaissance Quarterly*, Vol. 60 (2007), 1257–90; and Adam Smyth, "Almanacs, Annotators, and Life Writing in Early Modern England", *English Literary Renaissance*, Vol. 38, No. 2 (2008).
17 Nashe is quoted in Capp, *Astrology*, 44.
18 Stuart Clark notes the Protestant distaste for the magical power of words in "The Rational Witchfinder: Conscience, Demonological Naturalism and Popular Superstitions", in Stephen Pumpfrey, Paolo Rossi and Maurice Slawinski, eds., *Science, Culture and Popular Belief in Renaissance Europe* (Manchester University Press: 1991). Genevieve Guenther has argued that English poets were careful to dissociate the effectual power of words from the taint of magic. See her *Magical Imaginations: Instrumental Aesthetics in the English Renaissance* (University of Toronto Press: 2012).
19 For the many applications of charms, see Owen Davies, *Popular Magic: Cunning Folk in English History* (Continuum: 2003), 83–6, chapter 6.
20 William Perkins, *A Discourse of the Damned Art of Witchcraft* (1608), 153.
21 Bodleian, MS Ash. 1447, IX, 6, 17.
22 Thomas Potts, *The Wonderfull Discoverie of Witches in the Countie of Lancaster* (1613), E2*v*-E3*r*.
23 For further analysis of this charm and others described in the Lancashire witch trials, see Jonathan Lumby, *The Lancashire Witch Craze: Jennet Preston and the Lancashire Witches, 1612* (Carnegie: 1995), chapter 17.
24 Keith Thomas, *Religion and the Decline of Magic* (Weidenfeld & Nicolson: 1971), 220.
25 Bodleian, MS Ash. 1790, 121*r*.
26 The deposition of the healer, Henry Baggilie, is reproduced in Lumby, *Lancashire Witch Craze*, 95–6.
27 Bodleian Library, Oxford, MS Ashmole 1406, 98*r*.
28 Bodleian Library, Oxford, MS Ashmole 1488, II, 8*v*.
29 Bodleian, MS Ash. 1406, 98*r*.
30 Ashmole also used a glass surface to conjure spirits in the seventeenth century. For the use of crystals by Wycherley and Dee, see Parry, *Arch Conjuror*, 36–7.
31 Bodleian, MS Ash. 1790, 118*r*. The writer may be the Richard Napier who continued his uncle's work as an astrological physician in the 1630s and whose patients are considered in chapter 2.
32 Ryrie, *Sorcerer's Tale*, 129–30.
33 Bodleian, MS Ash. 1406, 52*v*.
34 William Perkins, *A Golden Chaine, or The Description of Theologie* (1591), H2*v*-H3*r*.
35 Chapman, "Marking Time", 1262.
36 Biblical condemnations of dealings with spirits include Leviticus 19:31, Dueteronomy 18:11, and 2 Kings 23:24.
37 Bodleian Library, Oxford, MS Ashmole 421, 231*v*, 232*r*.

38 Stephen Clucas, "False Illuding Spirits & Cownterfeiting Deuills: John Dee's Angelic Conversations and Religious Anxiety", in Joad Raymond, ed., *Conversations with Angels* (Palgrave Macmillan: 2011).

39 The quotation is from an incantation in MS Ash. 1790, 124*v*.

40 Bodleian, MS Ash. 1406, 52*r*, 52*v*.

41 In 1563 it became a capital crime to cause death by bewitchment. The 1604 Witchcraft Act extended this punishment to trafficking with spirits; but in practice this offence was secondary to the act of bewitchment, and very few cases were brought on this basis alone.

42 In the period 1560–1680, 291 people faced accusations of witchcraft at the Essex Assizes. Of these, 151 either had the bill of presentment against them dismissed by the grand jury or were sent to trial and acquitted. These figures are taken from Alan Macfarlane, *Witchcraft in Tudor and Stuart England* (Routledge: 2nd ed. 1999), 57.

43 Chapter 2 surveys some of the cases of bewitchment dealt with by the younger Richard Napier.

44 Bodleian, MS Ash. 1447, IX, 5.

45 Bodleian Library, Oxford, MS Ashmole 412, 201*v*.

46 Ibid.

47 Scholars have noted the importance of framing plausible narratives in cases of witchcraft, as direct evidence of *maleficium* was extremely hard to obtain. See, for example, Peter Rushton, "Texts of Authority: Witchcraft Accusations and the Demonstration of Truth in Early Modern England", in Stuart Clark, ed., *Languages of Witchcraft: Narrative, Ideology and Meaning in Early Modern Culture* (Macmillan: 2001).

48 Bodleian, Ash. 412, 209*v*.

49 Bodleian, Ash. 412, 255*v*.

50 The practice of scratching featured often in contemporary witchcraft pamphlets. These accounts are examined in their legal and religious context in Orna Alyagon Darr, *Marks of an Absolute Witch: Evidentiary Dilemmas in Early Modern England* (Ashgate: 2011), chapter 8.

51 Marion Gibson, ed., *Early Modern Witches: Witchcraft Cases in Contemporary Writing* (Routledge: 2000), 39.

52 Scot makes this famous assertion in the opening pages of *The Discoverie of Witchcraft* (1584). See below for the implications of his providentialism.

53 William Perkins, *A Discourse of the Damned Art of Witchcraft* (Cambridge: 1608), 3–4; Richard Bernard, *A Guide to Grand-Jury Men* (London 1627), 3.

54 Perkins, *Discourse*, 173–5.

55 George Gifford, *Discourse of the Subtill Practises of Devilles by Witches and Sorcerers* (1587), Dedication, D*r*, I*v*.

56 See chapter 6 for the relationship between these creatures and fairies.

57 Gifford, *Discourse*, I*r*-*v*.

58 Perkins distinguished between "express and manifest" compacts with the Devil, in which the witch openly professed allegiance to an evil spirit, and "implicit compacts" that involved the use of superstitious invocations or charms. Perkins, *Discourse*, 47–53.

59 Thomas Cooper, *The Mystery of Witch-Craft* (1617), 64–7; Richard Bernard, *A Guide to Grand-Jurymen* (1627), 108–14. On the role of the demonic pact in the East Anglian witch trials of 1645, see Malcolm Gaskill, *Witchfinders: A Seventeenth-Century English Tragedy* (John Murray: 2005), 47–8, 107–8, 138.

60 These encounters were recorded in *The Examination and Confession of Certaine Wytches* (1566). The text is reproduced in Gibson, *Early Modern Witches*; quotation, 20.
61 Henry Holland, *Treatise Against Witchcraft* (1590), C1r.
62 Bernard, *Guide*, 156.
63 Clive Holmes, "Women: Witnesses and Witches", *Past & Present*, Vol. 140, No. 1 (1993), 70.
64 *A True and Just Recorde* (1582), reproduced in Gibson, *Early Modern Witches*, 94.
65 The same document observed that witches often "have some extraordinary dog or cat". Yorkshire Archaeological Society, Leeds, DD146/12/2/19.
66 Bernard, *Guide*, 111–2.
67 Orna Alyagon Darr points out that witchcraft in England was both a serious crime and one that was unusually hard to prove. Such crimes created particular dilemmas for the judicial system. The desire for supernatural "proofs" of various kinds was one response to this situation. Darr, *Marks*, 4–5; see chapter 5 for the Devil's mark.
68 Macfarlane, *Witchcraft*, 57–60.
69 It is notable that William Perkins included the Devil's mark among the "presumptions" against alleged witches but denied that such tokens were sufficient for a conviction. Perkins, *Discourse*, 202–4.
70 Approximately 250 witches were investigated or tried during the East Anglian witch hunt, the great majority between July and December 1645. James Sharpe has estimated that at least a hundred were executed, and he notes that the real total may have been considerably more. James Sharpe, *Instruments of Darkness: Witchcraft in England, 1550–1750* (Hamish Hamilton: 1996), 128–9.
71 John Stearne, *A Confirmation and Discovery of Witchcraft* (1648), A2.
72 *A True and Exact Relation of the Severall Informations, Examinations, and Confessions of the Late Witches* (1645), 30.
73 See Darren Oldridge, *The Devil in Tudor and Stuart England* (History Press: 2nd ed. 2010), 189–90.
74 Gaskill, *Witchfinders*, 273.
75 Gaskill, *Witchfinders*, 217–8.
76 Scot, *Discoverie*, 3.
77 Thomas Ady, *A Candle in the Dark* (1655), 113.
78 John Webster, *The Displaying of Supposed Witchcraft* (1677), 97.
79 Scot also denied that spirits could manifest themselves in physical things, a doctrine that hardened the naturalism implicit in his view of providence. For this aspect of his thought, see Philip Almond, *England's First Demonologist: Reginald Scot and The Discoverie of Witchcraft* (I. B. Taurus: 2011), especially 114–6.
80 Scot, *Discoverie*, 3.
81 Thomas Hobbes, *Leviathan*, part two, chapter 31.
82 For Hobbes' treatment of wonders and miracles, see Michael Funk Deckard, "A Sudden Surprise of the Soul: The Passion of Wonder in Hobbes and Descartes", *Heythrop Journal*, Vol. XLIX, No. VI (2008), especially 953–5.
83 Ludwig Lavater, *Of Ghostes and Spirites Walking by Nyght* (1572), 9, 14, 16, 23, 49.
84 Edward Topsell, *The Historie of Serpents. Or, the Second Booke of Liuing Creatures* (1608), 14–5.
85 Sadly, English lizards do not shelter in the roots of birch trees. The spread of birch on heathland actually destroys their habitat.

86 Thomas Wright, *William Harvey: A Life in Circulation* (Oxford University Press: 2012), essay five.

87 For Boyle's association with alchemy, see William R. Newman and Lawrence M. Principe, *Alchemy Tried in the Fire: Starkey, Boyle, and the Fate of Helmontian Chymistry* (University of Chicago Press: 2002).

88 Newton is quoted in Simon Schaffer, "Newtonian Angels", in Raymond, ed., *Conversations*, 93.

89 Wright, *Harvey*, essay six.

90 William Harvey, "A Second Essay to Jean Riolan", in Andrew Wear, ed., *The Circulation of the Blood and other Writings* (Everyman: 1993), 118.

91 See Newman and Principe, *Alchemy*, for Boyle's collaboration with Starkey; especially 208–36.

92 Cornelius Agrippa, *De Occulta Philosophia* (1531), in P. G. Maxwell-Stuart, *The Occult in Early Modern Europe: A Documentary History* (Macmillan: 1999), 116.

93 To give one example, chemistry was not consistently distinguished from alchemy until the early eighteenth century, when the latter acquired the meaning of gold making. William R. Newman and Lawrence M. Principe, "Alchemy vs. Chemistry: The Etymological Origins of a Historiographic Mistake", *Early Science and Medicine*, Vol. 3, No. 1 (1998), 32–65.

94 The ointment was made from linseed oil, human blood and the "moss of a dead man's head". Napier noted that it was effective at a distance of thirty miles. Bodleian, Ash. 1488, II, 73r.

95 Catherine Wilson, *The Invisible World: Early Modern Philosophy and the Invention of the Microscope* (Princeton University Press: 1995), 54–7, 252.

96 Robert Hooke, *Micrographia* (1665), 176–7, 189, 190–1, 197.

97 John Wilkins, *A Discourse Concerning the Beauty of Providence* (1649), 52.

98 Jane Shaw, *Miracles in Enlightenment England* (Yale University Press: 2006), especially chapters 4 and 6.

99 This led to the extraordinary proposition that each microscopic embryo had a still smaller foetus inside it, and so *ad infinitum*. See Clara Pinto-Correia, *The Ovary of Eve: Egg and Sperm and Preformation* (University of Chicago Press: 1997).

100 Wilson, *Invisible World*, 254.

REFLECTIONS AND CONCLUSIONS

In December 1706 Robert Withers, the vicar of Gateley in Norfolk, described an unexpected meeting between two of his acquaintances. The meeting was unexpected because one of them, Mr Naylor, had been dead for four years. According to Wither's account, Naylor visited his old friend, Mr Shaw, as the latter was reading and smoking in his study on a late September evening. They conversed for an hour, in which time Naylor told his unlucky host that both he and another man, Mr Orchard, would soon be dead. The spirit departed, and shortly afterwards Mr Orchard died as predicted. This apparently prompted Shaw to seek advice from the Reverend Withers, who seems to have accepted the facts of the case. As he noted in an addendum to the parish register, "I have all the moral certainty of the truth of it [that is] possible".[1]

Withers' story is one small instance, among many, of the continued vitality of supernatural beliefs at the dawn of the "age of reason". It is notable that Withers and the participants in his tale were educated men: even Mr Shaw's surprising guest was once a fellow of St John's College, Cambridge. The inclusion of a ghost in the tale is also striking, as appearances of the returning dead were officially discredited by the English church. It is not clear whether Withers regarded the spirit as truly a ghost or a demon; but his account of the affair resembled the traditional narratives of visits from the grave, glossed by the doctrine of providence, that were described in chapter 6 of this book.

It was once widely assumed that Protestantism dispensed with the supernatural assumptions of medieval culture and inaugurated a naturalistic view of the world that corresponded, broadly, with the emergence of modern science. This view is now hard to sustain. While the reformers inveighed against what they perceived as non-biblical superstition, they did little to divest the world of its supernatural elements; nor was this their intention. Rather, they sought to reformulate the terms in which otherworldly phenomena were understood, by winnowing the inhabitants of the kingdom of spirits and redrawing the border between the living and the dead. The result was a simplified model of supernatural intervention, but one that left ample scope for the deeds of angels and demons and the judgements of a busy and immanent God. The apocalyptic expectations that attended the Reformation probably heightened the belief that such manifestations were likely. Moreover, as Alexandra Walsham has noted, the Protestant emphasis on divine sovereignty actively encouraged the acceptance of "constant providential intervention in temporal affairs".[2]

The supernatural currents in English culture flowed deeply into the era of "Enlightenment". In her study of miracles in later Stuart and Georgian England, Jane Shaw has revealed a lively interest in the movements of the divine hand among educated observers and ordinary people alike.[3] The work of Owen Davies and others has shown that anxieties about harmful magic extended long beyond the formal suppression of witch trials in 1736, and these anxieties were not confined to the unenlightened masses.[4] Reports of ghosts remained compelling in the same period; and English Catholics sustained a distinctive culture of the supernatural into the nineteenth century.[5] There is even some evidence that Protestant thinkers softened their objections to supernatural beliefs once viewed as superstitious. Towards the end of his life, Richard Baxter mused that God might, after all, permit the spirits of the dead to return to earth.[6] According to a pamphlet in 1696, even the fairies that had communed with Anne Jeffries during the civil war demonstrated the "great and marvellous works" of God.[7]

Rather than seeking a transition from a supernatural to a "scientific" understanding of the world, historians of early modern England, and beyond, can more fruitfully examine the shifts that occurred within a system of beliefs that maintained a fundamental role for occult powers. In the period covered by this book, three broad reformulations can be observed. The first was the expulsion of non-biblical spirits – intercessory saints, ghosts, fairies and a jumble of folkloric "bugs" – from the cosmos acknowledged by the Protestant church. This unsettled the traditional economy of the otherworldly and emphasised the importance of those forces that remained. An implacably sovereign God commanded legions of angels and allowed, within limits, the depredations of the satanic "prince of this world". The second shift, analogous to the reformed concern with inward religious experience, was a new emphasis on the unseen and interior manifestations of supernatural forces. Both angels and demons were presented as hidden movers within the human mind, as "secret physicians" and poisoners respectively. This tendency was not entirely new: it channelled a tradition of thought that was established within the panoply of late medieval religion. Nor was it absolute: as Robert Withers' story indicates, many educated people accepted that spirits could sometimes, if rarely, appear in embodied form, and popular representations of supernatural beings often acknowledged their corporeality.

The third major shift was the emergence, and development, of the doctrine of divine providence as the dominant model for explaining the operation of supernatural powers. Again, this doctrine had deep roots in the Christian past; but it achieved renewed significance because of the Protestant insistence on the sovereignty of God. The application of the doctrine evolved in the sixteenth and seventeenth centuries. Broadly speaking, there was a drift from the concept of "general providence", by which God ordered all earthly events to fulfil His sovereign and inscrutable will, to the interpretation of "special providences", or particular signs by which this will could be discerned. The tide of special providences reached its peak during the civil wars and began to subside after the Restoration. This process can be illustrated, in miniature, by the pattern of one particular kind of "divine judgement": the birth of deformed or "monstrous" children. In Elizabethan England there were sporadic reports of these sad events, such as the conjoined twins that were presented in 1565 as "a warning from God to move all people to amendment of life".[8] The genre became more popular in the early decades of the seventeenth century; and after 1640 it was a staple of cheap print.[9]

Many reasons can be advanced for this development. The interest in special providences coincided with a larger movement in English Protestantism towards an "experimental" style of piety, in which the devout scrutinised their lives and consciences for signs of grace.[10] The search for heavenly warnings, judgements and approbations in the wider world was, perhaps, a natural extension of this tendency. Great political events also encouraged speculations about the divine messages they contained; and the violent insecurity of the mid-seventeenth century probably increased the need to find indications of God's will. The relative decline of special providences after 1660 can also be attributed to numerous factors. The use of signs and wonders in political propaganda during the civil wars may have encouraged scepticism, as multiple and conflicting interpretations were placed on allegedly marvellous events. It is also possible that the sheer number of "wonders" reported in the 1640s and 1650s exhausted the market. Following the Restoration, the desire to avoid allegations of "fanaticism" discouraged incautious attempts to decipher the purposes of God. Glyn Parry has argued that the government of Charles II identified prophecy with political extremism, and sought to suppress supernatural speculations more generally.[11]

Crucially, the rise and long retreat of special providences did not undermine the belief in God's benevolent oversight of the world. This concept remained central to intellectual life and wider culture in late Stuart and Georgian England, and beyond. It is in this context that the development of physical and mathematical sciences during the Enlightenment should be understood. The doctrine of general providence was compatible with the "scientific revolution", and it certainly encouraged its most luminous contributor, Isaac Newton. The elucidation of patterns and laws in nature could be, and frequently was, used to show God's regular and perfect government of the physical world. As late as 1797, the Baptist theologian John

Fawcett observed that the "laws of nature, as they are called, are no other than the uniform agency of providence".[12] Similar principles applied in the emerging social sciences of psychology and economics. In 1749 David Hartley's extremely influential theory of the mind was premised on God's "system of benevolence", which assured that individuals exposed to education would use knowledge for the benefit of others.[13] Adam Smith's "invisible hand", which delivered prosperity for all from the myriad choices of private men and women, was also presented in explicitly providential terms.[14] From the larger perspective of early modern theology, Enlightenment science extended the tendency to emphasise general providence instead of specific interventions from God.

There are historical ironies here. The regular working of providence imagined by Hartley and Smith was similar, in some fundamental ways, to the vision of much earlier Protestant thinkers. In its most radical iteration by Reginald Scot in 1584, the doctrine of general providence effectively expelled magic from the world. Some later writers compared God's dispensation of earthly things to the mechanism of an infinitely complex clock, anticipating the concept of a "clock-work universe" that is sometimes held to have undermined supernatural beliefs.[15] If the doctrine of providence permitted an orderly and regular view of nature before the Enlightenment, the belief that earthly events are arranged according to a superhuman and benevolent plan also survived long into the modern age. Even today, the persistence of this way of thinking is remarkable: in the words of Blair Worden, "if God is dead, then providence may be said to have outlived him".[16] A version of the doctrine seems to underpin the idea that nature maintains a desirable "balance", and lurks behind appeals to the "wisdom of the market".[17] It is common for individuals to believe that the apparently random events of their lives conform to some kind of pattern, and to find in this pattern signs of a higher purpose: this is explicit in the idea that some things are "not meant to be". These examples suggest that providential assumptions may be far from obsolete, though they are not always explicitly acknowledged. As Tudor and Stuart writers often observed of the Devil, our continuing trust in unseen powers may be strongest when it is hidden from view.

Notes

1 Withers inserted the story in the register of the adjoining parish of Brisley. The episode is discussed in Owen Davies, *The Haunted: A Social History of Ghosts* (Palgrave Macmillan: 2007), 6–7; and Sasha Handley, *Visions of an Unseen World: Ghost Beliefs and Ghost Stories in Eighteenth-Century England* (Pickering & Chatto: 2007), chapter 5.

2 Alexandra Walsham, "Sermons in the Sky: Apparitions in Early Modern Europe", *History Today*, Vol. 51, No. 4 (2001), 59.

3 Jane Shaw, *Miracles in Enlightenment England* (Yale University Press: 2006).

4 Owen Davies, *Witchcraft, Magic and Culture, 1736–1951* (Manchester University Press: 1999); Willem de Blécourt and Owen Davies, eds., *Beyond the Witch Trials: Witchcraft*

and Magic in Enlightenment Europe (Manchester University Press: 2004); Willem de Blécourt and Owen Davies, eds., *Witchcraft Continued: Popular Magic in Modern Europe* (Manchester University Press: 2004).

5 For ghosts see Handley, *Visions*; for Catholics see Francis Young, *English Catholics and the Supernatural, 1553–1829* (Ashgate: 2013).

6 Baxter speculated that spirits that manifestly did good were sometimes the souls of the dead allowed by God to assist the living, though such matters were "uncertain to us". Richard Baxter, *The Certainty of the Worlds of Spirits* (1692), 7.

7 Anne Jeffries' commerce with fairies is described in chapter 6. Moses Pitt, *An Account of one Ann Jeffries, Now Living in the County of Cornwall* (1696), 5.

8 *The True Fourme and Shape of a Monsterous Child* (1565).

9 For the proliferation of "monsters" in this period, see Jerome Friedman, *Miracles and the Pulp Press During the English Revolution* (UCL Press: 1993), 48–56.

10 R. T. Kendall identified the "experimental" turn in English theology with William Perkins, whose work was immensely influential from the turn of the sixteenth century. See R. T. Kendall, *Calvin and English Calvinism to 1649* (Oxford University Press: 1979).

11 Glyn Parry, "John Dee, Alchemy and Authority in Elizabethan England", in Marcus Harmes and Victoria Bladen, eds., *Supernatural and Secular Power in Early Modern England* (Ashgate: 2015), 40.

12 Fawcett is quoted in J. C. D. Clark, "Providence, Predestination and Progress", *Albion*, 35:4 (2003), 569.

13 For Hartley see Isaac Kramnick, *Republicanism and Bourgeois Radicalism* (Cornell University Press: 1990), especially 84–6.

14 In 1759 Smith referred to God's beneficent oversight immediately after introducing the invisible hand: "When providence divided the earth among a few lordly masters, it neither forgot nor abandoned those who seemed to have been left out in the partition. These last too enjoy their share of all that it produces". Adam Smith, *Theory of Moral Sentiments* (1759), part 4, chapter 1, paragraph 10.

15 Wilkins used this metaphor to indicate the bewildering complexity of God's plan as well as its precision. John Wilkins, *A Discourse Concerning the Beauty of Providence* (1649), 52.

16 Blair Worden, "Providence and Politics in Cromwellian England", *Past & Present*, 109 (1985), 98.

17 In both examples, a this-worldly force has acquired some of the attributes of God. The benevolent purpose that was once believed to have been imposed by God on nature now resides in nature itself; and Smith's "invisible hand", outside its original context, now belongs to the market economy. Since neither nature nor the economy is an intelligent being, these formulations lack the coherence of the early modern ideas from which they emerged.

SELECT BIBLIOGRAPHY

Primary sources

Manuscripts

The notes after each chapter provide detailed references to manuscripts. Those most frequently used are listed below. All are held in the Bodleian Library, Oxford.

Astrological papers of Simon Forman: MS Ashmole 205
Magical papers, including Simon Forman's treatise "Of the Plague": MS Ashmole 1432
Papers of Simon Forman, including "A Discourse of the Plague": MS Ashmole 208
Simon Forman's commonplaces of occult philosophy: MS Ashmole 1430

Casebooks of the younger Richard Napier, 1634–7: MS Ashmole 412
Magical and medical papers, including cases "excerpted out of Dr Napier's books of horary questions for diseases": MS Ashmole 1790
Magical papers and medical treatments, and consultations by the younger Richard Napier: MS Ashmole 1447

Magical and medical papers, including medical charms: MS Ashmole 1408
Magical and medical papers, including advice on love spells: MS Ashmole 1417
Magical papers of Elias Ashmole, including astrological schemes by William Lilly and Lilly's autobiography: MS Ashmole 421
Magical papers of Elias Ashmole, including conjurations of fairies: MS Ashmole 1406
Magical papers including procedures for discovering treasure, and notes on the weapon salve: MS Ashmole 1488

Correspondence of Daniel Featly: MS Rawlinson D 47

Early modern printed texts

Thomas Adams, *Five Sermons Preached upon Sundry Especiall Occasions* (1626)
Thomas Ady, *A Candle in the Dark* (1655)
Thomas Alfield, *A True Reporte of the Death & Martyrdom of M. Campion* (1582)
Isaac Ambrose, *The Compleat Works* (1674)

John Aubrey, *Miscellanies upon the Following Subjects* (1696)
William Austin, *Devotionis Augustinianæ Flamma, or Certayne Devout, Godly, and Learned Meditations* (1635)
John Bainbridge, *An Astronomicall Description of the Late Comet* (1618)
John Bale, *The Image of Both Churches* (1548)
Richard Baxter, *The Certainty of the Worlds of Spirits* (1691)
Thomas Beard, *The Theatre of Gods Judgements* (1597)
Richard Bernard, *A Guide to Grand Jury Men* (1627)
Edmond Bicknoll, *A Swoord Agaynst Swearing* (1579)
The Black and Terrible Warning Piece (1653)
The Blacke Dogge of Newgate (1596)
Blanket-Fair (1684)
A Blazing Starre Seene in the West (1642)
The Blessed State of England (1591)
Thomas Blount, *A Natural History: Containing Many not Common Observations* (1696)
The Brideling, Sadling and Ryding, of a Rich Churle in Hampshire (1594)
Richard Bristow, *A Briefe Treatise of Divers Plaine and Sure Waies to Finde out the Truth* (1574)
Robert Burton, *The Anatomy of Melancholy* (1621)
George Carlton, *A Thankfull Remembrance of Gods Mercies* (1624)
Bezaleel Carter, *A Sermon of Gods Omnipotencie and Providence* (1615)
George Chapman, *The Shadow of Night: Containing Two Poetical Hymnes* (1594)
The Children's Example (1700)
Samuel Clarke, *A Mirrour or Looking Glasse, Both for Saints and Sinners* (1646)
Samuel Clarke, *A Generall Martyrologie* (1651)
Thomas Cooper, *Certaine Sermons wherin is Contained the Defense of the Gospell* (1580)
Thomas Cooper, *The Mystery of Witch-Craft* (1617)
Edward Cradock, *The Shippe of Assured Safetie* (1572)
John Darrell, *A True Narration of the Strange and Grevous Vexation by the Devil of 7 Persons in Lancashire* (1600)
A Declaration From Oxford (1651)
Arthur Dent, *The Plaine Mans Pathway to Heaven* (1601)
Arthur Dent, *A Sermon of Gods Providence* (1609)
A Detection of That Sinnful, Shamful, Lying and Ridiculous Discours of Samuel Harshnet (1600)
The Devils Oak (c 1683)
Dirty Dolls Farewel (1684)
The Distressed Gentlewoman; or Satan's Implacable Malice (1691)
The Divils Cruelty to Mankind (1662)
Thomas Drant, *The Divine Lanthorne* (1637)
Jeremias Drexel, *The Angel-Guardians Clock* (1630)
James Durham, *A Commentary upon the Book of the Revelation* (1658)
Englands New Bellman. Ringing into all Peoples Ears Gods Dreadful Judgement Against this Land (c 1663)
Desiderius Erasmus, *A Booke Called in Latyn Enchiridion* (1533)
The Examination of John Walsh (1566)
The Fairy Queene (1648)
Fearefull Apparitions or The Strangest Visions That Ever Have Been Heard Of (1647)
Fire from Heaven (1613)
John Fisher, *A Sermon had at Paulis by the Commandment of the Most Reverent Father in God my Lorde Legate* (1526)
Abraham Fleming, *A Straunge and Terrible Wunder Wrought Very Late in the Parish Church of Bongay* (1577)
John Foxe, *Christ Jesus Triumphant* (1579)
John Foxe, *Actes and Monuments of These Latter and Perillous Days* (1583 ed.)
John Frith, *A Pistle to the Christian Reader* (1529)

John Frith, *A Disputacion of Purgatorye* (1531)
A Full and True Relation of the Examination and Confession of W. Barwick and E. Mangall (1690)
William Gamage, *Linsi-Woolsie or Two Centuries of Epigrammes* (1621)
John Gaule, *Select Cases of Conscience* (1646)
George Gifford, *A Cathechisme Conteining the Summe of Christian Religion* (1583)
George Gifford, *A Discourse of the Subtill Practises of Deuilles by Witches and Sorcerers* (1587)
George Gifford, *A Dialogue Concerning Witches and Witchcraftes* (1593)
Gods Great and Wonderful Work in Somerset-shire (1674)
Gods Voice to Christendom (1693)
The Good Angel of Stamford (1659)
Thomas Gouge, *Gods Call to England for Thankfulness after Gracious Deliverances* (1680)
William Gouge, *The Whole-Armor of God* (1619)
Great Britains Wonder: or Londons Admiration (1684)
A Great Wonder in Heaven (1643)
John Gumbleden, *Christ Tempted: The Divel Conquered* (1657)
William Gurnall, *The Christian in Compleat Armour* (1655)
Joseph Hall, *The Invisible World Discovered to Spirituall Eyes* (1659)
Samuel Harsnett, *A Discovery of the Fraudulent Practises of John Darrell* (1599)
Samuel Harsnett, *A Declaration of Egregious Popish Impostures* (1603)
Thomas Hide, *A Consolatorie Epistle to the Afflicted Catholikes* (1579)
Thomas Hill, *A Quartron of Reasons of Catholike Religion* (1600)
An Historical Account of the Late Great Frost (1684)
The Historie of the Damnable Life and Deserved Death of Doctor John Faustus (1592)
Henry Holland, *Treatise Against Witchcraft* (1590)
Robert Holland, *The Holie Historie of our Lord and Saviour* (1594)
Robert Hooke, *Micrographia* (1665)
Robert Horne, *Of the Rich Man and Lazarus* (1619)
A Horrible Creuel and Bloudy Murther (1614)
Henry Howard, *A Defensative Against the Poison of Supposed Prophecies* (1583)
Immortality in Mortality Magnifi'd (1646)
Injunctions for the Clerge (1538)
James VI, *Daemonologie* (1597)
William James, *A Sermon Preached before the Queenes Maiestie* (1578)
Ben Jonson, *The Sad Shepherd: or A Tale of Robin-Hood* (1641)
Joyfull Newes From Plimouth (1646)
The Just Judgment of God Shew'd on Doctor John Faustus (c 1640)
The Kentish Miracle: or A Seasonable Warning to All Sinners (1684)
John King, *Lectures upon Jonas Delivered at Yorke* (1599)
William Langham, *The Garden of Health* (1597)
Ludwig Lavater, *Of Ghostes and Spirites Walking by Nyght* (1572)
Henry Lawrence, *Of Our Communion and Warre with Angels* (1646)
The Life and Death of the Merry Devil of Edmonton (1631)
William Lilly, *Christian Astrology Modestly Treated of in Three Books* (1647)
William Lilly, *Mr William Lilly's History of His Life and Times* (1715)
Londons Wonder (1684)
Thomas Lupton, *A Thousand Notable Things of Sundry Sortes* (1579)
Martin Luther, *Colloquia Mensalia* (1652)
The Mad Merry Pranks of Robin Good-fellow (c 1640)
The Mathematicall Divine (1642)
Merry Drollery Complete (1670)
John Milton, *Of Reformation Touching Church-Discipline in England* (1641)
Mirabile Pecci: or The Non-Such Wonder of the Peak in Darby-shire (1669)
George More, *A True Discourse Concerning the Certaine Possession and Dispossession of 7 persons in one Familie in Lancashire* (1600)

Henry More, *The Immortality of the Soul* (1659)
Most Certaine Report of a Monster Borne at Oteringham in Holdernesse (1595)
The Most Strange and Admirable Discoverie of the Three Witches of Warboys (1593)
A Most Strange and Rare Example of the Just Judgement of God (1577)
The Most Wonderfull and True Storie of a Certaine Witch Named Alse Gooderige of Stapen Hill (1597)
The Mowing Devil: or Strange News out of Hartford-shire (1678)
The New Help to Discourse, or Wit, Mirth, and Jollity (1680)
A New Song of Father Petre and the Devil (1689)
The New Yeares Wonder (1642)
News from Frost Fair (1683)
News From St John Street (1676)
Thomas Newton, *Aprooved Medicines and Cordiall Receiptes* (1580)
John Nicholls, *Pilgrimage, Wherin is Displayed the Lives of the Proude Popes* (1581)
The Norfolke Gentleman his Last Will and Testament (1595)
Philippe Numan, *Miracles Lately Wrought by the Intercession of the Glorious Virgin Marie* (1606)
Robert Parsons, *The First Booke of the Christian Exercise* (1582)
Robert Parsons, *The Seconde Parte of the Booke of Christian Exercise* (1590)
Robert Parsons, *A Treatise Tending to Mitigation Towardes Catholike-Subiectes in England* (1607)
William Perkins, *The Foundation of Christian Religion, Gathered into Sixe Principles* (1590)
William Perkins, *A Golden Chaine, or The Description of Theologie* (1591)
William Perkins, *Of the Calling of the Ministerie* (1605)
William Perkins, *The Combat Betweene Christ and the Divell Displayed* (1606)
William Perkins, *A Discourse of the Damned Art of Witchcraft* (1608)
John Peter, *A Philosophical Account of This Hard Frost* (1684)
Edward Phillips, *The New World of English Words* (1658)
George Phillips, *The Embassage of Gods Angell* (1597)
Moses Pitt, *An Account of one Ann Jeffries, now Living in the County of Cornwall* (1696)
The Politick Wife, or The Devil Outwitted by a Woman (c 1660)
John Pordage, *Innocencie Appearing Through the Dark Mists of Pretended Guilt* (1655)
Thomas Potts, *The Wonderfull Discoverie of Witches in the Countie of Lancaster* (1613)
Vavasour Powell, *Spirituall Experiences of Sundry Beleevers* (1652)
John Prime, *A Short Treatise of the Sacraments* (1582)
Samuel Purchas, *A Theatre of Politicall Flying-Insects* (1657)
The Quakers Shaken, or A Warning Against Quaking (1655)
The Ranters Monster (1652)
Francis Raworth, *Jacobs Ladder, or the Protectorship of Sion* (1655)
A Relation of a Strange Apparition (1641)
A Relation of a Terrible Monster Taken by a Fisherman Neere Wollage (1642)
John Reynolds, *The Triumphes of Gods Revenge* (1635 ed.)
John Reynolds, *A Discourse Upon Prodigious Abstinence* (1669)
Barnaby Rich, *The True Report of a Late Practise Enterprised by a Papist* (1582)
Robin Goodfellow his Mad Merry Pranks (1628)
Thomas Robins, *Newes from Darby-shire: or the Wonder of all Wonders* (1668)
Thomas Robins, *The Wonder of the World* (1669)
A Sad Caveat for All Quakers (1657)
Edwin Sandys, *Sermons made by the most Reuerende Father in God, Edwin, Archbishop of Yorke* (1585)
Reginald Scot, *The Discovery of Witchcraft* (1584)
The Severall Notorious and Lewd Cousenages of John West and Alice West (1613)
The Sheepherd's New Kalender (1700)
Richard Sibbes, *The Saints Safetie in Evil Times* (1634)
Signes and Wonders From Heaven (1645)
Edmund Skipp, *The Worlds Wonder, or The Quakers Blazing Starr* (1655)
Adam Smith, *Theory of Moral Sentiments* (1759)
Henry Smith, *Three Prayers, One for the Morning, Another for the Evening: the Third for a Sick-man* (1591)
Henry Smith, *The Sermons of Master Henrie Smith* (1592)

Edmund Spenser, *The Faerie Queene* (1590)
John Stearne, *A Confirmation and Discovery of Witchcraft* (1648)
A Strange and Miraculous Accident (1599)
Strange and Terrible Newes From the North (1648)
Strange and Wonderful News from Linconshire (1679)
A Strange and Wonderful Relation from Shadwel, or the Devil Visible (1674)
Strange Newes of a Prodigious Monster (1613)
Strange News from Westmoreland (1663)
A Strange Wonder, or The Cities Amazement (1642)
Tarltons Newes out of Purgatorie (1588)
Jean Thibaut, *Pronostycacyon of Maister John Thybault* (1533)
This Horyble Monster is Cast of a Sowe (1531)
Edward Topsell, *The Historie of Serpents* (1608)
A True and Exact Relation of the Severall Informations, Examinations, and Confessions of the Late Witches (1645)
True and Wonderfull. A Discourse Relating a Strange and Monstrous Serpent (1614)
The True Fourme and Shape of a Monsterous Child (1565)
The True Lamentable Discourse of the Burning of Teverton in Devon-shire (1598)
True Newes from Mecare and also out of Worcestershire (1598)
A True Relation of a Very Strange and Wonderful Thing That was Heard in the Air (1658)
A True Relation of Gods Wonderfull Mercies (1605)
A True Relation of the Queenes Majesties Returne out of Holland (1643)
A True Report and Exact Description of a Mighty Sea Monster or Whale (1617)
Thomas Tryon, *Modest Observations on the Present Extraordinary Frost* (1684)
Two Most Strange Wonders (1662)
Thomas Twyne, *A View of Certain Wonderful Effects of Late Dayes Come to Pass* (1578)
William Tyndale, *The Exposition of the Fyrste Epistle of Seynt John* (1531)
John Vicars, *Prodigies & Apparitions, or Englands Warning Piece* (1642)
Edmund Waller, *Upon the Late Storm, and of the Death of His Highness* (1658)
A Warning Piece for Ingroosers of Corne (c 1650)
Richard Watkins, *Newes From the Dead* (1651)
Richard Watkins, *The Storme Rais'd by Mr Waller* (1659)
John Webster, *The Displaying of Supposed Witchcraft* (1677)
The Westminster Wonder (1695)
Thomas White, *A Treatise of the Power of Godlinesse* (1658)
John Wilkins, *A Discourse Concerning the Beauty of Providence* (1649)
George Wither, *Campo-Musae: or The Field-Musings of major George Wither* (1643)
A Wonder in Stafford-shire (1661)
The Wonder of the Age (1635)
The Wonder of this Age: or God's Miraculous Revenge Against Murder (1677)
A Wonder of Wonders (1651)
The Wonder of Wonders, or a True Relation of a Late Strange and Miraculous Accident (1659)
Wonders on the Deep; or The Most Exact Description of the Frozen River of Thames (1684)
A Wonder Worth the Reading (1617)
The Wonderful Recompence of Faith (1675)
Nathaniel Woodes, *An Excellent New Commedie Intitutled The Conflict of Conscience* (1581)
The Worlds Wonder (1659)
Robert Yarrington, *Two Lamentable Tragedies* (1601)
The Young-Mans Second Warning-Peece (1643)

Early modern texts in later editions

Philip C. Almond, ed., *Demonic Possession and Exorcism in Early Modern England: Contemporary Texts and Their Cultural Contexts* (Cambridge University Press: 2004)

John Bale, *The Vocacyon of Johan Bale*, ed. Peter Happé and John King (Renaissance English Text Society: 1990)

Sir Thomas Browne, *The Major Works*, ed. C. A. Patrides (Penguin: 1977)

John Bunyan, *Grace Abounding to the Chief of Sinners*, ed. W. R. Owens (Penguin: 1987)

John Bunyan, *The Life and Death of Mr Badman* (Hesperus Press: 2007)

John Bunyan, *The Pilgrim's Progress*, ed. Roger Pooley (Penguin: 2008)

Thomas Cranmer, *Miscellaneous Writings and Letters of Thomas Cranmer, Archbishop of Canterbury*, ed. John Edmund Cox (Cambridge: 1846)

William Dowsing, *The Journal of William Dowsing: Iconoclasm in East Anglia*, ed. Trevor Cooper (Boydell Press: 2001)

David Englander, Diana Norman, Rosemary O'Day, and William Owens, eds., *Culture and Belief in Europe, 1450–1600* (Blackwell: 1990)

Edward Fairfax, *Daemonologia: A Discourse on Witchcraft*, ed. William Grainge (R. Ackrill: 1882)

Marion Gibson, ed., *Early Modern Witches: Witchcraft Cases in Contemporary Writing* (Routledge: 2000)

William Harvey, *The Circulation of the Blood and other Writings*, ed. Andrew Wear (Everyman: 1993)

Thomas Hobbes, *Leviathan*, ed. Ian Shapiro (Yale University Press: 2010)

Ralph Josselin, *The Diary of Ralph Josselin, 1616–1683*, ed. Alan Macfarlane (Oxford University Press: 1976)

W. P. M. Kennedy, "A Declaration before the Ecclesiastical Commission, 1562", *English Historical Review*, Vol. 47, No. 146 (1922)

Christopher Marlowe, *Doctor Faustus and Other Plays*, ed. David Bevington and Eric Rasmussen (Oxford University Press: 1995)

P. G. Maxwell-Stuart, *The Occult in Early Modern Europe: A Documentary History* (Macmillan: 1999)

John Milton, *The Complete Poems*, ed. John Leonard (Penguin: 1998)

Joanna Moody, ed., *The Private Life of an Elizabethan Lady: The Diary of Lady Margaret Hoby, 1599–1605* (Sutton: 1998)

Thomas Nashe, *The Unfortunate Traveller and Other Works*, ed. J. B. Steane (Penguin: 1972)

Joad Raymond, ed., *Making the News: An Anthology of the Newsbooks of Revolutionary England, 1641–1660* (Windrush Press: 1993)

Edmund Spenser, *The Shorter Poems*, ed. Richard A. McCabe (Penguin: 1999)

Alice Thornton, *The Autobiography of Mrs Alice Thornton of East Newton*, ed. C. Jackson (Surtees Society: 1875)

Jacobus de Voragine, *The Golden Legend*, trans. William Granger Ryan (Princeton University Press: 1993)

William Weston, *The Autobiography of an Elizabethan*, trans. Philip Caraman (Longmans, Green and Co: 1955)

Selected secondary works

Mary Abbott, *Life Cycles in England* (Routledge: 1996)

Philip C. Almond, *England's First Demonologist: Reginald Scot and The Discoverie of Witchcraft* (I. B. Taurus: 2011)

Robert Bartlett, *Trial by Fire and Water: The Medieval Judicial Ordeal* (Oxford University Press: 1986)

Robert Bartlett, *The Natural and the Supernatural in the Middle Ages* (Cambridge University Press: 2008)

Rudolph M. Bell, *Holy Anorexia* (University of Chicago Press: 1985)

G. W. Bernard and S. J. Gunn, eds., *Authority and Consent in Tudor England* (Ashgate: 2002)

Edward Bever, "Witchcraft Fears and Psychosocial Factors in Disease", *Journal of Interdisciplinary History*, Vol. 30, No. 4 (2000)

Edward Bever, *The Realities of Witchcraft and Popular Magic in Early Modern Europe* (Palgrave Macmillan: 2008)

Willem de Blécourt and Owen Davies, eds., *Beyond the Witch Trials: Witchcraft and Magic in Enlightenment Europe* (Manchester University Press: 2004)

Willem de Blécourt and Owen Davies, eds., *Witchcraft Continued: Popular Magic in Modern Europe* (Manchester University Press: 2004)

Katherine Briggs, *The Anatomy of Puck: An Examination of Fairy Beliefs among Shakespeare's Contemporaries and Successors* (Routledge: 2003; 1st ed. 1959)

Robin Briggs, *Witches and Neighbours* (HarperCollins: 1996)

Elizabeth M. Butler, *The Fortunes of Faust* (Cambridge University Press: 1952)

T. G. S. Cain and Ken Robinson, eds., *Into Another Mould: Change and Continuity in English Culture, 1625–1700* (Routledge: 1992)

Euan Cameron, *Enchanted Europe* (Oxford University Press: 2010)

Bernard Capp, *Astrology and the Popular Press: English Almanacs, 1500–1800* (Faber: 1979)

Charles Carlton, *This Seat of Mars: War and the British Isles, 1485–1746* (Yale University Press: 2011)

E. H. Carr, *What Is History?* (Macmillan: 1961)

Alison Chapman, "Marking Time: Astrology Almanacs, and English Protestantism", *Renaissance Quarterly*, 60 (2007)

J. C. D. Clark, "Providence, Predestination and Progress", *Albion*, Vol. 35, No. 4 (2003)

Stuart Clark, *Thinking with Demons: The Idea of Witchcraft in Early Modern Europe* (Oxford University Press: 1997)

Stuart Clark, ed., *Languages of Witchcraft: Narrative, Ideology and Meaning in Early Modern Culture* (Macmillan: 2001)

Stuart Clark, *Vanities of the Eye: Vision in Early Modern European Culture* (Oxford University Press: 2007)

David Cressy, *Bonfires and Bells: National Memory and the Protestant Calendar in Elizabethan and Stuart England* (Weidenfeld & Nicolson: 1989)

David Cressy, *Agnes Bowker's Cat: Travesties and Transgressions in Tudor and Stuart England* (Oxford University Press: 2000)

Patrick Curry, *Prophecy and Power: Astrology in Early Modern England* (Polity Press: 1989)

Orna Alyagon Darr, *Marks of an Absolute Witch: Evidentiary Dilemmas in Early Modern England* (Ashgate: 2011)

Lorraine Daston and Katharine Park, *Wonders and the Order of Nature, 1150–1750* (Zone Books: 2001)

Owen Davies, *Witchcraft, Magic and Culture, 1736–1951* (Manchester University Press: 1999)

Owen Davies, "The Nightmare Experience, Sleep Paralysis, and Witchcraft Accusations", *Folklore*, Vol. 114, No. 2 (2003)

Owen Davies, *Popular Magic: Cunning Folk in English History* (Continuum: 2003)

Owen Davies, *The Haunted: A Social History of Ghosts* (Palgrave Macmillan: 2007)

Owen Davies, *Grimoires: A History of Magic Books* (Oxford University Press: 2010)

S. F. Davies, "The Reception of Reginald Scot's *Discovery of Witchcraft*: Witchcraft, Magic, and Radical Religion", *Journal of the History of Ideas*, Vol. 74, No. 3 (2013)

Michael Funk Deckard, "A Sudden Surprise of the Soul: The Passion of Wonder in Hobbes and Descartes", *Heythrop Journal*, Vol. 49, Issue 6 (2008)

C. Scott Dixon, Dagmar Freist and Mark Greengrass, eds, *Living with Religious Diversity in Early Modern Europe* (Ashgate: 2009)

Richard M. Dorson, *The British Folklorists: A History* (University of Chicago Press: 1968)

Eamon Duffy, *The Stripping of the Altars: Traditional Religion in England, 1400–1580* (Yale University Press: 1992)

Jacqueline Eales, "Thomas Pierson and the Transmission of the Moderate Puritan Tradition", *Midland History*, 20 (1995)

Richard Kenneth Emmerson, *Antichrist in the Middle Ages* (Manchester University Press: 1981)

C. L'Estrange Ewen, *Witch Hunting and Witch Trials* (Dial Press: 1929)

C. L'Estrange Ewen, ed., *Witchcraft and Demonianism* (Heath Cranton: 1933)

Brian Fagan, *The Little Ice Age* (Basic Books: 2000)

Ronald C. Finucane, *Miracles and Pilgrims: Popular Beliefs in Medieval England* (Macmillan: 1995)

Tor Egil Førland, "God, Science, and Historical Explanation", *History and Theory*, 47 (December 2008)

Adam Fox and Daniel Woolf, eds., *The Spoken Word: Oral Culture in Britain, 1500–1850* (Manchester University Press: 2002)

Anna French, *Children of Wrath: Possession, Prophecy and the Young in Early Modern England* (Ashgate: 2015)

Jerome Friedman, *Miracles and the Pulp Press in the English Revolution* (UCL Press: 1993)

Malcolm Gaskill, *Witchfinders: A Seventeenth-Century English Tragedy* (John Murray: 2005)

Ann Geneva, *Astrology and the Seventeenth-Century Mind: William Lilly and the Language of the Stars* (Manchester University Press: 1995)

Marion Gibson, *Possession, Puritanism and Print: Darrell, Harsnett, Shakespeare and the Elizabethan Exorcism Controversy* (Pickering & Chatto: 2006)

Hal Gladfelder, *Criminality and Narrative in Eighteenth-Century England* (Johns Hopkins University Press: 2001)

Laura Gowing, "The Haunting of Susan Lay: Servants and Mistresses in Seventeenth-Century England", *Gender & History*, Vol. 14, No. 2 (2002)

Angus Gowland, *The Worlds of Renaissance Melancholy: Robert Burton in Context* (Cambridge University Press: 2006)

Brad S. Gregory, "The Other Confessional History: On Secular Bias in the Study of Religion", *History and Theory*, Vol. 45 (December 2006)

Paul Griffiths, Adam Fox and Steve Hindle, eds., *The Experience of Authority in Early Modern England* (Macmillan: 1996)

Genevieve Guenther, *Magical Imaginations: Instrumental Aesthetics in the English Reformation* (University of Toronto Press: 2012)

Sasha Handley, *Visions of an Unseen World: Ghost Beliefs and Ghost Stories in Eighteenth-Century England* (Pickering & Chatto: 2007)

Marcus Harmes and Victoria Bladen, eds., *Supernatural and Secular Power in Early Modern England* (Ashgate: 2015)

Christopher Hill, *Antichrist in Seventeenth-Century England* (Oxford University Press: 1971)

Clive Holmes, "Women: Witnesses and Witches", *Past & Present*, Vol. 140, Issue 1 (1993)

Sharon Howard, "Imagining the Pain and Peril of Seventeenth-Century Childbirth", *Social History of Medicine*, Vol. 16, No. 3 (2003)

Michael Hunter, "New Light on the 'Drummer of Tedworth': Conflicting Narratives of Witchcraft in Restoration England", *Historical Research*, Vol. 78, Issue 201 (2005)

Ronald Hutton, "The Making of the Early Modern British Fairy Tradition", *Historical Journal*, Vol. 57, No. 4 (2014)

Mark S. R. Jenner and Patrick Wallis, eds., *Medicine and the Market in England and Its Colonies, c. 1450–1850* (Palgrave Macmillan: 2007)

Nathan Johnstone, *The Devil and Demonism in Early Modern England* (Cambridge University Press: 2006)

Lauren Kassell, *Medicine and Magic in Elizabethan London* (Oxford University Press: 2005)

Lauren Kassell, "'All was this Land Fill'd of Faerie', or Magic and the Past in Early Modern England", *Journal of the History of Ideas*, Vol. 67, No. 1 (2006)

Lauren Kassell, "Casebooks in Early Modern England: Medicine, Astrology and Written Records", *Bulletin of the History of Medicine*, Vol. 88, No. 4 (2014)

David Keck, *Angels and Angelology in the Middle Ages* (Oxford University Press: 1998)

R. T. Kendall, *Calvin and English Calvinism to 1649* (Oxford University Press: 1979)

Isaac Kramnick, *Republicanism and Bourgeois Radicalism* (Cornell University Press: 1990)

Minor White Latham, *The Elizabethan Fairies: The Fairies of Folklore and the Fairies of Shakespeare* (Columbia University Press: 1930)

Joep Leerssen, *National Thought in Europe: A Cultural History* (Amsterdam University Press: 2001)

Brian P. Levack, *The Devil Within: Possession and Exorcism in the Christian West* (Yale University Press: 2013)

Julian Lock, "How Many Tercios has the Pope? The Spanish War and the Sublimation of Elizabethan Anti-Popery", *History*, Vol. 81, Issue 262 (1996)

Jonathan Lumby, *The Lancashire Witch Craze: Jennet Preston and the Lancashire Witches, 1612* (Carnegie: 1995)

Michael MacDonald, *Mystical Bedlam: Madness, Anxiety and Healing in Seventeenth-Century England* (Cambridge University Press: 1981)

Alan Macfarlane, *Witchcraft in Tudor and Stuart England* (Routledge: 2nd ed. 1999)

Peter Marshall, *Beliefs and the Dead in Reformation England* (Oxford University Press: 2002)

Peter Marshall and Alexandra Walsham, eds., *Angels in the Early Modern World* (Cambridge University Press: 2006)

Peter Marshall, *Mother Leakey and the Bishop* (Oxford University Press: 2007)

Timothy Scott McGinnis, *George Gifford and the Reformation of the Common Sort* (Truman State University Press: 2004)

H. F. McMains, *The Death of Oliver Cromwell* (University of Kentucky Press: 2000)

Angela McShane and Garthine Walker, eds., *The Extraordinary and the Everyday in Early Modern England* (Palgrave Macmillan: 2010)

Ralph Merrifield, *The Archaeology of Ritual and Magic* (B. T. Batsford: 1987)

S. I. Mintz, *The Hunting of Leviathan: Seventeenth-Century Reactions to the Materialism and Moral Philosophy of Thomas Hobbes* (Cambridge University Press: 1962)

Susannah Brietz Monta, *Martyrdom and Literature in Early Modern England* (Cambridge University Press: 2009)

William R. Newman and Anthony Grafton, eds., *Secrets of Nature: Astrology and Alchemy in Early Modern Europe* (MIT Press: 2001)

William R. Newman and Lawrence M. Principe, "Alchemy vs. Chemistry: The Etymological Origins of a Historiographic Mistake", *Early Science and Medicine*, Vol. 3, No. 1 (1998)

William R. Newman and Lawrence M. Principe, *Alchemy Tried in the Fire: Starkey, Boyle, and the Fate of Helmontian Chymistry* (University of Chicago Press: 2002)

Darren Oldridge, ed., *The Witchcraft Reader* (Routledge: 2nd ed. 2008)

Darren Oldridge, *The Devil in Tudor and Stuart England* (History Press: 2010)

Darren Oldridge, "Light from Darkness: The Problem of Evil in Early Modern England", *The Seventeenth Century*, Vol. 27, No. 4 (2012)

Darren Oldridge, "Fairies and the Devil in Early Modern England", *The Seventeenth Century*, Vol. 31, No. 1 (2016)

Glyn Parry, *The Arch Conjuror of England* (Yale University Press: 2011)

Graham Parry, *Seventeenth-Century Poetry: The Social Context* (Hutchinson: 1985)

Jacqueline Pearson, "Then she asked it, what were its sister's names?": Reading Between the lines in Seventeenth-Century Pamphlets of the Supernatural", *The Seventeenth Century*, Vol. 28, No. 1 (2013)

Clara Pinto-Correia, *The Ovary of Eve: Egg and Sperm and Preformation* (University of Chicago Press: 1997)

Stephen Pumfrey, Paolo Rossi and Maurice Slawinski, *Science, Culture and Popular Belief in Renaissance Europe* (Manchester University Press: 1991)

Diane Purkiss, *Fairies and Fairy Stories: A History* (Allen Lane: 2000)

Joad Raymond, ed., *Conversations with Angels: Essays Towards a History of Spiritual Communication, 1100–1700* (Palgrave Macmillan: 2011)

Richard Rex, *Henry VIII and the English Reformation* (Macmillan: 1993)

David Riggs, *The World of Christopher Marlowe* (Faber & Faber: 2004)

Roger Rosewell, *Medieval Wall Paintings* (Boydell Press: 2008)

Alec Ryrie, *The Sorcerer's Tale* (Oxford University Press: 2008)

Laura Sangha, *Angels and Belief in England, 1480–1700* (Pickering & Chatto: 2012)

James Sharpe, *Instruments of Darkness: Witchcraft in England, 1550–1750* (Hamish Hamilton: 1996)

Kevin Sharpe, *Reading Authority and Representing Rule in Early Modern England* (Bloomsbury: 2013)

Jane Shaw, *Miracles in Enlightenment England* (Yale University Press: 2006)

Jacqueline Simpson, "The Local Legend: A Product of Popular Culture", *Rural History*, Vol. 2, No. 1 (1991)

Adam Smyth, "Almanacs, Annotators, and Life Writing in Early Modern England", *English Literary Renaissance*, Vol. 38, Issue 2 (2008)

Jennifer Spinks and Dagmar Eichberger, eds., *Religion, the Supernatural and Visual Culture in Early Modern Europe* (Brill: 2015)

Charles Taylor, *A Secular Age* (Harvard University Press: 2007)

Verena Theile and Andrew McCarthy, eds., *Staging the Superstitions of Early Modern Europe* (Ashgate: 2013)

Keith Thomas, *Religion and the Decline of Magic* (Weidenfeld & Nicolson: 1971)

Keith Thomas, *Man and the Natural World* (Allen Lane: 1983)

Walter Vandereycken and Ron Van Deth, "Miraculous Maids? Self-Starvation and Fasting Girls", *History Today*, Vol. 43, Issue 8 (1993)

Walter Vandereycken and Ron van Deth, *From Fasting Saints to Anorexic Girls: The History of Self-Starvation* (Athlone Press: 1994)

Alexandra Walsham, *Providence in Early Modern England* (Oxford University Press: 1999)

Alexandra Walsham, "*Vox Piscis: or The Book Fish*: Providence and the Uses of the Reformation Past in Caroline Cambridge", *English Historical Review*, Vol. 114, No. 457 (1999)

Alexandra Walsham, "Sermons in the Sky: Apparitions in Early Modern Europe", *History Today*, Vol. 51, Issue 4 (2001)

Alexandra Walsham, "Miracles and the Counter Reformation Mission to England", *Historical Journal*, Vol. 46, Issue 4 (December 2003)

Alexandra Walsham, *The Reformation of the Landscape* (Oxford University Press: 2011)

Diane Watt, *Secretaries of God: Women Prophets in Late Medieval and Early Modern England* (Cambridge University Press: 1997)

Emma Wilby, "The Witch's Familiar and the Fairy", *Folklore*, Vol. 111, Issue 2 (2000)

Emma Wilby, *Cunning Folk and Familiar Spirits: Shamanistic Visionary Traditions in Early Modern British Witchcraft and Magic* (Sussex Academic Press: 2005)

Jonathan Willis, ed., *Sin and Salvation in Early Modern England* (Ashgate: 2015)

Catherine Wilson, *The Invisible World: Early Modern Philosophy and the Invention of the Microscope* (Princeton University Press: 1995)

Stephen Wilson, *The Magical Universe: Everyday Ritual and Magic in Pre-Modern Europe* (Hambledon: 2000)

Blair Worden, "Providence and Politics in Cromwellian England", *Past & Present*, Vol. 109, Issue 1 (November 1985)

Thomas Wright, *William Harvey: A Life in Circulation* (Oxford University Press: 2012)

Francis Young, *English Catholics and the Supernatural, 1553–1829* (Ashgate: 2013)

INDEX